DI064443

Flynn begins by examining the uses of "responsibility" in *Being and Nothingness* and in several postwar essays. He then concentrates on the *Critique of Dialectical Reason*, offering a thorough analysis of the remarkable social theory Sartre constructs there. Flynn considers how Sartre's theory of social wholes meshes with his understanding of collective responsibility, and he speculates about the possibilities of an existentialist, dialectical social philosophy.

Sartre and Marxist Existentialism offers a new view of Sartre's work and of the issue of collective responsibility, and it confirms Sartre's reputation as a social philosopher of the first magnitude. A masterful contribution to Sartre scholarship, this book will also be welcome to social and political philosophers involved in the debate over collective responsibility.

THOMAS R. FLYNN is associate professor of philosophy at Emory University. He has contributed widely to volumes on Sartre and to scholarly journals.

SARTRE AND MARXIST EXISTENTIALISM

SARTRE AND MARXIST EXISTENTIALISM

the test case of collective responsibility

THOMAS R. FLYNN

the university of chicago press · chicago & london

Thomas R. Flynn is associate professor of philosophy
at Emory University. He has contributed widely to volumes on
Sartre and to scholarly journals.

THE UNIVERSITY OF CHICAGO PRESS, CHICAGO 60637
THE UNIVERSITY OF CHICAGO PRESS, LTD., LONDON

Library of Congress Cataloging in Publication Data

Flynn, Thomas R.
    Sartre and Marxist existentialism.

    Bibliography: p.
    Includes index.
    1. Sartre, Jean Paul, 1905–80.   2. Existentialism
—History.   3. Philosophy, Marxist.   I. Title.
B2430.S34F58   1984   194   83-4994
ISBN 0-226-25465-8

For John

Contents

CONTENTS

Abbreviations

Where the French original of one of these works is cited, the abbreviation will add the suffix "F" to the abbreviation. Thus *L'Être et le néant* is cited as "BN-F."

AJ	*Anti-Semite and Jew*
BEM	*Between Existentialism and Marxism*
BN	*Being and Nothingness*
CA	*The Condemned of Altona*
CDR˙	*Critique of Dialectical Reason*
CM	*Cahiers pour une morale*
CP	*The Communists and Peace*
CSKS	"Consciousness of Self and Knowledge of Self"
EA	*The Ethics of Ambiguity* (de Beauvoir)
EH	"Existentialism Is a Humanism"
EMO	*The Emotions: Outline of a Theory*
EP	*Entretiens sur la politique*
IF	*L'Idiot de la famille*
L/S	*Life/Situations*
MR	"Materialism and Revolution"
ORR	*On a raison de se révolter*
PI	*The Psychology of Imagination*
SG	*Saint Genet*
SM	*Search for a Method*
ST	*Sartre on Theatre*
TE	*The Transcendence of the Ego*
WE	Preface to *The Wretched of the Earth*

Introduction

An existentialist *social* philosophy? The expression strikes many as a contradiction in terms, especially when the existentialism is that of Jean-Paul Sartre. Who, after all, is a greater champion of the solitary individual than the author of *Nausea?* And what more fitting epitaph for the tomb of a social theory than his menacing judgment, "Hell is other people"?

Yet we know that Sartre was the very model of the *philosophe engagé.* As one headline put it at the time of his death, he was the conscience of his age and, we might add, its social conscience at that. It is unlikely that his practice and his theory were so at odds. If he was not afflicted with double vision, how did his focus shift from the individual to society? Where did this existentialist turn in pursuit of the social dimension of human reality? And what did he find?

The issue centers on Sartre's Marxism. His years of fellow-traveling, his double standard for assessing East and West, the *gauchiste* politics of his later years—do these represent a volte-face, one more conversion story out of the war years? Or is there something richer and more profound at work in Sartre's social thought, perhaps the dawning of a synthesis of two of the most dynamic and influential philosophies of our times?

In what follows, I hope to make evident the uniqueness of Sartre's response to the perennial question of the relationship between individual and society, the ground problem for any social theory. The instrument I have chosen to bring this to the fore is the matter of collective responsibility. Sartrean existentialism is renowned for holding individuals to an extreme sense of moral responsibility and for dismissing their counter-protestations as "bad faith." Marxism, on the other hand, is just as noted for its sense of the collective subject and in particular for concentrating on the socioeconomic class in its historical evolution. In fact, the French Marxist philosopher, Lucien Goldmann, has argued that it is the collective subject, not economic determinism, which is the defining characteristic of Marxism.[1] The existentialist seems committed to the claim that the individual is all that matters; the Marxist to the thesis that impersonal forces and relations are responsible for the alienation of humankind.

I intend to show how Sartre, by developing a coherent and adequate theory of collective responsibility, has combined salient features of each philosophy into a new and challenging social theory. As the following chapters will attest, this theory, though not the natural outgrowth of *Being and Nothingness,* raises the incipient social aspects of that individualist classic to a higher, historical viewpoint. It also grounds and articulates a pattern of ascriptions of responsibility to collectives that Sartre had been employing in his popular writings since the war. Finally, I shall situate these theories of collective responsibility and of society in general in the context of Sartre's own life-project as moralist and philosopher of the imagination.

My prime intent, therefore, is to confirm Sartre's reputation as a social theorist. But in the process I wish to make more accessible his original contributions to what in recent years has been termed "theory of responsibility." Although the expression is taken from Anglo-American philosophy, the ideas are scarcely foreign to Continental, especially existentialist, thought. Consider the works of Jaspers and Ingarden, for example.[2] As we shall see, Sartre's is a unique and powerful voice in that discussion.

The originality of his social theory is brought home by dialogue with his critics. Aside from his contemporaries, people who matured with him and enjoyed almost equal renown like Raymond Aron and Maurice Merleau-Ponty, whose remarks figure in the body of my text, I must mention more recent commentators whose observations and objections demand a response such as the work I have written. Their criticisms settle on four issues of relevance to my topic and their opinions cover the political spectrum.

The first issue concerns the unity of Sartre's early and later work, specifically, the relation of *Being and Nothingness* to the *Critique of Dialectical Reason*. Some, like Mary Warnock and George Kline, claim that the latter is a complete repudiation of the former.[3] James Sheridan agrees that there is a "radical conversion" afoot in the move from early to later Sartre.[4] On the other hand, Marjorie Grene charges that "the *Critique* could be translated without significant residue into the dialectic of for-itself/in-itself," the basic ontology of his earlier work.[5] Similarly, Ronald Aronson asks himself whether Sartre has moved "decisively beyond his individualist, dualist and aestheticist starting point" and concludes he has not: "Even at their most penetrating, the analyses of the *Critique* remain wholly within the preexisting limits of Sartre's thought."[6] This view is shared by orthodox Marxists.[7] More moderate positions are supported by Hazel Barnes, who notes merely a "shift of emphasis,"[8] by Istvan Mészáros, who sees "change inside permanence,"[9] and by Fredric Jameson, who insists that the *Critique* completes and transforms the existentialist opus.[10] In this regard I shall indicate how the categories of the *Critique* are different from and irreducible to those of *Being and Nothingness,* which they nonetheless subsume. The later work, therefore, moved beyond but not counter to the earlier.

The next and related point of dispute concerns the authenticity of Sartre's Marxism. Has he simply "sold out" to his erstwhile foes as the "conversion" theorists maintain? Or is he rather a bourgeois fox in the socialist hen-house ("anarcho-syndicalist" is the received term) as his Communist critics warn? Specifically, how can the defender of absolute freedom subscribe to economic determinism, even determinism "in the last instance"? The challenge is to respect economic "necessity" while preserving enough *Spielraum* for individual freedom-responsibiity. And does Sartre accept the notion of a collective "subject of History," if such is a defining characteristic of Marxism? Of course, much depends on one's definition of "Marxism." If one limits "revisionism" to Bernstein's classical form, as does Fredric Jameson, then Sartre does not merit the label.[11] But I shall argue that Sartre's is an authentic, though "revisionist," Marxism, which grants a major role to economic conditioning and collective action while reserving pride of place for individual choice, a stance that William McBride, Hazel Barnes, and Mark Poster term "neo-Marxism." But precisely because of the primacy of individual praxis in his social ontology— what Poster decries as Sartre's tendency "to privilege individual reality over social experience"[12]—we must admit that Sartre's Marxism is adjectival to his existentialism.

The third point at issue pertains to social ontology. Is Sartre an individualist or a holist in this area? Raymond Aron claims the former, Warnock and Kline imply the latter.[13] I shall exhibit how Sartre's "dialectical nominalism" opens a via media between these two extremes in social theory precisely to avoid what Mészáros criticizes as a "characteristically Sartrean" conflation of the individual and the collective subject.[14]

Finally, there is the matter of collective responsibility itself. With the exceptions of Fredric Jameson, Ronald Aronson, and Wilfrid Desan, no Sartrean commentators, to my knowledge, have addressed the matter, and even the remarks of the men just mentioned are cursory.[15] But the question has received rather extensive treatment in the analytic literature,[16] and Jaspers dealt with it in a book which influenced Sartre.[17] Here Sartre's contribution lies in his sophisticated concepts of the *practico-inert* and the *mediating Third*, pivotal ideas in his social theory and each accounting for a distinct kind of responsibility that is collective but distributed across the individual members. The explanatory force and novelty of Sartre's existential social philosophy lie chiefly with these two concepts. By accounting for two basic forms of collective identity and responsibility, they convey an understanding of class-being in its many facets, which should remain a permanent acquisition in the literature on the subject. Sartre's theory is not immune to criticism, as we shall see. But its superiority to orthodox Marxism and reductionist individualism lies in its ready incorporation of the morally responsible individual into the sociohistorical context.

My statement of the question derives from Lucien Goldmann and a challenge he leveled at me on the Columbia University campus the year before his death. If it is lack of a collective subject that prevents Sartre from being a genuine Marxist, then Sartre must arrive at a theory of collective responsibility without aid of a collective subject or else fashion a concept of collective subject that somehow preserves the moral responsibility that existentialists attach to individuals. In other words, our test case in social ethics rides on the back of a more basic issue in social ontology, and it is primarily at this level that I shall argue the matter. So the subtitle to this book could just as well have read: "A Study in Social Ontology."

The posthumous notes for Sartre's existentialist ethics, *Cahiers pour une morale,* 1947–48 (Paris: Gallimard, 1983; hereafter cited as CM) appeared as this book was in press. In general, these working papers reveal Sartre laboring under the limitations of the existentialist social model but aware of the socioeconomic context of the analyses of *Being and Nothingness.* He does not yet possess the praxis philosophy that his growing sense of objective possibility demands. The value of positive reciprocity (good faith, authentic love) is stressed and the role of an end-goal of history is emphasized—theses of my study. I refer to relevant passages in the footnotes.

At this point, before undertaking this study, some acknowledgments are in order. First I wish to thank Professor Robert D. Cumming, who encouraged me to pursue this topic and whose own research continues to serve as a model. I am grateful to Professor Hazel E. Barnes for continuous support of my work over the years. Next I should recognize grants from the National Endowment for the Humanities (#FT-00236-80-0693) and from the Emory University Faculty Research Committee. I appreciate the efforts of my colleague and then chairman, William Edwards, to obtain for me the leisure to write a complete draft of this text. Professors John McDermott, Arthur Danto, Michel Rybalka, Ronald Aronson, and especially William McBride have read and made helpful comments on the manuscript, though they incur no responsibility for its defects. Finally, I owe a debt to my typist, Mrs. Pat Redford, for her expert assistance in bringing this work to completion.

Contrary to the cliché, one *can* choose one's relatives, at least in the Sartrean sense. I have never regretted having "chosen" my brother John, to whom this book is dedicated.

PART ONE

Freedom and Responsibility in Sartrean Existentialism

The Existentialist Anthropology of *Being and Nothingness:* Freedoms and Responsibilities

Existentialist anthropos, even rid of its reference to a human nature, would remain an arrogant anthropos who would take himself as the unique souce of meaning.

Jean-Marie Benoist, *La Révolution structurale*

A distinctive feature of that family of thinkers called "existentialist" is their desire to humanize, indeed to "personalize," a world disenchanted by the rise of modern science and rendered impersonal by technology and the mass culture it fosters. As Socrates reputedly shifted the focus of speculation in ancient Greece from nature to man, the existentialists in our day have sought to draw attention away from the dehumanizing values of a positivist and mechanistic society toward the human individual and his distinctive way of being. What, for example, even in our post-Einsteinian age, is more commonly held to be objective and impersonal than space and time? Yet Heidegger, following a clue from Kierkegaard,[1] formulates a personal, qualitative concept of time (ekstatic temporality), to which Sartre joins Lewin's personal (hodological) space, drawing both into the realm of the specifically human.[2]

Within the limits of this personalizing viewpoint, each existentialist has fashioned a vision peculiarly his own. Sartre's focuses on the free, responsible agent who can make something out of what has been made of him. This thesis is a constant in Sartre's thinking and remains the touchstone of his humanism. In the halcyon days of existentialism it earned him recognition as *the* philosopher of individual freedom and responsibility. Yet this very distinction made his subsequent "conversion" to Marxism unlikely, indeed, scandalous. So let us begin our discussion of these problematic concepts with Sartre's own point of departure, the existentialist anthropology of *Being and Nothingness.*

A Phenomenology of Freedom

The "oppressive freedom" which haunts the characters in Sartre's novels, plays, and short stories of the late thirties and forties finds its theoretical

3

justification in his phenomenological writings of the same period. From his first significant philosophical publication, *The Transcendence of the Ego*,[3] to the extended descriptions of *Being and Nothingness,* Sartre proceeds to empty consciousness of whatever might resemble Cartesian substance, transcendental subject, or inner "content" of any kind. His conceptual tools for this clearing project are basically two. The first is a radical application of the principle of intentionality whereby consciousness is defined as uniquely relational to an object which is formally other than consciousness.[4] This leaves consciousness totally in-the-world, self-transparent, and without a shadowy side, whether id, superego, or even ego, where awareness and hence responsibility might be lessened. His second instrument is a conception of the specific "action" of consciousness as an internal negation (Sartre coins the word "nihilation" *néantisation*) of this object term, thereby accounting for both the difference and the inseparability of consciousness (the for-itself, *le pour-soi*) and its negated term (the in-itself, *l'en-soi*). This precludes any two-substance ontology while supporting a functional dualism of spontaneity-inertia which will remain a Sartrean hallmark. In sum, consciousness stands to the nonconscious as the empty to the full, as otherness to the same, as negation to the negated, and as the free to the nonfree. How Sartre arrives at these dichotomies using intentionality and "nihilation" is illustrated by his theory of the imagination.

The cardinal thesis of his important study *The Psychology of Imagination,*[5] published in 1940, is that the imagination is not a faculty of the mind but is consciousness itself "intending" the world in a specific way, namely, as unreal, as a nothingness. Hence we should speak of imaging consciousness rather than of some "power" of a mental substance. Indeed, the act of imaging is characterized by negativity, possibility, and lack—features which Sartre will later extend to consciousness in general.[6]

He establishes a close relation between imaging consciousness and freedom in a move from phenomenological description to Kantian "regressive" argument, typical of his general method, when he asks: "What must a consciousness be in order for it to possess the power to imagine?" (PI, 234). His conclusion, which summarizes the theory of that volume, is that consciousness must be able to "posit the world in its synthetic totality" (an anticipation of what he will term "totalization" in the *Critique*) and to "posit the world as a nothingness [*néant*] in relation to the image" (PI, 239–40; F, 353). He calls these actions "constitution" and "nihilation" (*néantisation*) respectively and concludes: "It is therefore enough to be able to posit reality as a synthetic whole in order to posit oneself as free from it; and this going-beyond [*dépassement*] is freedom itself, since it could not happen if consciousness were not free. Thus to

4

posit the world as world or to 'nihilate' [*néantir*] it is one and the same thing" (PI, 240; F, 354). In a series of rough equivalencies typical of many Sartrean "demonstrations," he links Husserlian world-constitution and Heideggerian transcendence (*dépassement*) with his own "nihilation" to reveal the nature of imaging consciousness: man can imagine "because he is transcendentally free" (PI, 243; F, 358). At this most basic level, therefore, man's freedom consists in his "nature" as world-constituting, world-nihilating, and world-surpassing.

In *Being and Nothingness* Sartre brings the relation between consciousness and freedom to full equivalence. "There is no difference," he urges, "between the being of man and his *being-free*" (BN, 25). To understand existentialist freedom at its most basic, we must consider these world-constituting, -surpassing, and -nihilating "activities" of consciousness as they are developed in *Being and Nothingness*.

The world-constituting activity, in the Husserlian thesis that consciousness brings it about that "there is" (*il y a*) a horizon of meanings which we call "the world," is an expression of freedom, because consciousness is "more" than that horizon and could constitute it otherwise. I shall call this power to constitute a circle of meanings *noetic* freedom. It figures centrally in Sartre's claims that we are responsible for our world, for our death, and even for (the meaning of) our birth. This is the freedom (and responsiblity) of the meaning-giving animal.[7] It is manifest likewise in the phenomenological *epoche* (Husserl's methodological "bracketing" of the question of the ontological status of the contents of our consciousness),[8] which Sartre takes to be a form of refusal and an act of freedom. Sartre makes the most radical claim for noetic freedom when he argues that consciousness constitutes the very motivating power of motives. In other words, it brings it about that motives motivate, a thesis whose implications I shall discuss later in this chapter.

The world-surpassing character of freedom (consciousness) will assume special importance for the politicized Sartre. He will call upon it to ground what he calls a "philosophy of revolution."[9] But here it is discussed primarily in the contexts of possibility and value, that nonbeing beyond being toward which one moves or can move. I mention this dimension of consciousness-freedom to indicate the complexity and conceptual wealth of Sartre's basic scheme.

It is primarily as "nihilating" that Sartre extends the properties of imaging consciousness to consciousness generally. He distinguishes three "primordial nihilations" which lie at the base of all expressions of negativity in human experience: interrogative consciousness, the prereflective *cogito,* and temporality. Each is a precision of existentialist freedom and expresses the negativity and otherness proper to consciousness. The first denotes our ability to question our world and the freedom which such a posture implies, especially in view of an ever possible negative reply.

The second nihilation, the prereflective *cogito*,[10] refers to our immediate experience of the world as well as to that implicit self-awareness which is a necessary condition for explicit consciousness of anything. Sartre designates that implicit self-awareness by the preposition "of" in parentheses. Thus explicit or thetic consciousness of anything entails implicit or nonthetic consciousness (of) self. Nihilation enters first-level awareness from different directions. It comes through the world itself via intentionality interpreted as a form of negation; this is how Sartre interprets the "otherness" inherent in all explicit knowing. Secondly, nihilation figures in the relation of consciousness to the empirical ego or self. The object of empirical psychology, Sartre insists, is not some ethereal subject at the back of experience but an object "in the world" almost like any other.[11] It follows that my explicit awareness of my empirical ego or self presumes a constitutive negation of that "quasi object," as does all my knowledge.[12] In other words (to introduce an infamous Sartrean locution) I am my self in the manner of not-being (i.e., nihilating) it. I am my self in the only way that consciousness can "be" anything. What seems paradoxical at first blush is merely the rigorous application of a more general thesis, that of the basic ontological structure of relations between consciousness and being (*en-soi*). It is likewise an expression of the Sartrean thesis that consciousness is nonself-identical, that the Leibnizian principle of identity applies to the in-itself but not to the for-itself. This is the meaning of Sartrean consciousness as "otherness." I shall consider the implications of this aspect of nihilating consciousness later in the chapter.

The third primordial nihilation of consciousness-freedom is temporality. Sartre accepts Heidegger's distinction between quantitative clock time and the ekstatic temporality or lived time that constitutes the very existence of human reality. Man exists or literally "stands out" from his self in each of three temporal dimensions: the past as facticity or "*no* longer," the future as possibility or "*not* yet," and the present as "presence-to but *not* identity with" self and world. The ground of the negative dimension which each temporal "ekstasis" carries is the nihilating character of consciousness itself.

The relation between the for-itself's nonidentity and its inherent temporality warrants Sartre's introduction of another neologism, "*est été*," literally, "is been," to characterize that nothingness (*rien*) at the heart of consciousness. An adequate translation is difficult.[13] But the oddity of the expression jars us into recognizing that consciousness, like Zeno's arrow, "is-not" at any point on its temporal trajectory. It is its past in the manner of not-being it, again the mode of being proper to Sartrean consciousness.

The goal of this first step in our tour of existential anthropology has been to uncover the root concept of freedom in Sartrean existentialism, namely, nihilating freedom, or freedom of nonidentity, as it might also be called. As the foregoing has made clear, this is not merely a kind of deep-level negative freedom, e.g., freedom from unconscious drives, from habit, or from ego. Rather, freedom as nihilation and nonself-identity constitutes the ontological basis for Sartre's claim that consciousness is "empty" of all "contents" (intentionality being the epistemic basis of that claim) and likewise is the immediate implication of the basic thesis that consciousness is the internal negation of the nonconscious, that it is a no-thingness.

Before pursuing the related issues of choice, self-presence, and responsibility in Sartrean anthropology, let me summarize my discussion of existentialist freedom thus far.

Human reality, the "everyman" of *Being and Nothingness,* is world-constituting, world-surpassing, and world-nihilating. These are extensionally equivalent and mutually implicative terms for Sartre. They are expressions of that ontological freedom which human reality is (not "has"). Because man is free in this ontological sense, he can be called to freedom in more mundane (ontic) senses. This will remain a basic premise of Sartre's later thought, especially when he turns to political polemics.

As world-constituting or meaning-giving, Sartrean consciousness is noetically free. It brings it about that "there is" (*il y a*) a world, not only in the descriptive sense but likewise in the evaluative sense of conferring on motives their motivating character.

As world-surpassing or always "more" than its circumstances, consciousness is transcendentally free. It transcends (*dépasse*) whatever conditions (facticity) may constitute its situation.[14]

Finally, as world-nihilating or always "other" than its world, its self, or other selves, consciousness is freedom of nihilation or nonself-identity. Human reality is a "being of distances," as Heidegger would phrase it, including that inner distance which we shall examine shortly as presence-to-self. This pervasive nihilating freedom is typically existentialist. It grounds the three primary nihilations of questioning, first-level awareness, and temporality. It is the expression of the fundamental fact of Sartrean ontology, namely, that the for-itself is the internal negation of the in-itself. Hence, it is the most basic form of ontological freedom: "nihilation [*néantisation*] is precisely the being of freedom" (BN, 443; F, 519).

Freedom, Spontaneity, and Original Choice

It is impossible to understand Sartre's notion of ontological freedom without grasping his concomitant concept of original choice. "Freedom" in its common usage implies "choice," and so it does for Sartre. But just as ontological freedom with its constitution, transcendence, and threefold nihilation is not the ordinary understanding of "freedom," so original choice, which Sartre takes to be coterminous with ontological freedom, is not the usual meaning of "choice."

Choice commonly assumes preexisting alternatives, at least the option of not choosing. For Sartre, this is true only at the second, reflective level of consciousness. There he allows the usual deliberation and acts of will normally ascribed to an empirical self. But his concern is with original choice, with that which constitutes the criteria according to which we deliberate and decide at the second level; in other words, with the "fundamental project" of popular existentialism. Clearly, original choice is a function of prereflective consciousness-freedom as world-constituting. What it adds to the latter concept is the notions of value-establishment and exclusion.

Sartre agrees with Hume, Kant, and other defenders of the fact/value dichotomy that no factual state of affairs can by itself ever motivate choice or action. But he rejects the "irrationalism" often attributed to him as a result. Defending a position which has often been compared to that of the analytical philosopher R. M. Hare,[15] Sartre argues that original choice is not arbitrary; every action is intentional and so has a meaning-direction (the twofold translation of *sens*). Original choice is not a random, purposeless event like the "clinamen" of Epicurus. To be sure, it is criterion-constituting and hence is without antecedent reason or necessity. But Sartre's claim is that any appeal to prior reasons or motives conceals a more basic "choice" of such standards beforehand. The decision to deliberate about a proposed course of action rather than simply rushing into the breach, for example, presupposes the prior choice of being "rational" in the first place. "When I deliberate," as he summarizes in a well-known remark, "the chips are down." When the will intervenes, it is merely for the purpose of "making the announcement" (BN, 451)

As Sartre sees it, his position rests midway between libertarianism and determinism. The libertarians, who defend basic choice without a motive, fall into the absurdity of positing an intentional (i.e., conscious) act without an intention (see BN, 450ff.). Sartre argues that every action is a complex of reason/motive (*motif/mobile*)-intention-act-end.[16] To extract one aspect without making implicit reference to the others is to falsify the account. But he avoids psychological determinism (the need to follow the "strongest" motive) by making end-value the correlate of constituting consciousness, seeing reason as the means to this end, and relegating motive to the status of a reflective phenomenon (of) which we are non-thetically aware in every prereflective "choice" of an end-value. The novelty of this response to a perennial philosophical question lies once more in the uniqueness of Sartrean consciousness. It gains ready application in the existential "hermeneutic" of Sartre's biographies which "read" an agent's sustaining project-end through the motives, reasons and actions that reveal it.

Besides value-establishment, the concept of original choice adds to world-constitution the notion of exclusion. We noted how Sartre denied that original choice was selection from preexisting alternatives. "There are" no alternatives in the technical sense of *il y a* prior to the original upsurge of consciousness. Yet he respects the intuition that choice involves selection when he explains that project or original choice entails the exclusion of other projects, values, criteria and the like. This is a translation into the language of choice of Spinoza's dictum, *omnis determinatio est negatio*. Typically, Sartre reads it as a sign of our finitude: "Every choice . . . presupposes elimination and selection [in the constitutive sense, for original choice]; every choice is a choice of finitude" (BN, 495). Years later he will still insist that existence insofar as it "projects us across a field of possibilities, some of which we realize to the exclusion of others," is what we call choice or freedom.[17]

Original choice is as unique as Sartrean consciousness itself. He reminds us of this by another of his rough equivalences: "One must be conscious in order to choose and must choose in order to be conscious. Choice and consciousness are one and the same thing" (BN, 462). That is why the neologisms which he feels constrained to coin for consciousness can equally describe original choice. Such choice, for example, is obviously a "nihilation" of the in-itself both by its establishment of values or ends (as nonbeing or lack) and by its exclusion of other projects and their attendant possibilities. As nihilation, original choice is the concomitant awareness that the choice "could have been otherwise." Sartre calls this "the feeling of unjustifiability" (BN, 480). It is an aspect of the famous nausea which Sartre's Roquentin felt in the novel by that name.

"Thus the fundamental act of freedom is discovered," Sartre announces. "This constantly renewed act is not distinct from my being; it is choice of myself in the world and by the same token it is a discovery of the world" (BN, 461). We have seen how original choice is constitutive of the world. But it is also "choice of self." So we must next review the problematic Sartrean self.

Presence-to-Self

"Man is free because he is not a self but a presence-to-self' (BN, 440; F, 516). This deceptively simple remark distills the essence of Sartre's ex-

9

istentialist anthropology and can serve as a conceptual bridge from the question of freedom to that of responsiblity in *Being and Nothingness*.

We know how intent Sartre is on "emptying" consciousness of any substance, content, or even inner life.[18] What remains from this clearing project is not a lunar landscape but what might best be termed a "productive void," a dynamic inner distance which reveals nihilation and otherness at the very center of consciousness. Of course, we use "center" metaphorically because Sartrean consciousness has neither center nor "inside," as his essay on intentionality makes graphically clear. To illustrate this, Sartre chooses the striking metaphor of a play of mirrors. The image is that of a reflection reflecting a reflection . . . in endless repetition—an example of what Hegel called the "bad" infinite precisely because it precluded synthesis of any kind.[19]

Sartre's basic thesis that the for-itself is an exception to the ontological principle of identity, namely, that something must be what it is and not another thing, binds him to a host of paradoxical consequences which he courageously pursues for the sake of bringing home the fact that consciousness is a reality sui generis. Not the least of these conclusions is that human reality is presence-to-self.

Traditionally, the ego or self has served three principal functions in the philosophical literature: (1) ontological unifier, or substance; (2) that of ultimate agent, or subject; (3) center of moral ascriptions, or person. Since Sartre has bifurcated reality by limiting applicability of the principle of identity to being-in-itself, the presence-to-itself as conscious cannot be an identity. Yet it must constitute more than a mere extrinsic unity, lest it collapse into senseless flux—at best, the Humean "bundles" to which Sartre's concept has been erroneously compared. Sartre must navigate between these shoals as he brings his peculiar concept of presence-to-self to bear on these traditional functions of the self.

1. The unity of consciousness (for-itself), as we have seen, comes not from any underlying substance or self, but from the original choice or project by which it nihilates its facticity (it is the nihilation of *this* being-in-itself and not of another).

Of course, Sartre hasn't escaped the standard answer to the problem of individuation entirely, for *this* en-soi is such, in at least a major sense, because it is individuated already. Commonly, that individuation is attributed to space-time or to "matter." But Sartre, we know, has "personalized" the former and he relegates the latter to the status of the purely inert. Yet he cannot have it both ways, though he tries valiantly to do so, at least until introducing the "practico-inert" in the *Critique*. Either this en-soi individualizes a project because it is *this* en-soi and not another, or it is this en-soi and not another precisely because it is correlative to

10

this project and not another, in which case the project is entirely responsible for individuating not only me and my world, but every item in it—a total denial of what I shall later discuss as "objective possibility."[20] The root of Sartre's difficulty lies in his inability to distinguish the given from the taken in any particular case. Although he often trades on this ambiguity, as in his use of the concept of situation, the problem is endemic to his system as it is to most systems spawned from philosophical idealism, and it remains unresolved throughout his career.

But our analysis need not stop here, for original choice is choice of self and of world. As "choice" of self, consciousness must be other-than-self. This otherness follows likewise from the essential intentionality of consciousness (it always "intends" an other) as well as from Sartre's concept of first-level awareness as nonthetic consciousness (of) self. His term, "presence-to-self," is supposed to capture this "immanent otherness," as we might call it. "All presence-to implies duality," Sartre explains, "and at least virtual separation" (BN, 77; F, 119).[21]

Note well how Sartre "resolves" the issue of the immanent unity-otherness of consciousness, because it anticipates and basically accounts for his subsequent treatment of the problem of unity-otherness in the group. If consciousness is nonself-identity, presence-to-self as a precision of this feature is a "perpetual, unstable equilibrium" between identity, as absolute cohesion without a trace of diversity, and unity, as some extrinsic collection of multiplicity. If I can betray others, as Sartre will later insist apropos of the pledged group, it is because I am "other" to my very self. In words that will be echoed in his discussion of group unity, Sartre concludes that presence-to-self is "not a unity which contains a duality, not a synthesis which surpasses and lifts up the abstract moments of the thesis and of the anti-thesis, but a duality which *is* a unity, a reflection [*reflet*] which *is* its own reflecting [*réflection*]" (BN, 76).

Clearly, what Sartre intends by "reflection" at this (paradoxically *pre*reflective) level is not the traditional "bending back" of introspective psychology but the kind of self-reference proper to consciousness which Kant and others have tried to capture in the expression, "the 'I think' which must accompany all my representations." He implies this when he refers to the "nullifying characteristic of existing for a witness, although the witness for which consciousness exists is itself" (BN, 74). Sartre's point is that in our most arrested moments of awareness, we are somewhat detached from (not identical with) ourselves. The most sincere belief, for example, is consciousness (of) belief and, as such, "troubled" (*troublée*) (BN, 75; F, 118).

Here lies the deepest root of Sartre's concept of bad faith. At this point it is sufficient that we grasp the link which Sartre forges between presence-to-self and ontological freedom. The former is the most perfect expression of the later as nihilation. It reveals the fact that consciousness not only nihilates the world as it constitutes and surpasses it, but that, in the process, it also nihilates itself (*se néantise*) (BN, 239; F, 295).

2. How does Sartre's presence-to-self fill the traditional role of ultimate agent or subject, which philosophy has assigned to the self? We know that *The Transcendence of the Ego* had reduced the ego to the status of ideal term of actions ascribed to the empirical self.[22] But this does not mean that Sartre has emptied consciousness of subjectivity. Indeed, he will later see his mission to Marxism precisely as an effort to defend the place of the subject from the inroads of "economism."[23] He simply removes the substance (en-soi) from subjectivity and is left with the "immanence of self to itself" (BN, lvii; F, 24). This, of course, is yet another description of prereflective consciousness as presence-to-self. But it adds the distinctive note of a *limit* to reflective withdrawal. For Sartre describes immanence as "the smallest recoil [*recul*] which can be made from self to itself" (BN, lxv; F, 32). In other words, "subjectivity" is another word for the impossibility of man's being an object for himself: "I am the one who cannot be an object for myself" (BN, 241).[24] But we should not read Sartre's "subject which cannot become an object" as a transcendental ego in the manner of Kant or Husserl, who used similar formulas, for he explicitly excludes the self-identity which such an ego requires. We are left with a revolving self-nihilation as Sartre's "ultimate subject."[25]

3. What is the definition of person, Sartre asks, if not "a free relationship to self?" (BN 104; F, 148). This free relationship is a self-nihilation whereby consciousness resists being grasped as a finished totality. The self so resisted is the ideal limit to the reflection-of-reflections merry-go-round, i.e., conscious self-identity. By one and the same reflective act, I posit the empirical ego and grasp the futility of trying to coincide with it. Consciousness "makes itself personal" by this pure, nihilating movement of reflection. Sartre argues that "what confers personal existence on a being is not the possession of an Ego—which is only the sign of personality— but it is the fact that the being exists for itself as a presence-to-self" (BN, 103).[26] So the inner distance proper to consciousness is a free, personalizing relationship to self as ideal term.

Sartre completes his complex analysis of personhood by moving from presence-to-self to its complement, what he calls the "circuit of selfness."[27] He is intent on showing that "myness" (*moïté*) permeates prereflective awareness. Fundamental choice is simultaneously "choice" of self and of world. If "self" is that ideal of conscious self-coincidence, "world" is the corresponding sum of possibilities and obstacles on the way to "cloture" as self or ultimate value. Sartre describes "world" in this context as "the totality of beings in so far as they exist within the compass of selfness" (BN, 104).[28] Hearkening back to his concept of consciousness as world-surpassing and joining this to the self as value, Sartre characterizes world as "that which human reality surpasses [dépasse] toward the self" (BN, 104; F, 148).

So the Sartrean world is not only humanized, it is personalized: *I have the kind of world which corresponds to the person I am*—always in the sense of not-being that person. Sartre summarizes the correlativity of these concepts succinctly: "Without the world, there is no selfness, no person; without selfness, without the person, there is no world" (BN, 104).

A consequence of major significance follows from the foregoing analysis of presence-to-self. If I "choose" the world, if it is thoroughly "mine," I am by the same token responsible for that world in the senses now to be discussed. So presence-to-self is not only the source of freedom in Sartrean existentialism, it is the basis of responsibility as well. We have discovered the link between freedom and responsibility in Sartrean anthropology: Man is responsible because he is not a self but a presence-to-self.

The Spectrum of Responsibilities

In his early essay on the emotions, Sartre voiced what was to become a commonplace in popular existentialism: "For human reality, to exist is always to assume its being; that is, to be responsible for it instead of receiving it from outside like a stone" (EMO, 12). Our survey of the philosophical anthropology which Sartre constructs to support this claim has revealed that the basic terms "freedom" and "choice," features of human reality which commonly imply "responsibility," are not being used in their usual (ontic) senses. So we can expect to find a corresponding concept of ontological or original responsibility. In fact, the basic concept generates several derivatives which I shall briefly review.

The only definition of "responsibility" that Sartre ever ventures is "consciousness (of) being the incontestable author of an event or of an object" (BN, 553). We may call this the authorship concept and take it as the basis for his other uses of the term. As the parentheses in the definition indicate, it is a characteristic of *pre*reflective consciousness. Hence it is prior to reflection, decision, and will but is simultaneous with original freedom and fundamental choice. We are responsible for deciding to deliberate. As with freedom and choice, "prereflective responsibility" is a presupposition of existential psychoanalysis. Much of what Freud buried in the unconscious, Sartre stores in the prereflective *cogito,* where

13

responsibility is preserved for revelation by the proper hermeneutic. Indeed, it constitutes a pervasive responsibility which leads us to expect it in every corner of the Sartrean world.[29] As pervasive, such responsibility serves as a kind of "moral glue," binding Sartre's world in a manner not unlike the unifying function of Heideggerian care (*Sorge*).

The authorship concept underscores what recent responsibility theorists call "imputability." The imputed situation is held to be dependent on a subject in a significant manner. But in Sartre's usage, imputability is not the result of causing something (causality being limited to natural processes, which Sartre tends to ignore); rather, it is a function of "choice" and of various more specific forms of action. Consequently, the range of imputability is simply staggering: it extends to all that I am or do, to the meaning (*sens*) of what others do, and indeed to the very fact that "there is" a world at all. Yet this claim is not so astounding when read in light of his theory of consciousness-freedom as world-constituting.[30]

There is another dimension to "responsibility," namely, accountability or liability for praise or blame, which might seem to be excluded by Sartre's authorship use.[31] Imputability and accountability, no doubt, are distinct uses of "responsibility" and can be separated as, for example, when a parent is held responsible (accountable) for the effects of his child's actions (imputability). Common usage regularly conflates these two meanings. But despite appearances, Sartre's definition does not overlook accountability. It is assumed, for example, by his remarks about the anguish of responsibility.

But it is especially by choosing "authorship" in place of "causality" that Sartre reserves a broadly moral sense for the term "responsibility." This important claim follows from at least four considerations. First, authorship is a properly human relationship; it does not obtain among physical or apparently even among merely biological entities. Second, as a phenomenon of the prereflective cogito, basic responsibility presupposes ontological freedom and original choice. Third, it is by that same token value-constituting. Whatever we "author" is always done under the aegis of our fundamental project which, in turn, is our way of choosing our ideal self. As Sartre will later argue explicitly, this choice of self is choice of an image of what we believe every person *should* be.[32] Finally, responsibility is broadly moral because it is *co*constitutive of personhood along with selfness and world. The "myness" of the world and of every feature in it implies that I am responsible (answerable) for it. Sartre underscores this by a challenging claim made in occupied France in 1943: "We have the war we deserve" (BN, 555).[33] As with ontological freedom, with which responsibility now seems coterminous, Sartre concludes that "I am condemned to be wholly responsible for myself" (BN, 556).

I refer to authorship responsibility as "broadly" moral to distinguish it from specific ethical judgments which it will be called on to justify at the ontic (everyday) level. Thus, I can be urged to "assume" responsibility for a state of affairs by my conduct in the world precisely because I am responsible in the ontological sense. Sartre's implicit invitations to good faith can thus be read as so many applications of the ancient moral adage: "Become what you are!"

Finally, by speaking of "incontestable" authorship, Sartre is appealing to the well-known existentialist absence of excuses: "The peculiar character of human reality is that it is without excuse" (BN, 555). This contradicts the claim of H. L. A. Hart that such words as "responsible" and "obligation" are defeasible, i.e., that they are by nature contestable.[34] On that view, an agent would be responsible as long as the ascription had not been successfully contested. But Sartre's "incontestable" means that responsibility can never allow excuses and hence that it cannot admit of degrees. He occasionally refers to this responsibility as absolute (see BN, 554). We have obviously come a long way from the ordinary meaning of "responsibility."

Given the authorship concept as fundamental, its derivatives can be briefly summarized. The first and most immediate of these is what I shall call noetic responsibility, the authorship of meanings. Corresponding to the noetic freedom discussed earlier, its limit, here as there, is Sartrean consciousness itself. It is as noetic that Sartrean responsibility attains the extreme scope mentioned above.

But these "meanings" are not merely cognitive. They include values and ends-in-view, to borrow an apt Deweyism. The "choice" of meanings like that of world or self is a practical undertaking which occurs in the context of original choice. The circuit of selfness constitutes the world as a field of action.

The claim that everything in the world assumes the meaning which I choose to give it commits Sartre to the very idealist notion of freedom (and responsibility) that he will criticize three years later as being "fundamentally reducible to a more or less clear affirmation of the autonomy of thought" (MR, 237). The vast extent of noetic freedom and responsibility is purchased at the price of being limited to the realm of consciousness—scarcely a promising position for a future Marxist.

Sartre sometimes uses "responsibility" in what we may call a dispositional sense, as "power to be" or "to make to be." Existentialist anthropos is a creature of the possible. The consciousness-freedom which makes him "more" than the actual entails responsibility for the "can be" as well as for the "already is." This form figures chiefly in Sartre's subsequent ascriptions of responsibility to those who "would have done X,

15

if only they had had the opportunity."[35]

We are arriving at more commonplace, ontic uses of "responsibility" than the noetic. Often Sartre considers a person responsible only if he "could have done otherwise," a standard libertarian expression. Responsibility in this sense is a form of self-determination (see BN, 453–54).[36] Such is his notorious example of someone "giving in" under sadistic torture: "The abjuration remains *free*. . . . He has *determined* the moment at which the pain became unbearable. The proof of this is the fact that he will live out his abjuration in remorse and shame. Thus he is entirely responsible for it" (BN, 403). Though Sartre will later renounce this simplistic assessment of the tortured person's condition, at this point he is virtually identifying freedom-responsibility with self-determination or choice.

True to the existentialists' regard for the emotions as revelatory of our world, Sartre notes that consciousness of choosing ourselves "is expressed by the twofold 'feeling' of anguish and responsibility. Anguish, abandonment, responsibility . . . constitute the *quality* of our consciousness in so far as this is pure and simple freedom" (BN, 464). This feeling of responsibility is a specific way of apprehending the world, namely, as mine, as incontestably dependent upon my sustaining choice.

To complete my survey, I should mention Sartre's appropriative use of "responsibility" when he describes it as something to be accepted authentically or fled from in bad faith.[37] Appropriative responsibility is a value to be assumed and enhanced. In Part II we shall observe it function in his popular exhortations of the public to assume a responsibility which de facto is theirs already.

Freedom and Responsibility as Correlatives

Our initial foray into Sartre's existential anthropology has demonstrated that, for him, freedom and responsibility are correlative terms in the strict sense that they imply each other. If and inasmuch as the for-itself is free, it must be responsible; the extent of its responsibility is precisely that of its freedom.

The reason for this relationship of mutual implication between freedom and responsibility lies in the fact that each is conceivable as an alternative description of consciousness itself. The upshot of Sartre's phenomenological descriptions and regressive arguments surveyed in this chapter is that "responsibility" means "consciousness as authorship" and that "freedom" signifies "consciousness as nihilating choice." What mediates the extensional equivalence of these two terms, enabling us to see them as alternative views of the same reality, is Sartre's theory of human reality as presence-to-self.

But this very bridge which allowed us to pass from freedom to responsibility and back, namely, the Sartrean concept of person as comprising presence-to-self, selfness, and world, seems to erect a barricade to any theory of collective responsibility. For the personal responsibility which pervades the world as "myness" (*moïté*) appears to resist collective responsibility understood as in some sense requiring "ourness." So perhaps Lucien Goldmann is correct. This first survey of Sartre's existentialist anthropology is not very promising for a coherent social philosophy. But before drawing a final conclusion, let us first examine some commonly neglected social aspects of Sartre's admittedly individualist masterpiece.

two

The Existentialist Anthropology of
Being and Nothingness
The Social Dimension

Each one [of Giacometti's sculptures] faces us with this truth: man does not exist first in order to be seen afterwards; rather, he is the being whose essence is to exist for others.

Situations, 3:302

Since a number of his critics insist that Sartre never overcomes the limitations of the "social" ontology of *Being and Nothingness,* we must examine the social doctrine of that existentialist classic. Whatever social theory we may expect to find there will be a dimension of what Sartre terms "being-for-others" (*l'être-pour-autrui*). He claims it is as fundamental as being-in-itself or being-for-itself and devotes fully a quarter of the text to its analysis. In its collective aspect, being-for-others has two foci, the "Us" and the "We." They, along with being-in-situation and the phenomena of techniques and collectivities, which accompany it, constitute the rudiments of a "social" theory in *Being and Nothingness.* The result, though less than adequate to our social experience, is more than Sartre is commonly given credit for. It will be subsumed, not rejected, in his later thought.

Being-for-Others

As Durkheim had warranted the infant enterprise of sociology by appeal to a unique subject matter properly its own, namely, the realm of "social facts,"[1] so Sartre justifies his turn to the social in *Being and Nothingness* by pointing to (in the phenomenological sense of "making evident") a specific dimension of human existence, being-for-others.[2] But how is this realm to be made evident? It stands or falls with the existence of other subjects. Aware of the weakness of analogical arguments for other minds, and suspicious of appeals to "empathy" made by his predecessors in the phenomenological movement, Sartre hits upon his well-known shame-experience as immediate, apodictic evidence of the other as subject: "I experience the Other's infinite freedom" (BN, 270). The details of his classic phenomenological description have been analyzed many times and

18

need not detain us here.³ It turns on being-seen-by-the-other (*le regard*) as an irreducible fact, the condition for the possibility of which is a "preontological comprehension" of the other's existence which renders it as certain to me as my own (see BN, 251). Once more, phenomenological description is being buttressed by "regressive" argument.

The expression "preontological comprehension" denotes my awareness of the other as a real or potential term in the looking/looked-at relationship which grounds all interpersonal relations in *Being and Nothingness*. "My certainty of the Other's existence is independent of these experiences [of individual others] and is . . . that which makes them possible" (BN, 280). It is this *original presence* of the other subject in general that makes the actual presence of this particular subject possible and, when it occurs, certain.⁴ "It is in relation to every living man," Sartre writes, "that every human reality is present or absent on the basis of an original presence. This original presence can have meaning only as a being-looked-at or as a being-looking-at; that is, according to whether the Other is an object for me or whether I myself am an object-for-the-Other" (BN, 279–80). Sartre takes this to be a "prenumerical" presence of the Other. But far from being a mere abstraction, it serves as the basis for our encounters with other individual subjects. In fact, he argues that "we do not apprehend a plural look." When I am performing before an audience, for example, I am aware of this prenumerical Other. But if I were to try to grasp it like some concrete, individualized being with a collective consciousness, it would decompose into a plurality of heads and eyes (BN, 282).

These remarks immediately introduce two major theses from Sartre's early social theory. The first is his claim that the basis of our knowledge of other subjects and, by implication, the fundamental interpersonal relation, is the looking/looked-at dyad. I shall call this his *existentialist model* of society. The remainder of this chapter will consist in working out the theoretical implications of this model.

His second substantial claim is that we do not grasp a plural look. He goes on immediately to conclude that this renders a collective consciousness impossible, a position which he will maintain rather consistently for the rest of his career. This claim is important for the social ontology, such as it is, that he is constructing at this point, for it helps explain his subsequent thesis that the We is a mere psychological phenomenon whereas the Us enjoys ontological status. "We" can be seen, he is arguing in effect, but only "I" can see, and *le regard* is the foundation of all interpersonal relations.

Since the ground of the interpersonal is the looking/looked-at relationship, another necessary condition for shame-consciousness is my embodied state. All my concrete relations with the Other are functions of the attitude I adopt toward my objectivity, my "outside" as known by another. I may either transcend or incorporate the Other's original transcendence. But in either case I must preserve the Other's freedom-subjectivity-transcendence; for, without it, the entire interpersonal relationship would collapse into one of for-itself and in-itself; in other words, it would spell the end of the "social."

Sartre illustrates this struggle of freedoms in his description of the sadomasochistic relations that lie at the heart of all interpersonal exchanges. His conclusion, which paints this theory in a particularly Hobbesian hue, is that "conflict is the original meaning of being-for-others" (BN, 364). In fact, he epitomizes the social relations of *Being and Nothingness* when he describes the project of being loved as "pure engagement without reciprocity" (BN, 375). We shall see that his discovery of mediated reciprocity marks a quantum leap in Sartre's social ontology.[5]

Because Sartre will later attempt to "historicize" these descriptions,[6] it is significant that the reasons offered in *Being and Nothingness* for the conflictive nature of interpersonal relations are ontological, not historical or socioeconomic. The first reason follows from the nature of Sartrean consciousness as internal negation of the in-itself. This nihilation applies equally to the object status conferred on it by the Other's look (original presence). My selfness is reenforced by the negation of my being-for-others, which I am, as always, in the manner of not-being it. So my selfness is intensified, for example, by the pride or shame with which I live my being-for-others (see BN, 289.)[7]

Second, the original contingency of the for-others relationship, depending on the brute facticity of the Other's upsurge, precludes any synthesis of the respective negations themselves, i.e., between the Other's negation and mine (see BN, 365). Another may suddenly appear on the scene or disappear, changing everything. These nihilations cannot be stabilized, much less subsumed.[8]

Contingency and internal negation, therefore, set the inner limit to possible unity within the social ontology of *Being and Nothingness*. Unity among for-itselfs in a common transcendence is impossible in principle because such an assimilation "would necessarily involve the disappearance of otherness in the Other" (BN, 366). At this point he believes that common transcendence (community) and individuality (plurality) are mutually exclusive. "We are always . . . in a state of instability in relation to the Other. We pursue the impossible ideal of the simultaneous apprehension of his freedom and of his objectivity." But we can never achieve equality, Sartre argues, "the plane where the recognition of the Other's freedom would involve the Other's recognition of our freedom" (BN,

408). Let us call this the *dilemma of equality*. It is important to note that Sartre recognizes this particular difficulty in his own social ontology at this stage. For we shall see him claiming to have achieved just this positive reciprocity of freedoms (equality) when he introduces the group-in-fusion in the *Critique*.

What we might term the Sartrean schism spreads from my individual life (presence-to-self) to my basic relations with others, making any true collective action ("common transcendence" in the words of BN) a futile ideal. As the would-be collective totality of self and other, Sartre offers us a kind of "shattered totality, always elsewhere, always at a distance, never in itself, but always maintained in being by the perpetual explosion of this totality" (BN, 300); a graphic anticipation of that social unit called the "collective" (*le collectif*) in the *Critique!* Such is the peak of social integration in *Being and Nothingness*.

It should now be evident that the fundamental difficulty in Sartre's social ontology at this stage, one which he never really faces up to, arises from the fact that the very conditions which generate interpersonal relations in *Being and Nothingness*, namely, internal negation and embodiedness, seem to preclude the possibility of positive mutuality among for-itselfs, and this for ontological reasons, not merely because of historical exigencies. He criticizes Heidegger for taking *Mitsein* as original and individual existence as derivative, when the opposite should be the case (see BN, 427–28). In Sartre's view, Heidegger overlooks the basic element of opposition among individuals which preserves their individuality. But Sartre thereby answers one excess with another, for he reduces the "We" (Heidegger's *Mitsein*) to merely psychological status. In so doing, I wish to argue, Sartre's existentialist classic affords us an ontology of the interpersonal, but not of the social properly speaking.

Mitsein and the "We"

The strengths and weaknesses of Sartre's would-be social ontology in *Being and Nothingness* are summarized in his claim that the We is not original but derivative: "The being-for-others precedes and founds the being-with-others" (BN, 414). This indicates that whatever social philosophy he attempts will be fundamentally an application of the dyadic relation, looking/looked-at, which I termed the "existentialist" social model.

Now such dyadic relations, while ideal for grounding the psychological contrasts and interpersonal conflicts characteristic of Sartre's existentialist writings generally, are quite incapable of supporting the qualitatively richer relations which Durkheim denotes by the expression, "social fact." Such phenomena as institutions with their statuses and roles, languages

21

with their impersonal rules and structures, and collective actions such as wars, treaties, and the rest, are scarcely reducible to functions of the looking/looked-at relationship. As Georg Simmel pointed out in his seminal study of quantitative aspects of the group, it is the essential feature of dyadic relations to preclude any superpersonal unit,[9] the very feature that characterizes a social fact for Durkheim. Indeed, he notes that "abandonment of absolute contrasts" is precisely what distinguishes the triad from the dyad in the social realm.[10] It is the inability of the dyadic relation to account for the mediating function upon which social facts are based that warrants our calling them interpersonal and not social, properly speaking. This will become increasingly evident as we now begin our analysis of the Us and the We in *Being and Nothingness*.

The Us

Sartre's point of departure for his brief excursion into social ontology in *Being and Nothingness* is, as we should expect, original presence—that prereflective awareness that each of us has of the existence of an unnumbered Other. As Sartre observes, my relation to the Other occurs "on the infinite ground of *my* relation and of *his* relation to *all Others;* that is, to the quasi-totality of consciousnesses" (BN, 415). He believes that this background is both necessary and, with the appearance of the Third, sufficient for me to experience myself and another as objects for yet another. Like the original looking/looked-at phenomenon, the Us experience is immediate and unique: our mutual relationship is itself modified by the advent of the Third. I shall call this function of the Third "objectifying" or "alienating," since it objectifies us and deadens our possibilities by removing their meaning (*sens*) from our total control.[11]

But the Third operates as such only in relation to a duality (self-other). What is the nature of this duality? Generically, of course, it too is a form of being-for-others, a type of looking/looked-at relation. But that will not suffice to account for the experience of the Us. For the Third's gaze must fix and objectify not me and then another, but both together; and more important, that "togetherness" must be experienced and assumed by us. The problem is to account for this mutuality.

Sartre finds his answer in what he calls an "objective situation form" of solidarity and equivalence with the other which I experience in the presence of the Third. The Us is discovered only by my *assuming* responsibility for a situation that includes responsibility for the other. But why should I assume this revealing responsibility in the first place? Sartre attributes the need to assume *common* responsibility to "the internal reciprocity of the situation" (BN, 418). True to the dilemma of equality, the situation is one of equivalence in the eyes of the Third, not of equality in each other's eyes: "I am fighting you" and "you are fighting me" become, in the presence of the Third, "we are fighting each other" (see BN, 418).

In fact, Sartre seems to be hedging on the purely extrinsic unity of the Us. What of that "internal reciprocity of the situation" just mentioned? Here we touch a factor which will lead Sartre to modify what at this point is a basically anti-Marxist social ontology. On the one hand, he claims that every human situation is felt as Us as soon as the Third appears. This seems to be a corollary to his theory of original presence. But, on the other hand, he admits that some occupations, e.g., assembly-line work and marching in columns, are especially apt to generate the Us experience. Consider how this uncertainty affects his understanding of class consciousness.

He interprets class consciousness as "the assuming of a particular 'us' on the occasion of a collective situation more plainly structured than usual" (BN, 420). Because Sartre still ignores the crucial concept of objective possibility,[12] he does not elaborate on the structure of this "collective situation" except to characterize it vaguely as "economic or political" (BN, 420) and to situate the oppressive and oppressed classes in the categories of the looking and the looked-at respectively. His argument is that these "objective" considerations, for example, economic exploitation, merely constitute the facticity of our situation and that I experience our condition as alienated *only* in the face of the Third (see BN, 421). This is a powerful insight into social psychology, but it fails to capture the ontological reality of socioeconomic class, a topic he will treat at length in the *Critique*. Class being is an objective limitation of a person's possibilities. Whether it is a matter of education, geographic or economic mobility, or health care, it makes a difference whether one is an owner, a manager, or a daylaborer. But Sartre's existentialist social model leads him to regard the facticity of the collective condition, the privilege of one class, for example, or the misery of another, as having merely "significative value" for the individual class member; it signifies the relative independence of the Third (see BN, 421).

We encounter another limit to his existentialist social model in Sartre's suggested means of liberating the oppressed class: the assumption of the Us in a class situation "implies . . . the project of freeing the whole 'us' from the object-state by transforming it into a We" (BN, 422). This repeats his earlier turning of the tables in the looking/looked-at relationship but presumes that another must assume the alienated position; the possible disalienation of everyone is not even suggested. So the experience of the Us, Sartre concludes, "presupposes that of being-for-others, of which it is only a more complex modality" (BN, 421).

23

The We

A leading characteristic of Sartre's social ontology at this time and a serious obstacle to his future philosophical Marxism is the ontological asymmetry which he maintains between the Us and the We. Whereas the former is as real as the for-others of which it is a mode, the latter is "a purely subjective experience (*Erlebnis*)" (BN, 429).[13]

The inadequacy of so constricting the We is another reason why his social model breaks down. Again, the issue centers on those factors which account for the mutuality of the We relationship. Are they merely psychological and/or symbolic?

Sartre admits that we experience a community of sorts. He attributes this to a "lateral awareness" that subjects have of their associates in a common undertaking. The oarsmen in a boat, for example, gradually become aware of merging their respective rhythms into "our" rhythm. Lateral awareness appears to be nondeliberate. Sartre cites the example of our consciousness (of) being a *co*spectator at a theatrical performance (see BN, 413). In fact, he characterizes this lateral awareness as nonthetic consciousness that accompanies our explicit (thetic) awareness of something else—of the plot's unfolding, for example, or the boat's advance.

While psychologically arresting and doubtless true, this account of the We in terms of individual psychology is defective in several respects. First and of greatest importance, it fails to explain that mutuality of relations that lateral awareness reveals. It is not solely my awareness of the others' rowing that constitutes our rhythm. It is also our mutual accommodation to a common goal, the shared desire for "the team" to win, not to mention such social facts as the regatta and its attendant rules, functionaries, statuses, and rewards. These factors mediate collective identity and common action. Sartre will come to admit this in the *Critique,* but at present he is bent on excluding any "super subject" from the ontological scene.

Sartre insists correctly that it is the object transcended in common and the bodies surrounding mine which I apprehend laterally that constitute my experience of the we-subject (see BN, 424–25). But there is no reason why my apprehension need stop with that object and with those bodies, for it is precisely via the movement of such bodies that I read their intentions in the context of a common situation.[14] As I rush for the 5:40 commuter train, for example, I am painfully aware of the strivings of others for the same object. Without reflection, I distinguish between them and yet others who are waiting for another train or are merely loitering in the station. This kind of lived hermeneutic will later reveal real, practical unities of multiple agents. But Sartre is not looking in that direction at the moment.

Nevertheless, he indicates a vague sense of collective identity and even of collective action. He speaks repeatedly of a "community of transcended transcendences" (BN, 415), of solidarity (BN, 418), and of the experience, though not the ontological reality, of a "common transcendence directed toward a unique end of which I am only an ephemeral particularization" (BN, 424). But his account of this community and mutuality constitutes a form of psychological reductionism popular with methodological individualists in social philosophy.[15] Sartre will later abandon this reductionism in the *Critique* and even now he appeals to nonpsychological determinations of our collective identity other than the look of the Third, though always subordinate to it. We must examine two such conditions, namely, being-in-situation and techniques for appropriating the world. They are the closest Sartre arrives to the concept of objective possibility in *Being and Nothingness* and thus they open the door to the next stage in the evolution of his social thought.

As his analysis of being-for-others ended with what I have called the equality dilemma, so his examination of the We and the Us repeats the stalemate: "It is useless for human reality to seek to escape this dilemma: one must either transcend the Other or allow oneself to be transcended by him. The essence of the relations between consciousnesses is not the *Mitsein;* it is conflict" (BN, 429; F, 502).

Recalling my earlier remarks about the interpersonal versus the social in *Being and Nothingness,* I reaffirm the thesis that the "collective" relations analyzed by Sartre under the rubrics of Us and We are not properly social at all. Rather, as the foregoing should have made clear, they are extrapolations of such dyadic relations as love, sadism, and masochism, which Sartre discusses earlier in the volume. The difference between the former, "collective" phenomena and the latter, admittedly individualistic, forms of being-for-others consists in the presence of the Third and certain problematic "objective situation forms." These situation forms could indeed turn out to be properly social if Sartre had pursued their analysis in depth; they will emerge as such in the *Critique.* But their importance for the Sartre of *Being and Nothingness* is clearly secondary. They possess an "indicative" value, pointing to the major source of social cohesion, the look of the Third.

It is this Third which could introduce the fully social realm of which Durkheim and Simmel speak but which fails to do so in the present work. The reason for its social inadequacy is threefold. First, the Third is an individual acting as an individual. There is no plural look. As Sartre describes it, the Third is in no sense a social agent. Second, the "unity" of the Us is entirely extrinsic (allowing for the basic ambiguity of "situation," which I shall examine shortly) and is imposed by the Third, exactly

as my individual being-for-others is imposed on me by the de facto upsurge
of the Other. The sole difference between the Other and this would-be
social Third is the plurality of for-itselfs which the latter objectifies, a
mere difference of degree. Objectification-alienation does not differ qualitatively when experienced as "me" or as "us." Finally, the relationships
of solidarity and equivalence are merely a translation into the plural of
quite individualistic phenomena; the relation, as Sartre describes it, is
one of juxtaposition, not synthesis. For these reasons one is justified in
characterizing the triadic relations in *Being and Nothingness* as really
covert dyads and in interpreting the Third introduced in that work as in
effect the Other writ large.

Being-in-Situation

Sketching a "philosophy of revolution" shortly after the war, Sartre remarked: "It is the elucidation of new ideas of 'situation' and of 'being in
the world' that revolutionary behavior specifically calls for" (MR, 235).
And in a quasi manifesto marking his entry into mass politics, he affirmed
that the existentialist concept of situation should serve as common ground
between theoreticians of the Communist and the non-Communist left.[16]
In fact, "situation" proves to be a major bridge concept between existentialism and Marxism. So we must determine to what extent it might
bear greater weight in Sartre's social ontology than he is willing to place
on it in *Being and Nothingness*.

The promise of "situation" paradoxically lies in its ambiguity. As Sartre
explains: "The *situation,* the common product of the contingency of the
in-itself and of freedom, is an ambiguous phenomenon in which it is
impossible for the for-itself to distinguish the contribution of freedom
from that of the brute existent" (BN, 488). Nowhere is the existentialist
project of "personalizing" the world more evident than in the concept of
situation, and nowhere does the endemic Sartrean ambiguity of the "given"
and the "taken" come more forcefully into play. Sartre's lengthy analyses
of the components of situation, e.g., my place, my past, my fellow man,
my death and the rest, beside providing some of the best-known passages
in *Being and Nothingness,* constitute as many variations on the basic
theme that "there is freedom only in a situation and there is a *situation*
only through freedom" (BN, 489). He later adds that this antinomy "will
give us the exact relation between freedom and facticity" (BN, 491).

The relation, of course, is anything but exact, and therein lies the
possibility for its development. Consider his well-known example of a
rock which is "too difficult to climb" only for someone whose project
includes its scaling. Such examples overstate the role of freedom-project

as distinct from facticity in "situation" and contribute to the popular belief that situation is entirely a function of noetic freedom. Of course, Sartre invites this impression when he claims: "There is no privileged situation. We mean by this that there is no situation in which the *given* would crush beneath its weight the freedom which constitutes it as such— and that conversely there is no situation in which the for-itself would be *more free* than in others" (BN, 549). By failing to qualify this freedom as ontological and noetic, Sartre leads us to believe that a simple Gestalt-shift would suffice to liberate us from an intolerable situation.[17]

Sartre is trading on the ambiguity of the "mix" of the given and the taken in any situation. His conceptual move toward Marxism after *Being and Nothingness* will consist chiefly in allowing greater weight to the "given," i.e., to facticity, in accounts of the existential situation. But to balance our understanding of situation and to ease Sartre's transit to philosophic Marxism, let us consider aspects of the situation that share the recalcitrance of the given.

First of all, Sartre admits that there remains in any situation an "unnamable and unthinkable [sic] *residuum* which belongs to the in-itself under consideration" (BN, 482; F, 562). Elsewhere he speaks of this as the "brute quid" of facticity against which freedom must define itself. In sum, "freedom is originally a relation to the given" (BN, 486). But we must try to make the nature of that relationship more precise. For it is directly relevant to the possibility of a consistent historical materialism.

Granted that the given draws its meaning-direction (*sens*) from original choice, the natural contours and "objective possibilities" of the in-itself, even if not decisive, cannot be ignored. And Sartre, perhaps sacrificing consistency to completeness, allows as much: "What my freedom can not determine is whether the rock 'to be scaled' will or will not lend itself to scaling. This is part of the brute being of the rock" (BN, 488). Discussing another example, Sartre admits that a slave's facticity is such that the world appears to him with another countenance from that of the master's world to him. Consequently, the slave has to posit and resolve different problems and thereby give meaning (*sens*) to "that obscure constraint" which is his slavery (BN, 550). So there does appear the glimmer of a concept of objective possibility even in *Being and Nothingness*, though it shines no brighter than an "obscure constraint." Having finally acknowledged that the "objective" qualities are given, not directly but "only as an *indication* . . . of an ungraspable *quid*," Sartre leaves us with a question: Is the world telling me about itself or myself? and his answer: I can never know (see BN, 488–89).[18]

In his study of Sartre, Pietro Chiodi judges that "the introduction of the connection between 'possibility' and 'conditioning' in the *Critique* constitutes the most important innovation in Sartre's theory of the possible."[19] I can only second this assessment, adding that "objective possibility" systematizes this new insight and links Sartre to Lukács, Weber, and Marx himself.[20] But I have been arguing that this relation is not without precedent in *Being and Nothingness*.

Finally, from the viewpoint of collective responsibility we should recall that both the Us and the We come to awareness only as we prereflectively assume responsibility for them. The for-itself is absolutely responsible for its situation (see BN, 554). But this must be true of its collective situation as well. The worker on the assembly line and the soldier on parade are as responsible for their situations as is the solitary individual; Sartre is committed to this thesis. But again it is this community of situation that he has not explained. For how can *I* be responsible for this crucial mutuality? By taking the We for a psychological phantom, Sartre undermines the objectivity of the collective situation as well. His last attempt in *Being and Nothingness* to shore up this objectivity is introduced under the rubric of techniques for appropriating the world.

Techniques and Collectivities

Our reflections on the We and the Us in Sartre's early "social" philosophy have revealed a kind of responsibility for a plurality in the face of the Third. But that responsibility is mediated by what Sartre calls "techniques for appropriating the world." I do not simply belong to a nation, a family, or a rowing team. I share in a myriad of meanings, customs, institutions, and the like, which I have not originated but to which I am committed and thus responsible. In fact, Sartre insists that there are only two positive ways for me to "exist" my membership in such "collectivities" as the human species, the nation, and professional and familial groups, namely, my being-for-others (that is, the Us and the We) and the use that I make of collective techniques (see BN, 512).

As I bring to a close my survey of the social dimension of *Being and Nothingness*, I must note the phenomenon of techniques. Not only does Sartre's treatment of them exhibit a pattern of responsibility that will recur frequently in his subsequent writings but they form the all-important mediating factors which Sartre at present underplays but which will emerge as crucial to his theory of collective responsibility. Consider that basic technique for appropriating the world, language.

Sartre orders language and the other techniques generically according to the Hegelian concepts of reality and truth. Thus the reality of speech (*langage*) is language (*langue*) and the reality of language is dialect, slang, and the like. Conversely, the truth of dialect is language; the truth of language speech.[21] The movement to truth is through abstraction toward order and rule; the movement to reality is through concretization. But the most concrete act of all is that of free, individual choice. Thus the reality of each and every technique is ultimately found at the level of the individual choice which concretizes it.[22]

I am interested in his conclusion, which is valid for all techniques and for all collectivities whatsoever: "Freedom is the only possible foundation of the laws of language" (BN, 517). In other words, the freedom-choice-responsibility of the individual for-itself makes concrete (real) an otherwise "abstract" ensemble of relations. In making the collectivity real, that is, by choosing itself in and through the ensemble, the for-itself assumes responsibility for the collectivity so constituted. In accepting his Jewishness, for example, the individual Jew, in Sartre's theory, accepts all who bear that designation, for he thereby accepts that abstract ensemble which the anti-Semite labels *the* Jew.[23] This concept of individual responsibility for collectives is as close as Sartre comes in *Being and Nothingness* to the notion of collective responsibility.

Sartre's discussion of techniques is valuable for our purposes, not only because it exhibits a pattern of argument, namely, appeal to underlying freedom, which will loom large in the *Critique,* but also because it underscores "techniques" as a factor that mediates collective identity and hence collective responsibility. After his Marxist "conversion," Sartre will draw on this insight to speak of class identity and interest in the social struggle as the backbone of various French revolutions. A kind of "objectivity" is thus secured for Sartrean situation even in its collective aspect, and an instrument for critical social analysis is at least partially fashioned even in Sartre's presocialist thought.

And yet these techniques and the collectivities they reveal are regarded by Sartre as forms of objectification, i.e., alienation, as is the Us of which they are modes (see BN, 521). Clearly, Sartre has only begun to travel on the road toward an adequate social philosophy.

This survey of the social dimension of Sartre's existential anthropology has indicated that he scarcely ignores "social" questions, indeed, that he subscribes to a kind of Hobbesian model of interpersonal relations. But this last observation pinpoints as well the major flaw in his position. Grounded on the existentialist model of looking/looked-at, the "social space" that his theory posits is not really social at all. (Even Hobbes appealed to a mythical social contract.) Rather, it is merely an extension of the self-other relationship that obtains between any two for-itselfs. As I argued above, the Third-dual relationship which is called upon to generate the social, is really a covert dyad. What could have made it more than this, namely, a thorough analysis of factors which mediate collective identity and which qualitatively distinguish the Third from the Other, are either discussed psychologically (e.g., techniques) or totally ignored. Nevertheless, the concept of collective situation and, specifically, the ideas of Us and We, of techniques, and of common instruments and ends, witness more than a dim awareness of the problem of collective identity, action, and responsibility. In sum, the collective dimension of Sartre's existentialist opus is real, though inchoate and problematic.

I have arrived at the major problem for my test case, one which will engage us for the remainder of this work, namely, that of reconciling any concept of collective responsibility which we may hope to find in Sartre's writings with an ontology of interpersonal relations that explicitly accords only a psychological and subjective status to the We. If we follow Lucien Goldmann in taking as the defining characteristic of Marxism the notion of a collective subject, the limits to Sartre's treatment of collective responsibility will indeed spell the limits of his Marxism.

As for the construction of a theory of collective responsibility itself, this survey has uncovered a broad spectrum of freedoms and responsibilities in Sartre's existentialist classic. But the closest he has come to our topic so far is reference to individual responsibility for such "collectivities" as family, class, nation, and linguistic community; in other words, individual responsibility for collective situations. Yet this ambiguous concept of situation precisely in its collective aspect attests an awareness of social issues in *Being and Nothingness* overlooked by the majority of Sartre's commentators. Moreover, it affords the conceptual bridge we are seeking toward a full-blown social ontology consonant with the existential anthropology of the early Sartre. While not simply the natural outgrowth of the latter, neither should Sartre's social philosophy henceforth be seen as excluded a priori by the categories of his early works.

And yet, by opting for the looking/looked-at model rather than for what I shall later term the "praxis" model of interpersonal relations, Sartre has in effect excluded co-*operation* in the literal sense of the term and hence the mutuality (reciprocity) requisite for properly social relations. "To see" is exclusively private and, strictly speaking, incommunicable, in a sense that "to do" is not. As Sartre admits, there is no plural look. We must conclude at this juncture that his social thought resembles an attempt to account for a line by appeal to its points: no concatenation of individual for-itselfs as Sartre now understands them will ever yield a social whole.

three

Beyond Authenticity
Social Responsibility
and the Committed Agent

Any Ethic which does not explicitly profess that it is *impossible today* contributes to the bamboozling and alienation of men. The ethical "problem" arises from the fact that Ethics is *for us* inevitable and at the same time impossible. Action must give itself ethical norms in this climate of nontranscendable impossibility. . . . To a mind that experienced this agony and that was at the same time forced to will and to decide, all high-minded rebellion, all outcries of refusal, all virtuous indignation would seem a kind of outworn rhetoric.

Saint Genet

Doubtless, Sartre was speaking from experience when he observed shortly after the war: "The young bourgeois can come to the revolution only upon the perception of social injustices" (MR, 254). He might have added, as he would later, that one responds as revolutionary and not as solitary rebel once he has had "the true experience, that of *society*."[1] The immediate postwar scramble of parties and governments to replace recent injustices with older ones distressed Sartre deeply. But if his moral sensitivities were offended by this sorry spectacle, his optimism was heightened by having just experienced the exhilaration of common threat and struggle in the Resistance movement—a courage, self-sacrifice, and camaraderie quite foreign to those creatures caught in the hermetic hell of *No Exit*. "Never were we more free," he protests, savoring the paradox, "than under the German occupation" (*Situations,* 3:11). This newfound ideal of common freedom, we shall see, gives focus to Sartre's political and social undertakings for the rest of his career.

Sartre's interest has always been primarily ethical.[2] The ethic developed, mostly by indirection, in *Being and Nothingness* and in Sartre's plays and novels of the forties is one of authenticity. Writing a year after *Being and Nothingness* appeared (1944), he remarks: "Authenticity . . . consists in having a true and lucid consciousness of the situation, in assuming the responsibility and risks that it involves, in accepting it in pride or humiliation, sometimes in horror and hate" (AJ, 90). This is the

31

morality that captured the enthusiasm of the public at large in the heyday of café existentialism. Its hero is Orestes of *The Flies*—doer of the deed, alone and free, fated to choose his path in a godless universe. Its chief disvalue, bad faith, seems as much a matter of moral psychology as of ethics properly speaking and leaves the impression that Sartre is offering us an ethical style, not a content. Indeed, Simone de Beauvoir warns: "Ethics does not furnish recipes" (EA, 134). Yet the very work which popularized this interpretation of the existentialist ethic, *Existentialism is a Humanism,* served to transcend it. It is this move beyond an ethic of authenticity that concerns us now.

Hints of another ethic occur already in *Being and Nothingness*. Recall the project of "freeing the whole 'Us' from its object-state by transforming it into a We-subject" (BN, 422). Let us call this new project Sartre's "ethic of disalienatior. " though he seems to regard it as a simple abandonment of ethics in fa or of revolutionary pragmatics.[3] In contrast to an ethic of authenticity, thi: new ethic is characterized by a heightened sense of collective identity or solidarity, an emphasis on the socioeconomic conditions for the exercise of free choice, appeal to freedom as concrete and social, and by the definition of "alienation" not only in terms of objectification but also as involving mystification, exploitation, and the narrowing of choice to the option "do or die." It finds immediate expression in Sartre's postwar activism; for example, in his decision to found a journal which would espouse "committed literature" and in his brief association with that nonparty of the non-Communist left, the Revolutionary People's Assembly (RDR).[4]

But this negative, critical phase of Sartre's ethic is guided by the positive moral vision of a "City of ends," of freedoms recognizing each other— in effect, by that very ideal of equality which he had dismissed as impossible in *Being and Nothingness*. This ideal is ingredient in what I shall call Sartre's third ethic, an ethic of freedom,[5] itself integral to that philosophy of freedom which Sartre hopes for but which, he claims, can scarcely be imagined in our present, alienated condition.[6]

The central issue of this chapter can be stated succinctly: How does what is described in *Being and Nothingness* as an option, as an alternative mode of appropriation, namely, "freeing the whole Us from its object-state," emerge in Sartre's subsequent works as an imperative, and a moral one at that? In other words, I am concerned with the conceptual moves by which Sartre justifies his social ethic, especially the foundational claim that none is free until all are and the correlative command: choose for all persons. What follows is a reconstruction of the argument as employed in *Existentialism Is a Humanism*, fortified by ancillary theses from other bridge essays of the period from 1945 to 1948.[7]

The Argument of *Existentialism Is a Humanism*

This transcript of a public lecture is the only piece which Sartre publicly regretted having published.[8] It exhibits the weakness of an informal address where ideas are expressed that are still in gestation. But for that very reason it affords a rare glimpse of Sartre's thought *in via* from individualist to social categories. Its most significant conclusion for his social ethic is doubtless the claim that "I am obliged to will the other's freedom at the same time as my own" (EH, 308). This ambiguous remark embodies the two major theses of the lecture, that in choosing myself I choose all men, and that I cannot be free in a concrete sense unless everyone is free—the maxim of Sartre's ethic of disalienation. Let us term these respectively Sartre's moral imperative (MI) and his universal freedom conditional (UFC), and consider his defense of each.

At the outset we must admit that the "argument" of this lecture is more a string of *aperçus* than a set of deductions from basic principles. Still, a certain loose logical progression can be established among them, enabling us to assess the strengths and weaknesses of Sartre's social ethic in its embryonic stage.[9] Eight such insights-premises can be delineated in a rational reconstruction of his stand.

1. Since there is no God (Sartre's atheism being a conclusion of his definition of God as "Being-in-itself-for-itself"), there is no human nature or essence which can serve as a priori norm. This is Sartre's objection to natural-law ethics. He believes it follows from his atheism.

2. Bereft of necessary norms, man is what he makes himself to be; his "existence" precedes his "essence." Sartre terms this "the first principle of existentialism" (EH, 290–91). He also calls it "subjectivity," an expansion of the "limit to reflective recoil" by which he had defined the term in *Being and Nothingness*.

3. If existence precedes essence, man is responsible for what he is. In choosing, he chooses himself and his world. (Thus far Sartre is merely restating the position elaborated in *Being and Nothingness*. Although the term "responsible" carries a more explicitly moral connotation in *Existentialism Is a Humanism,* it clearly builds on the ontological and the noetic responsibility of the earlier work. We now reach his threshold-crossing claim.)

4. Each man is likewise responsible for all men, because "in choosing himself, he chooses all men" (EH, 291; F, 25). I noted a precedent for this in Sartre's discussion of situation and especially of ethnic and class consciousness.[10] But the claim must now bear the major weight of Sartre's social ethic. So he buttresses it with two arguments, the second of which

has occasioned a great deal of criticism both of this lecture and of his social ethic in general.

4.1 His first subsidiary argument has been underrated, if not totally ignored, by commentators whose fire has been drawn to the second, Kantian position. Yet it evinces a characteristically Sartrean regard for imaginative consciousness as value-constituting. In the language of *The Psychology of Imagination,* it conceives of value as image demanding to be realized.[11]

It is on this value-image that Sartre's first subsidiary argument rests: "For in effect, there is not one of our acts that, in creating the man we wish to be, does not at the same time create an *image* of man such as we judge he *ought* to be" (EH, 291; F, 25; emphasis mine). And later on: "What is at the very heart and center of existentialism is the absolute character of the free commitment, by which every man realizes himself in realizing a *type* of humanity" (EH, 304; emphasis mine). This normative image figures in Sartre's writings from then on.[12] Without further defense, he appeals to what has become a commonplace in axiological ethics such as that of Max Scheler, with which Sartre was familiar,[13] namely, that in choosing we affirm the value of what we choose (its aspect as good); but he gives it a Kantian twist that Scheler would have resisted, when he adds that "nothing can be good for us without being [considered] good for everyone" (EH, 292; F, 25–26).

In this first argument, therefore, it is the value-image which invests individual choice with collective import: "I create a certain image of the man that I choose; choosing myself, I choose man" (EH, 292; F, 27). This image, I am arguing, constitutes a general ethical ideal, not a universal principle. It serves as a moral paradigm or concrete model of how the moral person ought to choose.[14] Accordingly, it will function in an integrative, not in a nomological, sense, unifying projects and allowing degrees of approximation.[15] So when Sartre writes: "I am obliged at every instant to perform actions which are examples" (EH, 293), he is not merely alluding to being-for-others as an inescapable dimension of human reality. He is also underscoring the imaginative articulation of an ideal theme occurrent in every moral choice: "That's how man ought to be!" Consider Sartre's reference to *image,* not rule, in the preceding paragraphs. It is the indirect communication of such value-images through imaginative literature that has become the hallmark of existentialism.

4.2. In what appears to be a bold and inconsistent appeal to Kant, Sartre restates his moral imperative in terms of the "universal legislator" formulation of the Categorical Imperative. He does so in the context of existential anguish: no longer does *Angst* denote merely the Kierkegaardian awareness of freedom, possibility, and individual choice; it now entails

34

a "feeling of total and profound responsibility" for all men, such as the commander experiences who must send others on a certain-death mission. Each man ought to say to himself: "Am I he who has the right to act such that humanity regulates itself by my acts?" (EH, 293; F, 31).

In view of the proverbial antilegalism of Sartre's ethical thought, this subordinate argument seems paradoxical at best. Even sympathetic critics have dismissed it as unwarranted.[16] To accept their assessment is to be satisfied with a de facto shift in Sartre's thought without seeking any justification for it in his existential anthropology.

But we now have reason to think that this is an inadequate reading of the text. First, it ignores the value-image argument just elucidated, with its basis in Sartre's early elevation of imaging consciousness to the status of paradigm for consciousness in general. Elements of that prior argument recur in the moral-legislator thesis as well, modifying considerably its formal, nomological character. Sartre expands this reasoning, for example, when he asks: "By what right do I impose my conception of man and my choice on humanity?" Indicating that "conception" is equilavent to what I have termed "value-image," he continues: "I am obliged at every instance to perform *exemplary* acts (EH, 293; F, 31; emphasis mine). The moral agent, even in this second, "Kantian" argument, is not so much legislating universal statutes as exemplifying an ethical ideal: this is how everyone ought to act.

So whether it is because of an ethical image or the mediation of a quasi-legislative act, in choosing himself, Sartre insists, the moral agent chooses for all.

5. Having offered a kind of defense of his moral imperative, Sartre must do the same for his universal freedom conditional. The latter is not a mere corollary to the former, since it is at least conceivable that one can will all men to be free while remaining among the few who in fact enjoy such freedom.

Sartre resumes his argument by appeal to what he terms "intersubjectivity." This elaborates the interpersonal realm of being-for-others in *Being and Nothingness*. "The man who discovers himself directly in the cogito," Sartre points out, "recognizes that he cannot be anything (in the sense in which one says one is spirited, or that one is wicked or jealous) unless others recognize him as such" (EH, 303). And he concludes: "Thus we immediately discover a world which we shall call intersubjectivity. It is in this world that a man decides what he is and what others are" (EH, 303; F, 67).[17]

The intersubjective is that public realm where each depends on the free recognition of the other for discovering such "truth" about himself as his moral character. Of course, whatever he is, the for-itself will be so in the manner of not-being it, that is, as conscious. Still, Sartre's appeal to the constitutive role of free recognition without mention of "objectification" suggests a more positive sense of the intersubjective than his earlier analysis of the Us and the We had allowed. Although the individuating power of original choice is not denied, we are now witnessing a socialization of those features that make me who I am. Another cautious step is taken toward the conclusion that my freedom requires that of all men (UFC).

6. Again, Sartre relies on the ambiguous concept of situation to bring to the fore a certain universality which adheres to every human choice, rendering each intelligible to every other. He retains the concept of a universal human condition while denying any normative essence to man. He defines "condition" as "all the *limitations* which a priori define man's fundamental situation in the universe" (EH, 303). He concludes that every project has "universal value" to the extent that, at a certain level, it comes to terms with such limits to our fundamental situation as being-in-the-world, work, being-for-others, and death. He adds that this condition makes the most diverse projects "comprehensible" to everyone (EH, 304; F, 69–70). It is fundamental situation which accounts for the "absolute" character of free commitment as distinct from its relative expression in diverse historical epochs. Thirty years later, Sartre will repeat this claim in a discussion with several young Maoists: "Freedom without alienation is an idea which transcends class lines and historical periods and [which] pertains to the very constitution of human reality."[18]

By speaking of "fundamental situation" as distinct from less basic, contingent determinations of human reality, Sartre acknowledges an a priori limit to the human and reserves a place for the idea of freedom without alienation—one of those ideas that transcend class lines and historical periods. This is a cardinal claim for the ethical theory he is in process of formulating. For it affords him critical leverage against the self-defeating thesis of historical relativism, an advantage he will press against the "mechanistic Marxists" after the mid fifties.

Yet this basic role of "fundamental situation" prompts us to ask just what is and what is not historically conditioned in Sartre's existentialist anthropology. Obviously, "freedom without alienation" is not so conditioned, and neither, presumably, is its ontological basis. But what about the looking/looked-at relationship, with its necessary objectification (alienation)? Unless the latter can somehow be relativized, Sartre's social theory will never rise above the barren We/Us relationships of *Being and Nothingness*. The fact that he undertakes the present series of moves aimed at grounding a social ethic and does so without referring either to shame-consciousness or to the looking/looked-at relationship, is significant. When this relationship does reappear, e.g., in *Saint Genet* and in the *Critique,* it will be as a product of certain cultural or socioeconomic conditions and will stand in contrast to another, nonalienated type of social relation.[19]

Our discussion of "situation" in terms of "techniques for appropriating the world" revealed that both "situation" and "being-for-others" require other freedoms. But in what sense and why do they require the freedom of *all?* That is the question whose answer we must try to reconstruct as we move to the last two premises of Sartre's "argument" in *Existentialism Is a Humanism.*

7. Sartre's next premise is that "freedom, in respect of concrete circumstances, can have no other end and aim but itself" (EH, 307). He sees this as another way of saying that existence precedes essence (see EH, 308; F, 84). It follows, he claims, from the major ontological thesis of *Being and Nothingness* that freedom (consciousness) is the basis of all values. Sartre appeals to this seventh premise to warrant the ethical conclusion that choice of freedom is the criterion for good faith: "The actions of men of good faith have, as their ultimate signification, the quest of freedom itself as such," that is, the willing of "freedom for freedom's sake in each particular circumstance" (EH, 307; F, 82–83). This in turn justifies his moral evaluations of the cowards (*les lâches*) and the skunks (*les salauds*) on his ethical blacklist. These are people who flee the choice of freedom as such. So this seventh proposition serves as a middle premise, mediating Sartre's move from (ontological) fact to (moral) value. Let us consider (*a*) his defense of the thesis and (*b*) its relevance to his social ethic.

Why does it follow from the ontological fact we are value-constituting that it is immoral, i.e., in bad faith, to act as if this were not the case? First of all, Sartre notes that this would involve us in a factual error: "I define [such] bad faith as an error" (EH, 307; F, 81).But worse, to choose as if such values imposed themselves on one places the agent "in contradiction" with himself: "I will these values and at the same time say that they impose themselves upon me." The contradiction is not a logical one but consists in a practical inconsistency, analogous to the famous "practical impossibility" in Kant of universalizing immoral maxims. Given the total awareness of Sartrean consciousness, his point seems to be that choosing as if such values imposed themselves is a kind of hypocrisy, the "lie" of bad faith (EH, 307).

At this point Sartre, the implacable foe of ethical naturalism, crosses the bridge from fact to value. Good faith is now seen to require not only consistency but that I acknowledge by my choices, e.g., by assuming the responsibility which accompanies them, that I am the foundation of all values. "Choosing freedom," the criterion of good faith, is not the same

37

as "maximizing" some value, for freedom is neither the object nor the specific content of our choice. Rather, it is what Sartre terms the form of our choice, the ultimate meaning (*sens*) of our actions (see EH, 308). Thus freedom is both fact and value for Sartre, a transcendental fact and a moral value, indeed, the "form" of all the values that make up what he calls the "authentic" life.

But characterizing freedom as the "form" of the authentic life does not mean that freedom is compatible with any content whatsoever, for example, with the choice of unfreedom or of bad faith. Numerous critics have argued that Sartre must allow this, even though he explicitly rejects it in the case of the anti-Semite.[20] I have just noted his appeal to the "lie" of choosing unfreedom, i.e., to the practical inconsistency involved in such a move. But his critics have insisted, Why not choose to be inconsistent and accept the consequences? Sartre's answer at this point is weak. He admits such choice is possible but implies that it would exclude one from the community of discussants who are concerned with such questions in the first place. In any case, the fact of freedom implies that one cannot consistently deny that one is free in the very act of freedom.[21]

Pondering Sartre's argument at this juncture, I should like to suggest that he could have made a stronger case against "choosing unfreedom" than he did; in other words, that he conceded too much when he granted that the anti-Semite, for example, could choose to be practically inconsistent. What I have in mind is an argument akin to Jaakko Hintikka's interpretation of Descartes' famous "I do not exist" as a *counterperformative*.[22] In the latter case, such an utterance, though grammatically impeccable, is "existentially inconsistent" in that it exhibits in its performance the very opposite of what it claims to be saying. In Sartre's case the statement might be "I hereby choose unfreedom." Once I am aware that my freedom is the foundation of all values, an important condition for Sartre (see EH, 307), I cannot mean what I say when I utter the sentence: "I hereby choose unfreedom." This would be a futile and empty gesture; in fact, a *non*act, one might say. For the relation of "choice" to "unfreedom" is not that of subject to predicate (as in a declarative sentence where logical consistency might be at stake), but one of process to product (or, more precisely, that of constitution to the constituted; for choice-consciousness "brings it about" that "there are" values at all). Consciousness-choice is the performance that brings value into being in the first place. Hence, to choose unfreedom is like choosing not to choose. And this has been unmasked as self-defeating by existentialists since Kierkegaard.

I am arguing that Sartre's theory of consciousness as value-constituting entitles him to exclude the choice of unfreedom as impossible in practice and suggesting that his critics would be on firmer ground were they to attack the ontology underlying the entire Sartrean project rather than concentrate on the choice of inconsistency as a counterexample.

It is a curious nonnaturalism that Sartre preserves, grounded on the (transcendental) fact that we are "condemned to be (ontologically) free," that is, to be value-constitutors. Coupled with this fact is the "choice of freedom" as the form of authenticity. Since we cannot consistently (or perhaps at all) choose unfreedom, we must acknowledge this condition, Sartre insists, as the ultimate meaning (*sens,* form) of whatever concrete choices we may effect. That freedom as fact is joined to freedom as form in Sartre's argument is clear. What still remains obscure is the precise nature of the linkage.

To appreciate the social relevance of Sartre's thesis that freedom must choose itself, we should look to Simone de Beauvoir's "official" commentary on his existentialist ethic, *The Ethics of Ambiguity.* She argues that "my freedom in order to fulfill itself requires that it emerge into an *open future:* it is other men who open the future to me" (EA, 82; emphasis mine). As she later explains: "A freedom wills itself genuinely only by willing itself as an *indefinite movement* through the freedom of others" (EA, 90; emphasis mine). This, for example, is the sole way for human reality to transcend the facticity of death and thus to realize itself as an indefinite unity (see EA, 32). But, granted that I need other freedoms to convey a kind of "immortality" to the meaning of my project, why should these others be free in more than the ontological sense? Her response is straightforward. On the assumption that choice of freedom/self is the criterion of authenticity, I could not consistently will that my project of authentic choice be perpetuated by for-itselfs who were less than authentic themselves. Such inauthentic perpetuation of a project (and both de Beauvoir and Sartre by this time have in mind the project of a socialist revolution) would constitute mere objectification and no perpetuation at all. The "indefinite" movement of my freedom would be halted.

De Beauvoir's "open future" argument is sketchy and its lines are circular. But it exhibits both authors' growing sense that one cannot be concretely free alone or merely here and now. Sartre expreses that insight in the final premise of his lecture.

8. Our freedom "depends entirely on the freedom of others and their freedom depends on ours" (EH, 307; F, 83). This is a version of what we have termed Sartre's "universal freedom conditional" (UFC). It forms the linchpin of his social ethic. Though it has antecedents in the ontology of *Being and Nothingness,* the principle is better read as an anticipation of the mutuality prized by the *Critique.*

Appeal to this principle marks a major shift in Sartre's argument from formal or abstract to concrete freedom. Hence the import of the concept of situation.[23] Freedom in the purely formal sense, that is, "freedom as the definition of man," Sartre allows, does not depend on the other. But as soon as there is commitment, i.e., once my particular project and its attendant situation enter the picture, "I am obliged to will the other's freedom as well as my own. I cannot take my freedom as an end [in the sense of his seventh principle] unless I equally take that of others for an end" (EH, 308; F, 83). Again, his critics challenge: "It may be true that I cannot consistently choose unfreedom, but why can't I simply 'choose' freedom for myself alone?"

In response, we must recall, first, that this universal freedom conditional is limited to "the plane of free commitment" (EH, 309), that is, to "the level of total authenticity" (EH, 308; F, 84). So it requires as a precondition that I admit the factual truth of my own presence-to-self and presence-to-world as well as that of *every other.*

Second, it follows that, as authentic, I must admit my being-in-situation-before-others. Just as in *Being and Nothingness* a kind of (ontological, so it seems) necessity requires "free submission" *of* other freedoms (sadism) or *to* other freedoms (masochism), so here my authentic situation requires that I acknowledge the fact of other freedoms' acknowledging my freedom. That is what it means to be "in-situation-before-others." *Freedom unrecognized remains abstract.* This last point is a corollary to Sartre's theory that being-for-others is constitutive of human reality as situated (no. 6) as well as to the newly stated formula that choice of self implies intersubjectivity (no. 5).

Third, the claim that my freedom depends on that of others and theirs on mine explicitly appeals to a new and henceforth paramount ideal, that of the human community, though it is only mentioned here (see EH, 309).

Sartre concludes his address by distinguishing two kinds of humanism, the classical with its appeal to some abstract human community, which he rejects, and the existential with its emphasis on man's constant transcending of his facticity and his continuous reshaping of the human universe, the intersubjective world. His brief mention of this idea, which will figure so prominently in his subsequent work, suggests that his new community and the humanism it embodies are already operative in the "argument" of *Existentialism Is a Humanism.* In fact, I now wish to indicate why any adequate reconstruction of this argument must incorporate the value-concepts of humanism, solidarity, and freedom that are developed in other bridge essays of the immediate postwar years.

40

Before considering these auxiliary concepts, let me summarize the reconstructed argument of the *Existentialism* lecture. As I have organized it, the argument turns on two basic premises, namely, that in choosing I choose for all people (MI) and that I cannot be concretely free unless everyone is free (UFC). Setting out from the ontology of *Being and Nothingness,* modified by an elaborated sense of "situation" and "being-for-others," Sartre intends to draw the social implications of the existentialist maxim that existence precedes essence. His choosing-for-all-men principle, I have claimed, thrusts human reality into the social ethical sphere less by use of a Kantian universalizability thesis than by appeal to the value-image of exemplary choices. This interpretation accords with his early elevation of imaging consciousness to paradigmatic status, with his preference for concrete thinking as exhibited in the phenomenological method, e.g., in Scheler's work on value theory, and with his own penchant for communicating existentialist themes through imaginative literature, i.e., with what Fredric Jameson calls Sartre's "novelistic vision."

He then undertakes a defense of the universal freedom conditional. He establishes that subjectivity (choice of self) implies intersubjectivity and that my personal characteristics, e.g., moral predicates and, presumably, authenticity itself, depend on the other's recognition. After designating fundamental situation as the referent for acts (and hence images) of universal, that is, transcultural, value, he argues that freedom can have no other choice but to will itself. This affords him a criterion for assessing bad faith and inauthenticity generally. It likewise constitutes the bridge from fact to value in this lecture. I defended this choice of freedom first in terms of the practical (not logical) inconsistency of willing anything contrary to its own freedom, and then by likening this inconsistency to a counterperformative in ordinary language philosophy.

But I am still left with the objection that willing one's own freedom need not entail willing that of everyone else. Sartre formulates his claim that it does entail the freedom of all in what I have called his universal freedom conditional (UFC). I introduced the defense of this principle by relevant remarks of Simone de Beauvoir regarding freedom's need for an open future and hence for the recognition of other freedoms. Sartre's own sketchy defense relies on distinguishing concrete from abstract freedom and on "situation" as entailing acknowledgment of my being-before-others. My concluding observation is that the "argument" in general and this final premise (UFC) in particular rely heavily on three value-concepts developed only in other bridge essays. To fill the conceptual gaps in the foregoing sequence, we must turn to these essays and to those concepts.

41

Three Auxiliary Value-Concepts

Unless fortified by considerations from other Sartrean works of about the same period, *Existentialism Is a Humanism* remains a kind of manifesto, more a statement of commitment than a coherent philosophical thesis. Its second major premise, that I cannot be free unless all men are free (UFC), is scarcely established, except in the formal sense that my freedom requires the mutual recognition of other freedoms. And even that, as we saw, leaves unanswered the objection that the recognition of everyone's freedom does not seem required. Yet aside from strictures against the inconsistency of choosing unfreedom and, during the question period, brief allusions to "situation" as involving the material and psychological conditions of an ensemble, no clear link is forged in this lecture between the ontological freedom that defines the individual in abstracto and the socioeconomic freedom of concrete, historical agents. As Sartre admits in the ensuing discussion, it is the conditions for universality, i.e., those factors which make his conclusions applicable to all persons here and now, that challenge his thinking at this juncture.[24]

Three master value-concepts emerge from his other essays of these years to form the theoretical framework for his answer to the problem of universality, namely, "humanism," "solidarity," and a new understanding of "freedom." Together they confer a cohesion on the transitional statements of *Existentialism Is a Humanism* that the lecture itself obviously lacks. As permanent acquisitions of Sartre's social thought, they figure prominently in his subsequent works. So, using these other bridge essays of the period, let us consider how each concept in turn might bolster the argument of *Existentialism Is a Humanism*.

Humanism

As its title suggests, the context for this lecture is Sartre's broader humanistic vision taking shape in the bridge essays of the period. We have just observed him espouse an existentialist humanism in opposition to the bourgeois variety he has always decried. This opposition relies on a distinction between analytic and synthetic reason first introduced in *Anti-Semite and Jew* (see AJ, 71). There he criticizes the social atomism that the analytic spirit generates. It "resolves collectivities into individual elements" and fails to see "synthetic realities" (AJ, 55–56). Later I shall discuss the flowering of his spirit of synthesis into "Dialectical Reason." What is of interest now is how his holistic reading of "situation" supports his claim of "choosing for all men."[25] It is because of the interrelatedness of our respective projects, Sartre argues in his inaugural essay for *Les Temps modernes,* that a person is "free to choose in one and the same movement his destiny, that of all men, and the value which one must ascribe to humanity. So he simultaneously chooses the worker and the man, while likewise giving meaning to the proletariat'' (*Situations,* 2:28).

It is in "Materialism and Revolution" (1946) that Sartre describes this new, revolutionary humanism as a "humanism of work." It is based on the conviction that "the liberating element for the oppressed person is work" (MR, 237). Work gives the worker his first sense of freedom (transcendence) in the overcoming and molding of physical nature. But the collective dimension of Sartre's humanism of work emerges fully with two further considerations, which usher in our remaining value concepts, namely, that collective work is the model or type of all human relations (solidarity) and that mutual recognition by other freedoms is necessary for concrete freedom.

Solidarity

The humanism of work which Sartre recommends not only views work as a primary kind of relation among men, it implies an ideal of mutual dependence and collective action: "What he [the worker] hopes for . . . is that the *relationship of solidarity* that he maintains with other workers *will become the very model of human relationships*. He hopes, therefore, for the liberation of the entire oppressed class; unlike the lonely rebel, the revolutionary understands himself only in his relationship of solidarity with his class" (MR, 226; emphasis mine). This is a far cry from that merely extrinsic denomination imposed on the Us by the look of the Third. Still, it continues and advances the earlier project of liberating the entire Us from object-status by insisting on the positive, internal mutuality (solidarity) of interpersonal relations. It should go without saying that neither Sartre nor the worker wants these relations to be modeled on the objectifying gaze of the Third. Rather, it is cooperative, group effort that is being held up as the model for human relationships.[26] Though Sartre will develop the social ontology needed to account for group unity only in the *Critique,* he now sees that such unity exemplifies the truly human social relationship; in effect, collective solidarity has become the norm.

In *What Is Literature?* he repeats his criticism of the analytical humanism of the bourgeoisie for denying the existence of a "proletariat" and for insisting that only individual proletarians exist; in other words, for denying that the proletarians "are united among themselves by an internal solidarity."[27] In what appears to be at least a revision, if not a rejection, of his earlier analysis of the We-subject, he continues, "the bourgeois . . . sees only *psychological* relations among the individuals whom his analytic propaganda has seduced and separated" (*Situations,* 2:159–60).

Elsewhere, Sartre distinguishes the revolutionary from the rebel in terms of synthetic or "holistic" versus analytic reasoning. To wish to better only oneself, he argues, is indicative of bourgeois, atomistic thought, which is ready to sacrifice others to oneself (see *Situations,* 3:187). Revolutionary thought, on the contrary, is synthetic thinking "in-situation" (*Situations,* 3:182); one thinks in terms of us, of our cadre, of our class. It is precisely this synthetic situational thinking (precursor to dialectical reason in the *Critique*) that lies behind Sartre's universal freedom conditional in the *Existentialism* lecture, namely, the claim that the freedom of one implies that of all. It is the oppressive situation itself which must be changed, if the worker is to be liberated.[28] And the fact of solidarity of situation requires the liberation of all who are in the same collective situation, namely, the entire working class, in the case of the proletarian revolution. This is a postulate of synthetic thinking in that all are enmeshed in the collective situation by interrelation and that there is no difference for such thinking between *my* freedom and *our* freedom.

There might well be a distinction between our freedom and yours, however, and Sartre at this point does not exclude a possible "dictatorship of the proletariat," an idea he will reject as absurd in the *Critique.*[29] Yet his emphasis on mutual recognition renders such a state incompatible with true freedom, as we shall now see.

Freedom

Already discussed ontologically and noetically in the context of Sartre's existentialist anthropology, the concept of freedom expands in denotation with Sartre's experience of the Resistance movement to the point that it includes group effort and socioeconomic liberation. In a remark which unites solidarity, concrete freedom, and the argument from mutual recognition, Sartre observes that "revolutionary demands" of the period taught him first of all that "the revolutionary act . . . [is] the free act par excellence," that this freedom, far from being anarchistic and individualistic, "springs from a recognition of other freedoms, and demands recognition on their part." So from the very start, Sartre concludes, freedom "places itself on the level of solidarity" (MR, 249–50). In other words, the free act par excellence is one of mutual recognition of freedoms, indeed, a communal effort as distinct from a solitary enterprise.

It is mutual recognition of concrete, i.e., situated, freedoms that ties "humanism," "solidarity," and "freedom" to Sartre's universal freedom conditional (UFC). It is no longer enough that the proletariat turn the tables. Pursuing Hegel's master/slave dialectic once more,[30] he urges that "the bourgeois oppressor is a victim of his own oppression" and that his freedom "can be asserted only by the *recognition* bestowed upon it by

44

other freedoms." When that time arrives, the oppressor will divest himself of the invidious panoply of rights and duties bequeathed him by bourgeois humanism and will finally "assert himself as a man among men" (MR, 254–55; Sartre's italics).

The egalitarian tone of these remarks bespeaks an implicit Sartrean conviction which will grow in intensity and expressiveness till his open espousal of the libertarian socialist cause after the events of May 1968. But his unstated premise is already evident, namely, that concrete freedom is possible only in a situation of solidarity, that is, in one where freedoms recognize each other. The inevitably objectifying (alienating) looking/ looked-at relation is set aside for another based on cooperative effort (on what I shall later call common praxis). If one accepts the Hegelio-Marxian thesis that oppression enslaves the oppressor, then Sartre's conclusion seems unexceptionable: we cannot be free so long as we are either oppressors or oppressed. Still, Sartre owes us a social ontology to accommodate this new (for him) insight.

What relevance does this understanding of mutual recognition as essential to concrete freedom have to the universal freedom conditional? Again, it is a matter of "situational thinking." I am basically a situated being, and one circle—perhaps the outermost—of my situation includes all persons with whom I currently inhabit this planet. Given the interrelatedness of people in this age of mass communication and high technology, it is unlikely that someone else's freedom is not diminished to some degree as long as inequality obtains with anyone.[31]

The coffee *finchiero* in Guatemala, for example, who pays his Indian workers barely subsistence wages, may be able to undersell another grower and, conceivably, offer a more attractive price to me, the consumer, who thus benefits from his exploitative practice. Such examples are commonplace these days. We shall observe Sartre employing similar ones when social responsibility is discussed in the next chapter.

But it would be a mistake and would weaken his case were we to regard the argument from being-in-situation as simply an empirical generalization from, say, economics or social anthropology. If concrete positive freedom demands a situation of solidarity, and if "situation" can be expanded dialectically (i.e., via relations among relations among relations . . .), then there is a rather clear sense in which one cannot be concretely free unless all are "free recognizers of freedom." It is in this context that we should reconstruct Sartre's universal freedom conditional. It amounts to taking seriously his claim that the revolutionary philosophy calls for "elucidation of the new ideas of 'situation' and of 'being-in-the-world' " (MR, 253). The equality called for at this juncture is equality of recognition; each must be free from the objectifying gaze of the Other; given the "humanism of work" which lies behind this ideal, each must be respected as a free agent in a common task.

We are now in a position to assess the role of these three value-concepts—(revolutionary) humanism, (situational) solidarity, and (concrete) freedom—in supporting the sketchy argument of *Existentialism Is a Humanism*. That lecture, as I remarked earlier, is as much a political act as a philosophical treatise. It is an expression of revolutionary thinking on the part of the newly politicized Sartre. Now revolutionary thinking, as we have seen, is synthetic and holistic. It understands the agent as in-situation. The situation which foments revolution is one of exploitation; that is, some freedoms not recognizing other freedoms, a practice often justified by appeal to a quasi-racist humanism of "rights and duties." In resisting exploitation, the revolutionary realizes that he is being victimized not as an individual but as a member of a particular race or socioeconomic class. What was an option in *Being and Nothingness,* namely, liberation of the entire Us (class, race, sex group) from its alienated condition, becomes an imperative for the holistic thinker, the true revolutionary. The new humanism that inspires this move is, in its negative phase, a form of antibourgeois thinking. But positively it is grounded on the ethical and social ideal of freedoms mutually recognizing each other, without hierarchy or privilege of any kind. Taking as the norm for truly human relations solidarity in a common project rather than some abstract "rights of Man and of the Citizen," this humanism concludes that, since man is free (ontologically), he can become free (ontically) and that no one can be free (concretely) unless all are free (the universal freedom conditional). Socialism, therefore, is but the means, not the end, of human action. The authentic end of all our projects, Sartre now insists, is the reign of freedom (see MR, 246).

Though the details of this disalienated state are necessarily unavailable to us in our present condition, *positive reciprocity of freedoms* is beginning to emerge as the prime value in Sartre's social ethic. It will permeate his subsequent writings, especially the *Critique* and *The Family Idiot,* conferring on them the unity of the project to realize this full flowering of Sartrean humanism. But the germ of this vision of positive freedom is already contained in the universal freedom conditional of *Existentialism Is a Humanism:* one cannot be concretely free unless all are free. That germ is a function of Sartre's newly acquired synthetic thinking and of the holistic sense of being-in-situation which such thought entails.

I have argued that if one accepts the situational, holistic, (later) "dialectical" thinking that Sartre is advocating and employing in *Existentialism Is a Humanism* and other bridge essays, then the universal freedom conditional seems possible and even plausible. But if this conditional receives independent corroboration, it in turn can strengthen the argument of the *Existentialism* lecture by a kind of reciprocal move not uncommon to dialectical thinking. Thus, if we assume the plausibility of the universal freedom conditional, the earlier premises, insofar as they are restatements of theses 1–3 or corollaries to theses 5–7 of *Being and Nothingness,* can be regarded as more abstract, i.e., less historically situated, statements of the situation of the committed agent. Thesis 4 would enunciate the formal condition of the commitment itself—that it involves a universal value-image—and thesis 8 would serve as the material or substantive condition for my concrete choice of freedom. These dialectical progressions from the abstract to the more concrete would culminate in the specific choice of freedom on the part of the committed agents such as those whom Sartre analyzes in his biographies.

As I remarked at the outset, this lecture is a transitional piece. It manifests all the inconsistencies and incompleteness of a thinker in process of reassessing his stand (if not changing his mind). As such, it calls for contextualization and completion. The former I have offered by reference to other bridge essays of the period; the latter is the subject of Part II of my study.

Conclusion to Part One

I began my examination of collective responsibility as a test-case for Sartre's Marxist existentialism with an analysis of the freedoms and responsibilities proper to his existentialist anthropology. We found that the terms were correlative and that freedom and responsibility pervaded the world, rendering it mine, a reflection of the choice which I am. Despite its individualist reputation, there is the beginning of a social dimension to Sartre's existentialist anthropology. It is a function of being-for-others, constituted by the Other's look. The concepts of Us and We, of collective situation, and of techniques for appropriating the world are the vehicles for carrying this social aspect forward. But the limits to its advance from a merely interpersonal to a truly social philosophy are precisely those of its existentialist model, the looking/looked-at. Hence, the Us is an extrinsic unity while the We dissolves into a purely psychological *Erlebnis.* As Sartre summarized his position with regard to a collective subject at this point: "There is no plural look."

But might not there be a plural praxis? This is the question with which I turn to the second half of Sartre's career and Part II of my inquiry. The sense of practical union, of common effort, as the model for social relations begins to take shape in *Existentialism Is a Humanism.* It advances along with the concepts of collective situation and concrete freedom toward a new articulation in what I have termed the universal freedom conditional: "No one can be free unless all are free." This statement must remain enigmatic until we realize that concrete freedom and the ideal of common effort converge in the concept of group praxis: we are free together and only as long as we remain in practical union. This is the message of the *Critique*. And it is a message of collective responsibility as well: we are responsible for each other's freedom, because the latter depends on our mutual, practical recognition. In this way, Sartre continues to respect the twin values of "socialism and freedom [*liberté*]" that have set the parameters of his political existentialism from the start.[32]

PART TWO

Collective Responsibility
The Emergence of a Theory

In this way [Goetz] discovers his moral law: separation is real and absolute unity is necessary. Here again we meet the express fact that the individual is the goal of the collectivity and at the same time the collectivity is the goal of the individual.

> Interview concerning *The Devil and the Good Lord,*
> in Contat and Rybalka, *The Writings of Jean-Paul Sartre*

four

Three Portraits of
Social Responsibility

> We feel that we are being judged by masked men who will succeed
> us and whose knowledge of all things will be such that we cannot
> have the slightest inkling of what it will be; our age will be an object
> for those future eyes whose gaze haunts us. And a guilty object. They
> will reveal to us our failure and guilt. . . . . What course is open to us?
> There is one which I perceive and which I shall discuss elsewhere.
>
> *Saint Genet*

If Sartre's social theory was checkmated by the existentialist model of
looking/looked-at in *Being and Nothingness,* this did not inhibit his ascriptions of responsibility to individuals and collectives for social ills,
which multiplied rapidly in the postwar decades. We have just witnessed
his incipient reassessment of the existentialist model in *Existentialism Is
a Humanism.* But his practical ascriptions outreached this new theoretical
base and called for more thorough grounding in a complete social ontology.
Leaving for the following chapters the sorting out of types of collective
responsibility and their relation to social responsibility, I wish at this point
merely to establish the nature and depth of Sartre's concern with the
generic issue of social responsibility. By brief phenomenological descriptions of three cases of such ascriptions, I hope to reveal the dawning of
a pattern in Sartre's practice that calls for the new social theory which
he elaborates in the *Critique.* I shall examine the elements of that theory
in the next three chapters—in a sense, the heart of my general investigation—returning to an extended application of this theory to the case of
the nineteenth-century industrial capitalist in chapter 8. So the flow of
argument in Part II moves from initial examples to the principles and
theory behind them and back to an explicit application of that theory to
the industrial capitalist; in other words, from intuitive practice to reflective
theory to comprehended practice.

The Anti-Semite

The first of Sartre's portraits of social responsibility occurs in his masterful
essay *Anti-Semite and Jew.*[1] Written in 1944, the year after *Being and*

51

Nothingness appeared, although not published in book form until 1946, this brief work raises the question of collective responsibility in concrete form, while offering in response several observations and arguments that will soon be standard features of Sartre's future analyses of social issues.

The historical context of this essay is, of course, the French Resistance. Petain's government had been echoing the anti-Jewish legislation of its Nazi masters without serious opposition from the citizenry. *L'affaire Dreyfus* had brought to the surface an undercurrent of anti-Semitism in a previous generation of Frenchmen. The Nazis were now directing a similar movement toward their own ends.[2] It is ultimately against this frame of mind rather than to its particular manifestations that Sartre raises his voice. He draws his portrait of *the* anti-Semite with the precision of a phenomenologist who would capture an essence in the concrete. Indeed, he will later enlarge this picture into an image of the racist as such. Here and in the next two portraits he is dealing with types, with concrete descriptions whose characteristics possess general applicability, like the value-images discussed in the previous chapter. Although a type per se is not a collective, *the* settler and *the* Jew, as Sartre will later observe, are "primarily serial unities" (CDR, 267), which, we shall see in the following chapters, entail a form of collective responsibility. By focusing on social types, Sartre's descriptions move beyond individual psychology to the social field and to what in an important insight he calls the "bases and structures" of choice. So in this relatively early work we discover a pattern of ascriptions of responsibility to racists which will recur throughout the next decades of Sartre's political writings.

Three characters figure in the essay. The first is the avowed anti-Semite. His choice of racial hatred has all the earmarks of inauthenticity according to the norms of *Being and Nothingness*. "In espousing anti-Semitism, he does not simply adopt an opinion," Sartre points out, "he chooses himself as a person. He chooses the permanence and impenetrability of a stone, the total irresponsibility of the warrior who obeys his leaders—and he has no leader" (AJ, 53). Sartre perceives that the anti-Semite *needs* the Jew: "If the Jew did not exist, the anti-Semite would invent him" (AJ, 13). "The Jew only serves him as a pretext; elsewhere his counterpart will make use of the Negro or the man of yellow skin. . . . Anti-Semitism, in short, is fear of the human condition" (AJ, 54). Thus in portraying the anti-Semite, Sartre is really characterizing the racist in general. In the language of *Being and Nothingness*, the racist lives in bad faith.

The specious solidarity of the anti-Semites, galvanized by their hatred of Jews and ultimately by their fear of freedom, is contrasted with that unity of situation with other Jews which marks *the* Jew himself, the second character in this essay. Sartre's description of the Jewish situation is an amalgam of concepts from *Being and Nothingness* and of ideas later expressed in *Existentialism Is a Humanism.*[3] The Jew, for example, cannot choose not to be a Jew; Jewishness is part of his facticity. "To be a Jew is . . . to be *abandoned to*—the situation of being a Jew; and at the same time . . . to be responsible in and through one's own person for the destiny and the very nature of the Jewish people" (AJ, 89). Just as one is condemned to be free-responsible in general in *Being and Nothingness,* so the Jew is condemned to be free-responsible for the nature and destiny of "his" people. Note that the situation is collective, like that of the Us in *Being and Nothingness,* and that the responsibility is both ontological and appropriative: "You are responsible," Sartre is advising us in the manner of a classical Greek moralist, "acknowledge that responsibility by the choices you make."

Why is the Jew so responsible? Primarily because of the look of the Third, the anti-Semite. In a quotable remark that returned to haunt him, Sartre insisted: "The Jew is one whom other men consider a Jew" (AJ, 69).[4] It pertains to his situation, his facticity, that he is part of a totality not of his own making but with which he must come to terms because he cannot do otherwise.

We know that in "Materialism and Revolution" Sartre will insist that the concept of situation must be developed to account for the new social philosophy which the postwar problems call for. The beginning of this development is already evident in the present essay. First, Sartre speaks of the Jews as sharing "a solidarity which is not one of action or interest, but of situation" (AJ, 100). The context implies that the former two are more complete types of solidarity, and we know from the previous chapter that "solidarity of action" is the model of human relations for the revolutionary philosopher. Moreover, in the *Critique* he will speak of the socioeconomic classes sharing mutually exclusive interests and destinies, interest being a form of serial unity for Sartre.

But of greater importance than hints of future development is the fact that Sartre actually introduces a topic which, when full-grown in later essays, will usher him into historical materialism. For the "situational solidarity" that makes *the* Jew responsible for all Jews is not only the product of the look of the Third. Ambiguous phenomenon that it is, "situation" includes reference to material conditions which help define the Jewishness of the Jew.

So the Jew, like the rest of us, is faced with the choice of authenticity or flight from freedom-responsibility. Recall that Sartre defines "authenticity" as "having a true and lucid consciousness of a situation, in assuming the responsibility and risks that it involves, in accepting it in pride or humiliation, sometimes in horror or hate" (AJ, 90). But what makes the Jew's choice intolerable is the objective necessity of choosing between a denial of his humanity in compliance with the demands of the anti-Semite (for example, by wearing a special insignia or simply by living in the ghetto) and a repudiation of his Jewishness for the sake of the liberal democrat whose egalitarian principles require the excision of concrete differences between individual men. In a way that will become standard to subsequent Sartrean criticism, the Jew's situation is shown to be oppressive: though each Jew must accept responsibility for his situation by facing up to the solidarity it confers, responsibility for the oppression lies with the anti-Semite and his liberal democratic accomplice.

Sartre's real target in this essay is precisely this would-be friend of the persecuted Jew, the liberal democrat. A victim of the analytic spirit, his passion for *l'égalité* blinds him to "the concrete syntheses with which history confronts him" (AJ, 55). He sees neither Arab nor Jew, neither bourgeois nor worker, but only man. The liberal democrat is an assimilationist, one who wants the Jews to be full members of the community— if only they will not insist on remaining Jews! While the anti-Semite overlooks the man for the Jew, the liberal democrat sacrifices the Jew to the man. As I noted in the previous chapter, what is called for is the kind of concrete reasoning that can overcome these defects of the analytic spirit, what Sartre terms "the spirit of synthesis," precursor to his dialectical reason in the *Critique*.

I have observed likewise that criticism of the analytic spirit is a permanent feature of Sartrean social thought and have noted how it grounds his opposition to the concept of abstract human nature and to the bourgeois humanism of "natural rights" which that concept supports. It is to Sartre's credit to have pointed out that the definition of man can serve as a weapon in social or political conflict. Doubtless this lies behind his frequent accusations of racism against settlers, capitalists, and others. For every such definition is normative, embodying what we may call "defining values" in terms of which the other group or class is judged. Thus, the anti-Semite decides what makes a man a "real" Frenchman, and the Jew by definition is unable to realize the value proposed. The humanism based on such a definition is accordingly antihumanistic for the excluded party. From this point on, Sartre's critical stance assumes that central to the social struggle is a conflict of humanisms.

The question of collective responsibility arises when Sartre asks who is at fault for this Jewish situation. Obviously, the avowed anti-Semite is partially to blame, as is the Jew himself (in view of the account of "situation" given in *Being and Nothingness*). But it is chiefly the misguided liberal democrat whom Sartre accuses and whom he urges to ameliorate the situation in its "objective" components. For the Jew's condition is

54

reduced to a hellish choice between inauthenticity, if he follows the liberal democrat, and martyrdom, if he faces up to the anti-Semite. Since few will admit to being anti-Semitic and yet most of us glory in our democratic convictions, Sartre concludes that all are at fault. Listen to his accusation because, mutatis mutandis, it will emerge as his basic criticism of the colonialist and the capitalist in each of us:

> It is our eyes that reflect to him the unacceptable image that he wishes to dissimulate. It is our words and our gestures— *all* our words and *all* our gestures—our anti-Semitism, but equally our condescending liberalism—that have poisoned him. It is we who constrain him to be a Jew whether through flight from himself or through self-assertion: it is we who force him into the dilemma of Jewish authenticity or inauthenticity. We have created this variety of men who have no meaning except as artificial products of a capitalist (or feudal) society, whose only reason for existing is to serve as scapegoat for a still pre-logical community. . . . *In this situation there is not one of us who is not totally guilty and even criminal;* the Jewish blood that the Nazis shed falls on all our heads. (AJ, 135–36; emphasis mine)

He will later refer to "our involuntary complicity with the anti-Semites who have made hangmen of us all" (AJ, 151).

Sartre is writing for rhetorical effect here but he nonetheless reveals several points crucial to a theory of collective responsibility. Chief among these is the notion of mediation. Setting aside those relatively unproblematic instances of collective responsibility where the effect is attributable to a team effort (i.e., cases of conscious, explicit, and deliberate cooperation), the crux of the problem is to determine what links a specific event or state of affairs with the group and/or individuals to whom it is collectively ascribed. In the present instance, Sartre sees this mediating element in the social climate, the entire value system which is oppressive of Jews (see AJ, 80). This is the point of his subsequent criticism of colonialist and capitalist antihumanism. We shall see in the other portraits as we do here that such a sharing in an oppressive value system is essential to Sartre's ascriptions of collective responsibility. It is for this reason that the concept of humanism will play such an important role in our discussion.

Perhaps the major lesson of this essay for my topic is that collective responsibility is always mediated responsibility, whether in the sense of responsibility of a group member qua member (in which case the group mediates) or in the more difficult sense of responsibility of an unspecified number of individuals (the present case) for a climate, atmosphere, or system that is itself exploitative or oppressive. The discovery and analysis of the basic forms of social mediation constitute the main task in my reconstruction of a Sartrean theory of collective responsibility. For according as the basic forms of social mediation can be unearthed, our understanding of collective responsibility will gain in clarity and precision.

When Sartre speaks of the "Jewish situation," I remarked earlier, he is referring to more than the unity imposed by the anti-Semite's gaze, though this existentialist model still dominates his social thinking. For he is beginning to respect that dimension of situation which he will later term "objective possibility."[5] The Jew is objectively constrained to choose between two alternatives neither of which is consonant with his concrete freedom, that is, with his freedom to be a Jewish man. Sartre's advocacy of "concrete liberalism," as he calls it, is proof of his awareness that this objective possibility must be modified if the Jew (and the anti-Semite) would be set free. For he insists:

> If we wish to make such a choice [anti-Semitism] impossible,
> . . . since he, like all men, exists as a free agent within a
> situation, *it is his situation which must be modified from top
> to bottom.* In short, if we can change the perspective of the
> choice, then the choice itself will change. Thus we do not attack
> freedom, but bring it about that freedom decides on other bases,
> and in terms of other structures. (AJ, 148; emphasis mine)

This last sentence could serve for the motto of political existentialism as it came to be practiced by Sartre, Merleau-Ponty, and others after the war. On the one hand, it respects the inviolable freedom of the individual (*la liberté*) while, on the other, it urges us to work on the bases and structures of the anti-Semite's situation so as to alter the perspective of his choice (*le socialisme*).

But this prescription of structural change as a remedy for social ills is as problematic as it is significant. Occurring so close in time to the appearance of *Being and Nothingness,* it suggests that some features of the latter, especially "facticity," be given a more "objectivist" reading than Sartre had seemed to allow at that stage. Of course, Sartre is far from adopting even the softest determinism. And yet we must admit that henceforth we are dealing with genuine *conditions,* however vaguely conceived, and not with mere occasions of choice.

Unfortunately, aside from general references to "economic and social causes" and specific mention of the system of private property (see AJ, 150), Sartre leaves unexplained the nature of these bases and structures, much less their precise relation to the perspective of choice. But one senses a fundamental acceptance of the concepts of economic base and ideological superstructure characteristic of historical materialism, even in this essay from his peak existentialist period. Indeed, he implicitly appeals to a socialist revolution as the means of making the choice of anti-Semitism impossible—a definite, if not well-thought-out, nod toward social conditioning.

Finally, when he mentions "our involuntary complicity with the anti-Semite," he is implying that in an anti-Semitic society each of us is responsible for anti-Semitism to the extent that we permit or even support those bases and structures which make possible the choice of anti-Semitism. Of course, it is incumbent upon him to explain the kind of conditioning and corresponding possibility he has in mind. To remove all possibility of inauthenticity (e.g., of choosing anti-Semitism) would be tantamount to destroying ontological freedom. He seems to mean positive conditions and "enabling" structures. But these are relevant to a different kind of freedom from the ontological, namely, to the concrete or situated freedom of his *Existentialism* lecture. And even there these concepts are scarcely analyzed with any precision, as we know.

Despite their imprecision, it is ultimately to the concepts of bases and structures that Sartre will appeal to justify his accusation that *all* our words and *all* our gestures make us racists. As his subsequent popular writings make clear, these bases and structures mediate our private lives and our public responsibilities. Clearly, this insight has applicability far beyond the boundaries of anti-Semitism in France. Along with the idea of situational solidarity, criticism of the spirit of abstraction, and emphasis on collective responsibility as mediated by such factors as racist humanism, the concepts of the bases and structures of choice form the fourth permanent feature of Sartre's social thought. They will develop under the rubric of objective possibility as his theoretical commitment to historical materialism deepens. But we can now speak of a pattern in Sartre's ascriptions of collective responsibility. He will follow it without substantial change throughout his subsequent popular writings on political and social issues.

The Neo-Colonialist

At the height of the Algerian crisis Sartre published a number of articles in *Les Temps modernes* and in *L'Express* as well as prefaces to two books wherein he proposed in concrete and popular style ideas on colonialism that he would treat systematically in the *Critique*. Ascriptions of collective responsibility abound in these journalistic writings, gathered into volume 5 of *Situations*.[6] Their common purpose is to move the stolid bourgeoisie to admit its complicity in the dirty work of colonial warfare. From them emerges a pattern of argument similar to that of *Anti-Semite and Jew,* based on a stable set of principles, exhibiting the rudiments of a theory of collective responsibility.

The first addition to Sartre's social theory that these essays make is the concept of system. This objective factor is dimly present but understated in *Anti-Semite,* which, with its emphasis on the psychology of bad faith, is still a product of Sartre's vintage existentialist years. But he sees a necessity written into colonialism that, once set in motion, operates independently of its agents' intentions. Thus in "Colonialism Is a System" he explains:

> Here is what I should like to show you apropos of Algeria which is, alas! the clearest and most legible example of the colonial system. I should like to make you see the rigor of colonialism, its internal necessity, how it had to lead us exactly where we are, and how the purest intention, if it is born in this infernal circle, dies immediately.
>
> For it is not true that there are good settlers and others who are wicked; there are settlers, that's all. (Note: I do not call settlers the petty functionaries nor the European workers who are at once victims and innocent beneficiaries of the regime.) (*Situations,* 5:27)

This is reminiscent of a passage from the preface to the first edition of *Capital* where Marx absolves the individual capitalist of responsibility "for relations whose creature he socially remains."[7] It immediately plunges us into a major dilemma of Marxist social thought, one especially painful for an existential libertarian like Sartre, namely, the reconciliation of responsibility and freedom with historical and social determinism. He does not face the issue here, and it plagues him in his Genet and Flaubert "biographies" as well. It is now raised in concrete fashion with implicit use of principles that will be formulated only in the *Critique.* So let us observe the issue *in praxi* the better to reconstruct its presuppositions later on. For this problem of freedom-determinism strikes at the heart of Sartre's theoretical and, so it seems, personal ambivalences.[8] He exposes his basic rationalist penchant by accentuating the rigor of colonialism, "its internal necessity." Thus he can speak of the purest intentions dying in its infernal circle, a claim reminiscent of the conditions-choice relationship alluded to in *Anti-Semite.* "The meanness is in the system," he wrote several years earlier, apropos of capitalism, "one must not see a national characteristic in it, but the collective situation which our lords have made for us."[9] This accords with his revolutionist's preference for an "ethic" of results over one of intentions, and exhibits what we have seen him term his brush with "amoral realism."

But the ambiguity of his position is heightened when he excludes from the class of settlers those who are at once victims and *innocent* beneficiaries of the system. The settlers themselves are by implication guilty beneficiaries of colonialism, and the guilt of the latter like the innocence of the former is a function of status within that system. All the settlers are guilty because they are settlers. Yet talk of innocence and guilt in such a context of social criticism bears a moral connotation difficult to reconcile with "internal necessity" or "amoral realism." For Sartre obviously is not speaking of innocence and guilt in any legal sense.

And so this essay faces us squarely with Sartre's version of the classical Marxist dilemma. On the one hand, his refusal to speak of good and bad settlers ranks him with the proponents of what we shall later call the *Marxist-determinist* concept of responsibility, one ostensibly free of moral significance, as the quotation from *Capital* indicates.[10] Yet on the other hand, his reference to innocence (and guilt) both in the immediate context of sociopolitical polemic and in the broader setting of his existential libertarianism and abiding ethical concerns witnesses the presence of another understanding of "responsibility," the *existentialist-moral* concept. As my reconstruction of Sartre's social ontology progresses in chapter 7, I shall study each of these concepts and their interrelation. For the present it suffices to note that the issue has been raised but scarcely settled in his polemical writings.

In order to defend responsibility in a moral sense, Sartre often seems constrained to exaggerate, as in his ascription of cynicism and premeditated brutality to the colonialist government (see *Situations*, 5:32) or the deliberate murder attributed to the Malthusian bourgeoisie (see CDR, 782–83). But he is merely applying an axiom from practical life, namely, that whoever wills the end wills the necessary means. In the final analysis, it is not the barbarism and brutality of the means that he is decrying but the choice of an end, colonialism, that necessitates such means. And the existentialist-moral responsibility which accompanies the colonialist project (the choice, for example, to be or to remain a settler) overflows into all the messy details of oppression and exploitation that such a project entails. To protest that one did not want this—the bloody quelling of a native uprising, for example—while not reacting violently against colonialism itself is in Sartre's eyes consummate bad faith.[11] To the extent that such a protest is true, it is irrelevant, being nothing but a matter of intentions; to the degree that it is relevant, being an expression of one's fundamental project, it is not true. For exploitation and oppression, Sartre is arguing, are part and parcel of what it means to be a settler. It is part of the objective reality of each and every colonialist.

In this way Sartre hopes to attach existential-moral responsibility not only to the originators of the oppressive system but to their heirs as well. If his application of the existential categories of fundamental project and bad faith to subsequent generations of colonialists is plausible, he will have succeeded in humanizing the Marxist understanding of collective responsibility. Let us observe his initial attempt at close range, for it will constitute the specifically Sartrean dimension of the question of collective responsibility.

Although he is somewhat careless about distinguishing kinds of responsibility, Sartre appeals to a rather straightforward concept of political liability to account for the responsibility that all Frenchmen inherit for a colonial policy which their government has pursued for generations in their name:

> By plunging us into a despicable undertaking, [our political leaders] have invested us from without with a *social culpability*. But we vote; and in a way we can revoke them. . . . The crimes which are committed in our name, it must be that we are personally a party to them, since it is in our power to stop them. This guilt which has remained inert and foreign in us must be assumed on our part—we must degrade ourselves so as to be able to bear it. (*Situations,* 5:58; emphasis mine)

If each generation of colonialists inherits its fathers' guilt as well as their colonial system, this is due to the mediation not only of the system itself but of their government which sustains it. The crucial concept of mediation is now familiar to us in this regard. But to refer to "social culpability" and "guilt," as he now does, involves us in evaluative terms. In the present context, as we observed, they are moral, not legal, ascriptions. Sartre must somehow find the cognitive and volitional conditions for moral culpability fulfilled in the case of French colonial policy. How he finally resolves this problem, again, must await the rational reconstruction of his finished position I undertake in chapter 7. At this stage, Sartre is satisfied (or more likely, believes his middle-class audience will be satisfied) with appeal to the power of the electorate: "It is in our power to stop them."[12]

The issue becomes more interesting and Sartre's claims bolder when he turns for a parallel to that paradigm of collective responsibility in our time: the atrocities of the Hitler regime. Commenting on the German people's supposed ignorance of the genocidal practices of their government, Sartre expands his concept of bad faith to proportions commensurate with the concept of collective responsibility which he is applying in the existentialist-moral sense. He insists that the Germans deliberately drove knowledge and suspicion of the Nazi atrocities from their minds. And he sees an analogy with the French in the Algerian situation.[13] This fear to investigate, to confirm one's dark suspicions, this truncated ignorance Sartre sees as "notre complicité" (*Situations*, 5:61). "In a word, the French have a bad conscience. . . . And that is what makes us guilty" (*Situations*, 5:65).

> False candor, flight, bad faith, solitude, speechlessness, complicity at once refused and accepted, that is what we called *collective responsibility* in 1945. At that time it was not proper for the German population to pretend to have been ignorant of the camps. "Come now," we used to say, "they know everything!" And we were right, they did know everything; and it's only today that we can understand it, for we too know everything. . . . They thought as do we that the information wasn't sure; they kept quiet; they distrusted each other. Dare we condemn them still? Will we dare yet to absolve ourselves? (*Situations*, 5:66)

In Sartre's eyes, the French collectively are as responsible for the massacres and tortures in Algeria as were their German neighbors for those of the Nazis. And the responsibility is more than merely Marxist-determinist or even just political. It is existentialist-moral, involving (collective) bad faith, the *mauvaise foi* of *Being and Nothingess:* an "infernal circle of . . . irresponsible responsibility, of culpable innocence and ignorance which is knowledge" (BN, 49). The crucial concept of collective bad faith, employed in this lengthy quotation, will receive extended analysis in my rational reconstruction of Sartre's complete theory of collective responsibility.

We know that for Sartre racism lies behind the inculpating "humanism" which mediates the responsibility of the capitalist and the colonialist as well as that of the anti-Semite. His remarks about the racist foundation of neocolonialism anticipate more recent discussions of "institutionalized racism":

> Racism is inscribed in the facts themselves, in the institutions, in the nature of production and distribution; political and social statuses mutually reenforce each other: since the native is a sub-human, the Declaration of the Rights of Man do not pertain to him; conversely, since he has no rights, he is abandoned without protection to the inhuman forces of nature, to the "iron laws" of economics. (*Situations*, 5:52)

61

Again, "the meanness is in the system." But a distinctive feature of Sartre's existentialist approach surfaces when he immediately adds that "racism is *already there,* carried by the colonialist praxis, engendered each minute by the colonialist apparatus" (*Situations,* 5:52). The point is that at the base of the most impersonal and inevitable racist situations stands a racist praxis—to which responsibility in the existentialist-moral sense can readily be ascribed. We are witnessing Sartre's practical appeal to what I shall call his principle of "the primacy of praxis." Its moral and regenerative use should already be clear: if praxis sustains these institutions, praxis can change them. Later I shall integrate this important principle into Sartre's social ontology as a whole.

It was evident in chapter 3 that a new and socialist humanism now sets the standard by which Sartre measures contemporary social and economic evils. The fact that his support of this criterion has all the earmarks of moral advocacy leads us to conclude that his humanism is a moral norm. Indeed, his references to the antihumanism of the racist, be he anti-Semite, settler, or capitalist, enjoy in Sartre's arguments the conclusiveness of an appeal to first principles. I pointed out in that same chapter that "choice of unfreedom" is a practical inconsistency but, further, that one can not choose freedom concretely without choosing the same for everyone.

Yet the argument supporting what I have called Sartre's "universal freedom conditional" is, at best, elliptical and obscure. The crucial link between abstract and concrete freedom, that is, between choosing freedom as self-presence and intending that all agents mutually recognize each other as self-presences, depends on a set of value-concepts and especially on the use of "situational thinking" which Sartre fails to integrate into a coherent argument in any single locus during that postwar decade. This is indeed ironic for someone who is in the process of discovering the power of synthesis. In any case, the basic premises of *Existentialism Is a Humanism,* the moral imperative and the universal freedom conditional, emerge as nonnegotiable principles of Sartre's socialist humanism from this period onward.

Support of this new humanism not only lends a certain moral earnestness to Sartre's essays but also supplies another component for his theory of collective responsibility. For he argues with almost monotonous regularity that the liberation of the exploited and the oppressed will entail freeing the exploiters and oppressors as well. The French, for example, must fight "to free *both* the Algerians and the French from colonial tyranny" (*Situations,* 5:48). Again, the new humanism supports his universal freedom conditional (UFC).

Since my concern at this stage of my investigation is to examine Sartre's practice of attributing responsibility to collectives, I shall analyze his powerful Preface to Frantz Fanon's *The Wretched of the Earth*. For it is a model of such ascriptions in his more popular writings, employing all the elements of the theory uncovered so far.[14]

He sets the accusatory tone when he urges: "For we in Europe too are being decolonized: that is to say that the settler which is in every one of us is being savagely rooted out" (WE, 24). To those who disclaim complicity in the plight of their former colonies because they live in the mother country and deplore her excesses, Sartre responds:

> It is true, you are not settlers, but you are no better. For the pioneers belonged to you; you sent them overseas, and it was you they enriched. You warned them that if they shed too much blood you would disown them, or say you did, in something of the same way any state maintains abroad a mob of agitators, *agents provocateurs,* and spies whom it disowns when they are caught. You who are so liberal . . . , men are massacred in your name. Fanon reveals to his comrades—above all to some of them who are too Westernized—the solidarity of the people of the mother country and of their representatives in the colonies. (WE, 13–14)

This is a case of what he has previously called the "objective reality" of the metropolitan Frenchman. Though talk of atrocities committed "in their name" and "by their settlers" suggests political liability, the solidarity between settler and homeland resident is more than political.

As Sartre ferrets out this "settler in each of us," the first bond of unity and hence of responsibility that he exposes is one of interest. Recall that the Jew lacked such unity to the extent that he was solely a product of the Third. But we are "settlers" in the sense that we have profited to some degree from the exploitative system ("It was you they enriched"). In more rhetorical terms, he claims: "With us, to be a man is to be an *accomplice* of colonialism, since all of us without exception have profited by colonial exploitation" (WE, 25; emphasis mine).

Second, in an obvious appeal to the moral consciousness of his audience, he emphasizes their awareness, despite pretended ignorance, of the human activities performed in their name. This is the collective bad faith mentioned earlier.

But the chief source of unity between settlers and those in the mother country is ideological—Sartre's bête noire, bourgeois humanism. The same humanism which "justified" mistreatment of the Jew and the native is now called upon to excuse the metropolitan Frenchman who appeals to nonviolence to salve his conscience. But Sartre's concept of situation has moved beyond the stage where desire not to be involved or appeal to good intentions will remove anyone from the ranks of the guilty. He states with accustomed bluntness:

> First we must face that unexpected revelation, the striptease of our humanism. There you can see it, quite nude, and it's not a pretty sight. It was nothing but an ideology of lies. . . . A fine sight they were too, the believers in nonviolence, saying that they were neither executioners nor victims. Very well then; if you're not victims when the government which you voted for, when the army in which your younger brothers are serving without hesitation or remorse, have undertaken race murder, you are without a doubt executioners. And if you choose to be victims and to risk being put in prison for a day or two, you are simply choosing to pull your irons out of the fire. But you will not be able to pull them out; they'll have to stay there till the end. (WE, 25)

Like the true revolutionary whose book he is prefacing, Sartre leaves no room for good intentions:

> Try to understand this at any rate: if violence began this very evening and if exploitation and oppression had never existed on the earth, perhaps the slogans of nonviolence might end the quarrel. But if the whole regime, even your nonviolent ideas, are conditioned by a thousand-year-old oppression, your *passivity serves only to place you in the ranks of the oppressors.* (WE, 25; emphasis mine)

In a sense, therefore, Sartre's pendulum has swung back to the Marxist-determinist concept of responsibility, refined by allusions to the sociology of knowledge, to the fact that the very idea of nonviolence in the present context is a product of the oppressive bourgeois value system. Once more, it is the bases and structures of exploitation, the colonialist system itself, which must be changed. Yet as a final tribute to completeness, if not consistency, Sartre's tacit appeal to the primacy of praxis warrants his exhortations to rise above a system whose internal necessity he has just been describing, with sufficient force to change it—a perennial inconsistency for more orthodox Marxists.[15]

The Torturer: *The Condemned of Altona*

I take my third portrait of social responsibility from Sartre's theater. Existentialism, with its stress on the revelatory power of such emotions as anguish and shame, its dramatic conception of existence, and its penchant for oblique communication, has always maintained a close relation

64

to imaginative literature and the fine arts. But even among existentialists Sartre is unique because of the quality and sheer extent of his literary output. As the consummate artist-philosopher, he has labored in each field with close regard for the other. He brings the artist's descriptive power to bear on many striking philosophical passages while extending the philosopher's acumen to literary endeavors that thereby gain an intelligence and decisiveness which fortify the mere pleasure of the text.

We have seen that Sartre has been a philosopher of the imagination from the start. His first thesis for the diploma in advanced studies (1926) was on the imagination, as were two of his subsequent philosophical studies. One of them, *The Psychology of Imagination,* is a masterwork on the subject. Small wonder that, when he first sought an explicit philosophic method, he would be drawn to phenomenology with its accent on "free, imaginative variation" of examples. The relation between the imaginary and the real continued to hold his attention through that momentary triumph of political imagination, the events of May 1968, to his extended study of the real-unreal relationship in Flaubert and his era.[16] His theory of committed literature justifies theater as social criticism—"reflecting in our mirrors the unhappy consciousness [of the bourgeoisie]" (WL, 276)—and warrants an appeal to his imaginative literature in pursuit of philosophical issues. For there is a continuous cross movement between Sartre's philosophy and his theater in particular, the latter often exhibiting concretely problems analyzed abstractly in the former.[17] Such a relation obtains between *Being and Nothingness* and *No Exit,* between *Saint Genet* and *The Devil and the Good Lord,* and between the *Critique* and *The Condemned of Altona.* The philosophic themes treated in each play are, respectively, the look and being-for-others, the dialectic of good and evil, and serial otherness. Since *The Condemned* is an artistic portrayal of a problem from the *Critique* as well as a response to a particular political situation, it can serve both as my final example of Sartre's practical ascriptions of collective responsibility and as an introduction to his systematic treatment of social philosophy in the *Critique.*

Someone who knows him well called 1958 "without doubt the most terrible year in Sartre's entire life."[18] Chief among its tragedies for Sartre, and one that enraged him, was the silent acquiescence of the bourgeois press in the increasing repression of the Algerian revolution with its inevitable torture and summary trials and executions. Setting aside the toilsome writing of the *Critique* in the summer of 1958, he began composing a play that would "give the bourgeoisie a guilty conscience" regarding the inhumane conduct of the Algerian war. This work raises in imaginative form the issue of collective responsibility with which Sartre had been wrestling both in his political essays and in the *Critique.*

65

The plot concerns a young soldier, Franz, son of a Hamburg shipbuilding magnate, who returns from the Russian front covered with glory and guilt. Unable to face the prospect of Germany's resurrection despite her war crimes, he sequesters himself in an upper room of the family mansion. There in his tattered officer's uniform he lives out a half-believed fable of Germany's destruction and current distress—a fitting payment for her crimes. But she will not suffer without a voice being raised. In an act which dramatically portrays Sartre's growing concern with the judgment of history and with the responsibility of one generation to another, Franz is making a series of tape recordings which will give the "true" story of Germany's treatment by the self-righteous victors whose hands are as bloody as her own. The tapes are addressed to the thirtieth century and those crablike creatures who will have survived our self-destruction. Franz is aided in this charade by his sister Leni, his only link with the outside world. His father, whose desire for Nazi support of his shipyard led him to inform on Franz, who had been harboring an escaped Jewish prisoner, thereby forcing his son to enlist in the army, has been denied access to the upper room for thirteen years. The two remaining characters are Werner, Franz's brother who has supplanted him as heir, and Werner's wife, Johanna, who pierces Franz's fortress and threatens to destroy it with the truth that he has long suspected: Germany is prospering and the firm is stronger than ever. But Johanna falls in love with Franz and is ready to share his fantasy when he reveals to her the source of his guilt: he had tortured two captured partisans in a vain effort to save the lives of his encircled men. In a reaction characteristic of the "beautiful souls" that Sartre detests, she peremptorily rejects Franz in revulsion, unwilling to accept any explanation of so barbarous an act.

Sartre's lesson is that *all* war is barbarous and that only those in bad faith would allow France (Franz) to conduct a war of repression as long as it did not dirty its hands with cruel and inhuman practices. As in the case of capitalism and colonialism generally, the meanness is part of the system. When someone, for example, the committed artist, unveils the system's underlying racism and the inhumane tactics it calls for, the sight is a shocking one. Like Johanna, we disavow it. Yet we all knew better or could have, if we had cared to.

Let us apply the pattern of ascriptions that has emerged in Sartre's polemical essays to this imaginative portrayal of collective responsibility. The basic issue is one of solidarity. Who is the "we" who are responsible? Franz has decided to assume the guilt of the entire German people for the atrocities committed by the Nazis. Motivated by fierce family and national pride that prohibits compromise—"We are all Luther's victims"—Franz opts for total responsibility: "I am your martyr."[19] But a martyr must have a cause: "Either Germany must die or I shall become a common criminal," he cries. "Precisely" is his father's perceptive reply (CA, 170). Hannah Arendt called it "the banality of evil" in her famous communiqués from the Eichmann trial.[20] It is this commonplace guilt that Franz seeks to avoid by such histrionic gestures. In an interview in *Der Spiegel* on the occasion of this play's first German production, Sartre insisted that its aim was "to show that torture is a practice which has become generalized during the last thirty years" (ST, 287–88). Franz is guilty, indeed, but so is everyone else.[21]

Solidarity among the generations has traditionally been captured in the biblical saying, "The fathers have eaten unripe grapes; the children's teeth are set on edge" (Jer. 31:29). When criticizing the anti-Semite, Sartre had rejected such a "prelogical concept of responsibility" (AJ, 67; see 16). But events led him to temper this wholesale dismissal. In our present case such "diachronic" responsibility is based on a solidarity of influence and interest: (Franz to father) "It's because you're an informer that I'm a torturer" (CA, 161). The father had groomed his son to succeed him in the firm, a process Sartre describes with biting irony in his short story, "The Childhood of a Leader."[22] The training includes realizing one's right to command and others' duty to obey—the implicit racism of "natural" leaders and followers, as Sartre reads it: (Franz) "Do you know that he made me into a rather formidable machine?" (Johanna) "Your father?" (Franz) "Yes. A machine to give orders" (CA, 136–37). Driven by the economic exigencies of the family enterprise,[23] the father informs on his son, who has sheltered a fugitive Jew. The son is likewise forced to "sacrifice" two captives for those under his command. In each case they are victims of circumstance; "the meanness is in the system," but again not entirely. If external necessity (history) has turned the elder Gerlach into an informer and his son into a torturer, "the Butcher of Smolensk," neither can escape entirely his part in the crime. The credo of Sartrean humanism reads: "I believe that a man can always make something out of what is made of him."[24] In the case at hand, it leads to the double suicide of father and son, but not before the elder Gerlach has admitted: "Tell your Court of Crabs that I alone am guilty—of everything" (CA, 172).[25]

Addressing his tapes, Franz extends responsibility to his generation as a whole: "Centuries of the future, here is my century, solitary and deformed—the accused" (CA, 177). Although these future judges function as a Third whose objectifying gaze steals our freedom to read our actions as we will, our solidarity is no longer imposed by their look. Our common guilt, Franz dramatically points out, is our rapaciousness: "One and one make one—that's our mystery." Man is a beast to man. The play concludes with the suicides completed and a recorded voice crying to an empty room: "Oh tribunal of the night—you who were, who will be, and who are—I have been! I, Franz von Gerlach, here in this room, have taken the century upon my shoulders and have said: 'I will answer for it. This day and forever!' " (CA, 178).

Of course, we find more illustration than argument in these feverish exchanges. One senses that, for Franz, collective responsibility is individual responsibility writ large, so large in fact that only the shoulders of a von Gerlach can bear it. But they instantiate what we now realize is Sartre's own theory of collective responsibility. This is made abundantly clear by the quasi-official commentary on *The Condemned,* his interview in *Der Spiegel,* mentioned earlier. "In our century of violence and bloodshed," he laments, "any adult . . . has a responsibility to assume [for what he has learned to live with]. In almost every country there exists active or passive complicity" (ST, 286; F, 334). "Notre complicité"is by now a well-worn Sartrean expression. When asked by *Der Spiegel* whether Franz's speeches to the Crabs are not some sort of plea against the accusation of collective guilt, Sartre responds:

> Yes, because collective guilt exists insofar as it represents a kind of indifference or a deliberate semi-evasion or toleration in each individual. You can see this in France every day, and in other countries too, if you read the newspapers. We are somewhat reluctant to learn the truth, and the result is that, strictly speaking, we are moving toward collective guilt. (ST, 297)

Here is the Sartrean pattern in a nutshell: *collective bad faith amidst an objectively incriminating situation* equals *collective responsibility.*

Simply to hold the leaders responsible and to excuse their obedient subordinates is to ignore the torments of conscience behind the latter's free decision to obey. As Sartre warns: "It is too easy to get rid of the leaders and not to take into consideration the problem of the collectivity" (ST, 297; F, 345). It is with this problem of the collectivity that he chooses to grapple in *The Condemned* and in the *Critique.* We have been examining his practical and almost ad hoc treatment of the issue since the war's end. In his remarks to the interviewer from *Der Spiegel,* Sartre allows a rare glimpse of his own understanding of the issue:

> We must see the problem of responsibility, not in its direct form, but [as] the problem of the solitary [*seul*] man who lives his responsibility individually while in fact it is tied to *collective structures.* . . . While showing Franz's crime, I have tried to portray it as almost inevitable. There was a brief instant of

freedom [Sartre's humanistic principle], but in fact everything conspired to lead Franz to his act. Naturally, he was free to choose otherwise, even if for only an instant. But *au fond* Franz is a man *so formed by his family,* so formed by the horrible experience of powerlessness, and who, moreover, had been so ill-prepared for human love, for human ties, that he *almost* necessarily had to do what he finally did. But, of course, he wasn't obliged to do it. It's there that the problem of freedom arises, to be sure. (ST, 298–99; F, 347; emphases mine)

Strange words from the father of existentialism as it is popularly conceived, but added evidence of his growing sense of the relatedness of human agents, their malleability especially at an early age, and the "almost" decisive influence of objective possibility and historical environment on their life projects. It is this sense of "objective possibility," as we may now call it, that enables him to dialogue theoretically with Marxists while easing his way into a complete and coherent theory of collective responsibility.[26]

From these three portraits as from a composite photo emerges the complete configuration of Sartre's theory: situational solidarity that includes socioeconomic interest as well as the look of the Third, mediation of a racist antihumanism set in motion by childhood socialization, an objectively oppressive and exploitative system of social and economic relations supported by governmental intervention, a Marxist-determinist and an existentialist-moral use of "responsibility," the last bolstered by appeal to collective bad faith and by at least a nod toward what I shall call the principle of the primacy of practice. More than ad hoc solutions to pressing social issues, these features express an underlying social ontology whose nature and scope I shall now examine.[27]

five

Freedom and Necessity
The Existentialist in the Court of History

> The other day, I re-read a prefatory note of mine to a collection of these plays—*Les Mouches, Huis Clos* and others— and was truly scandalized. I had written: "Whatever the circumstances, and whatever the site, a man is always free to choose to be a traitor or not. . . ." When I read this, I said to myself: it's incredible, I actually believed that!
>
> *Between Existentialism and Marxism*

Franz's concern to justify himself before future generations should not be dismissed as a mere symptom of cosmic paranoia. We have noted Sartre's growing sensitivity to the historical dimension of responsibility. Viewed as a broadening of the existentialist category "being-for-others," this comes as no surprise. In *Being and Nothingness* Sartre allows that only the living give meaning to an otherwise dead past. This is a major lesson of *No Exit*. Yet the Other's look in these works, as we know, is always singular; the Us is constituted by that alienating gaze. For the existentialist Sartre, in other words, there is no subject of history, only an object: the curdled consciousness of the Us. Hence, history will be a chronicle of alienation narrated by one freedom to another. True freedom (subjectivity) must be sought in biography, the attempt to decipher another's project via a hermeneutic briefly sketched at the close of *Being and Nothingness*.[1]

Aristotle recommended that we desert the historian for the poet if we would learn the truth about human nature. Sartre at this stage seems to concur: the existential psychoanalysis that he practices in his biographies is much closer to creative literature than to historiography properly speaking. He ratifies this assessment himself when characterizing his three-volume Flaubert study as "a *true* novel" (with somewhat muted ambiguity in the French, "un roman *vrai*").[2]

But something has changed in Sartre's approach to the panorama of human actions, and that shift is reflected in his biographies. We have noted an increasing awareness of cultural, social, and economic condi-

70

tioning in his accounts of collective situation. His biographies exhibit a concomitant evolution in his attitude toward both the unconscious and the role of the family in a child's psychosocial development. Moreover, as these works incorporate his newly acquired consciousness of socio-economic conditioning, they broaden into cultural history and social criticism.[3] They are immediate applications of what we have described as the motto of Sartrean humanism: "A man can always make something out of what is made of him" (BEM, 35). If the first part of this formula voices his abiding existentialist conviction, the second expresses his awareness of the forces that militate against what he now calls concrete freedom. This interplay of optimism and pessimism, of the comic and the tragic, of freedom and necessity, dominates the second half of Sartre's productive life. It is epitomized in the issue of collective responsibility: we are condemned to a responsibility which surpasses our individual actions, yet each must bear the burden himself.

At the very time when Sartre was wrestling with social theory in the *Critique,* two of his leading critics were pointing out the inadequacies of *Being and Nothingness* as a social ontology. Roger Garaudy, then reigning philosopher of the French Communist party, dismissed Sartre's existentialism as "voluntaristic idealism" because, in the present-past relationship, it gives priority to the present. The true Marxist perspective, according to Garaudy, requires "that project be subordinated to situation as superstructure to base."[4]

Two years earlier, Sartre's erstwhile friend and cofounder of *Les Temps modernes,* Maurice Merleau-Ponty, had criticized him for reducing all social relations to those of looking/looked-at, that is, to what I have called the "existentialist" model.[5] Merleau-Ponty argues that what results is a world of "pure action," of action-at-a-distance, which undermines the Marxist dialectic: "We are in a magical or moral universe." Summarizing the weaknesses of *Being and Nothingness,* he notes perceptively that "the social cannot enter into [Sartre's] philosophy of the *cogito* except via the *alter ego,*" and that it then does so as a kind of scandal—the infamous scandal of the Other for Sartre. He adds that "what continues to distinguish Sartre from Marxism even in recent times, is therefore his philosophy of the *cogito.* Men are mentally attached to history. The *cogito* perseveres in its claim to be everything that we are, taking as its own even our situation before others." But this simply lands us in the obscurity of "pure action" and leaves us with a society that is merely a relationship of consciousnesses.[6]

What both critics are marking is a defect in the social ontology and in the method of *Being and Nothingness,* which Sartre is trying to remedy in *Search for a Method* and the *Critique.*[7] In these subsequent works he gives greater weight to the "facticity" dimension of being-in-situation in response to Garaudy and enters wholeheartedly into the realm of dialectical reason in meeting Merleau-Ponty's challenge. So at this first stage of our rational reconstruction of Sartre's social ontology, let us examine at length the two key concepts of objective possibility and dialectical reason.

Objective Possibility

"Life taught me *la force des choses*—the power of circumstances," Sartre admitted in the late 60s (BEM, 33). And it is as "objective possibility" that he incorporates this power into his systematic thought. Since that concept or its equivalent figures centrally in the thought of Marx, Weber, and Lukács as well, writers with whose work Sartre was familiar, in order to appreciate his adaptation of the concept to his own purposes let us briefly follow its career in his three predecessors.

Marx

In his brilliant pamphlet, *The Eighteenth Brumaire of Louis Bonaparte,* Marx succinctly states this question in terms which will profoundly affect Sartre: "Men make their own history, but they do not make it as they please; they do not make it under circumstances chosen by themselves, but under circumstances directly encountered, given, and transmitted from the past."[8] Elsewhere, he elaborates those circumstances as the "forces" and "relations" of production that determine the possibility of change in the "ideological superstructure" of civil society.[9] Though he never employs the term, it is the objective possibility of ideological change that is being described by his "materialist conception of history."[10] This concept frees Marx, as it will later free Sartre, from his early idealist tendencies while preserving a scientific respectability for his theory of history. Thus, Napoleon III is described in *The Eighteenth Brumaire* as the natural leader of the small-holding peasants, the largest class in France at the time, whose mode of productive life kept them from thinking in universalist, much less in revolutionary, terms.[11] That Marx would have supported Plekhanov's extreme view of economic determinism, ridiculed by Sartre,[12] is unlikely. He does allow that men make their own history. But the link between consciousness and economics is sufficiently tight to count as "scientific"—and therein lies the problem of reconciling freedom and necessity in Marx. In rough fashion it can be said that he resolves the issue in Hegelian terms, by defining "freedom" as the recognition of necessity, which translates into a kind of "soft" determinism in William James's sense.

Weber

Max Weber was perhaps the leading social theorist of his day, but it is unclear how directly his work was known to Sartre. Sartre's early friend, Raymond Aron, did much to introduce *Verstehende Soziologie* into France at a time when Sartre was deeply interested in German thought.[13] Weber seems to be the first sociologist to use the expression "objective possibility."[14] It serves a double function in his work: as constitutive of his famous ideal types, it expresses the notion of rationality, the rationality of the effective means to real or presumptive ends; as a form of causal imputation (*Kausalzurechnung*), it supports the counterfactuals ("what would have happened if . . .") to which Weber appeals in attempting to distinguish "adequate" from merely "accidental" causes of historical events.[15] Thus the winning of the battle of Marathon was an adequate cause of the subsequent rise of Greek culture whereas the shots fired in Munich on a day in March 1848 were accidental to the Bavarian revolution because we can conclude from an assessment of objective possibility that, unlike the former, the latter "would have happened anyway." "Objective possibility" is thus a nomological concept for Weber. It presumes factual knowledge of conditions at the time in question, and knowledge of relevant empirical laws. What it yields is not absolute necessity but various degrees of probability, a notion that Weber fails to clarify.

It is by appeal to probability that Weber seeks to resolve the freedom-necessity dilemma which Marx escaped in a Hegelian manner. Thus he argues that we take as the opposite of "chance" not "necessity" but "adequacy," in the sense just explained.[16] Weber was too alive to the irrational element in history to opt for a "natural science of society" as Plekhanov and other Marxist enthusiasts were advocating. In his search for social intelligibility, he concentrates on ideal typologies and objective possibilities to yield probabilities, "adequate causes," and comprehension of the agents' own understanding both of the end-in-view and of the rational means thereto. As W. G. Runciman notes, a further difference from the Marxist and one which must have appealed to Sartre was Weber's insistence that "sociological explanations must relate to the self-conscious actions of individual people."[17] But an underlying assumption separates Weber from Marx, Lukács, and Sartre, namely, that "reality cannot be objectively grasped by the human mind as a meaningful whole."[18] Totalization, as Sartre terms it, and hence dialectical reason, are excluded on principle.

Lukács

It is precisely in this concept of totalization that one can see the greatest similarity between Lukács and Sartre.[19] Lukács claims that what distinguishes Marxism from other social theories is not economic determinism—others have proposed such views—but the concept of concrete totality: "concrete totality is . . . the category that governs reality."[20] Judging everything *sub specie totalitatis* enables Lukács (and Marx) to distinguish, for example, between false consciousness and the real, progressive consciousness of a socioeconomic class. It is only in relation to society as a whole and to the social process in its totality that the objective interests of a class can be determined and assessed. Lukács weds Marxian economic and holistic factors to Weberian objective possibility to yield a normative concept of "real" class consciousness that Weber would have repudiated.[21]

He summarizes his methodological use of "objective possibility" concisely:

> The relation [of consciousness] with concrete totality and the dialectical determinants arising from it transcend pure description and yield the category of objective possibility. By relating consciousness to the whole of society, it becomes possible to infer the thoughts and feelings that men would have in a particular situation if they were *able* to assess both it and the interests arising from it in their impact on immediate action and on the whole structure of society. That is to say, it would be possible to infer the thoughts and feelings appropriate to their objective situation.[22]

In a sense, Lukács, like Marx, is equally concerned with objective *impossibility*, with why it is, for example, that the French peasants could not have conceived of socioeconomic change. And he can speak of "objective historical necessities" as "nuances in the objective possibilities of consciousness." Indeed, the focus of his attention in this regard is class consciousness as it reflects class interest, and this presumes a conception of the social process as a whole. He emphasizes that "the objective theory of class consciousness is the theory of its objective possibility."[23] It is here that talk of the "destiny" or the "historical mission" of a particular class is deemed appropriate. By referring to necessities rather than to probabilities, Lukács sides with Marx against Weber. In fact, he speaks of the determining influence of economic structures: they are "the focal points of man's interaction with [the] environment at any given moment and . . . determine the objective nature of both his inner and his outer life."[24]

74

Yet, despite these holistic and necessitarian emphases, Lukács is strongly opposed to the reification of social forms. Echoing words which Sartre will often cite from Marx, he writes: "History is precisely the history of the unceasing overthrow of the objective forms that shape the life of man. . . . From this standpoint alone does history really become a history of mankind. For it contains nothing that does not lead back ultimately to men and to the relations between men."[25] On the face of it, this is a statement worthy of Weber. But in Lukács's holistic and dialectical context it translates into a wholehearted endorsement of the relations between individuals.

Nowhere is this endorsement more evident than in his remarks on freedom: "Above all, one thing must be made clear: freedom does *not* mean freedom of the individual." Such a conception, in his view, is bourgeois and egotistical. Rather, "it implies the conscious subordination of the self to that collective will that is destined to bring real freedom into being . . . [viz.] the Communist Party." The party, Lukács believes, anticipates the goal it aims to achieve, "freedom in solidarity."[26] Small wonder that Merleau-Ponty, when he noted the similarities between Lukács and Sartre, could do so in a chapter entitled "Sartre and Ultrabolshevism." It seems safe to conclude that Sartre's *Critique* is written partially in answer to Merleau's charge. It too must address the freedom-necessity issue.

As we review Sartre's predecessors in the use of "objective possibility" we can say that Marx anticipates the term by appeal to objective contradictions and impossibilities and to the material conditions of life. Weber introduces the concept as a heuristic device. Lukács returns to Marx's normative use, which he expands especially in terms of class consciousness, but retains the Weberian heuristic.

With these intellectual antecedents in mind, let us turn to Sartre's adaptation of the concept of objective possibility, tracing its roots in *Being and Nothingness,* surveying its employment in the postwar decades, and assessing its theoretical elaboration in the *Critique.* Our general aim, of course, is to examine the fundamental components in Sartre's broadening concepts of freedom and responsibility.

Being and Nothingness

"Objective possibility" is more than a heuristic device for Sartre; it has solid grounding in his social ontology. Even in this existentialist work he leans in its direction in order to free himself from an "idealist" understanding of "possibility" which haunts his humanization of world, space, and time. In search of a more "realist" conception of "possibility" in

Sartrean existentialism, we naturally turn to the limits of existentialist freedom itself, the limits of facticity and other freedoms.

Our earlier survey of the social dimension of *Being and Nothingness* underscored the collective aspect of being-in-situation under the rubric of "techniques" and the collectivities they reveal. It likewise brought to light the ambiguity of "situation" itself and the potential for further conceptual development which that ambiguity harbored.[27] It was in the analysis of "facticity" that we found the seeds of his subsequent understanding of objective possibility. And yet they were well buried. So acute a critic as Merleau-Ponty could conclude as recently as the mid fifties that for Sartre "possibilities are all equally distant—in a sense at zero distance, since all there is to do is to will, in another sense infinitely distant, since we will never be *them,* and *they* will never be what we have to be."[28]

Sartre, as we know, was chiefly responsible for such interpretations of this work. By failing to distinguish concrete freedom from freedom "as the definition of man" as he would later do, he could support such arresting, if seemingly outlandish claims, as that we are equally free in whatever situation (see BN, 548). But we know that he conceded an importance to facticity: "this brute and unthinkable 'quid' is that without which freedom could not be freedom" (BN, 494). As internal negation of being-in-itself, freedom (consciousness, the for-itself) is intrinsically dependent upon the "things" that it nihilates. We are not free except in situation. And in this ontological sense, we are indeed free in any situation whatsoever. But the brute being of the rock, for example, either lends itself to easy scaling or not (see BN, 488). It was not Sartre's intention to question that fact. He simply wished to urge that ontological freedom-responsibility was not compromised by such facticities: "Thus, although brute things (what Heidegger calls 'brute existents') can from the start limit *our freedom of action,* it is our freedom itself which must first constitute the framework, the technique, and the ends in relation to which they will manifest themselves as limits" (BN, 482; emphasis mine).

"Our freedom of action" was not Sartre's concern when he wrote those lines. As it began to interest him, it came to occupy the center of his attention. If we summarize those features of "facticity" discussed thus far to which Sartre could subsequently appeal in his formulation of objective possibility, we must include whatever contributes to the "coefficient of adversity" of a particular project: for example, the brute givenness of the in-itself, its "qualities" which aid, resist, or are indifferent to our undertakings, the distribution of factual elements and their interrelation according to objective rules, and the like,[29] all of which contribute to "that obscure constraint" that we experience in the formulation and undertaking of our projects (BN, 550).

Three more aspects of facticity discussed in *Being and Nothingness* inch us closer to objective possibility properly speaking: collective techniques, economic and political structures, and the so-called "unrealizables" (*irréalisables*). The first two features were examined in chapter 2. The third feature is also a form of limitation by other freedoms. As a dimension of facticity, these "unrealizables" are the external limits to my freedom imposed by the Other for me to interiorize as I will. These include such familiar items as my being courageous or cowardly, my being Jewish, and even that archetypal limit situation, my death. They are real, not imaginary. But they are "other" for the one who ascribes them to me, while becoming mine, though unrealizable, to the degree that I interiorize them, that is, insofar as I take a stand in their regard. It is as an unrealizable, for example, that Sartre can claim that *the* Jew is a product of the anti-Semite. In the broader context of looking/looked-at, the unrealizables denote the way in which I figure in others' projects, in their situations. It is in this sense that Sartre maintains that "they represent the reverse side of situation" (BN, 528). Of course, as being-for-others generally, the unrealizables are precisely such only as long as my project assumes them. But "facticity" means that I cannot not assume them, even if it be via indifference or refusal. The unrealizables are "an a priori limit given to my situation" (BN, 529).

The best summary of the foregoing as an anticipation of objective possibility is found in Sartre's own characterization of "situation": "[It] reflects to me at once both my facticity and my freedom; on the occasion of a certain objective structure of the world which surrounds me, it refers my freedom to me in the form of tasks to be freely done. *There is no constraint here* since my freedom eats into my possibilities and since correlatively the potentialities of the world *only indicate and offer* themselves" (BN, 259–60—emphasis mine; F, 317–18). Thus far in the freedom-necessity debate we can say that, whereas Weber sees objective possibility as justifying judgments of probability and Lukács (Marx) draws from it historical necessity, Sartrean facticity leaves us with "obscure constraint" which translates into "indications" and "offers."

To be precise, facticity does not so much limit freedom as enable it to define itself (as *this* no-thingness). To repeat, Sartre has not yet distinguished abstract from concrete freedom. The sole limit to my freedom in this existentialist period is another freedom: "It is for and by means of a freedom and only for and by means of it that my possibilities can be limited and fixed" (BN, 270). Only the Other's objectifying gaze can rob me of my possibilities by incorporating them into a set of possibilities not of my own choosing. Sartre will not reject this thesis even in the *Critique*, though he will modify its exclusivity. It remains as the implicit, objectifying gaze of the Other as alienating Third.

Writings of the Immediate Postwar Decade

The first indication of a change in Sartre's understanding of the related concepts of "possibility," "necessity," and "freedom" occurs in the *Comoedia* interview (1944) mentioned earlier, where he distinguishes freedom-in-consciousness and freedom-in-situation, the latter requiring others' freedom. He expands this view shortly thereafter in *Anti-Semite and Jew* by calling for a change in the "bases and structures of choice" which would render anti-Semitism impossible (see AJ, 148–49). It is in order to change these bases and structures of choice that he enters briefly into a political nonparty of the non-Communist left, *Le Rassemblement Démocratique Révolutionnaire* (RDR).[30] In a quasi manifesto for that group he reveals his growing sense of objective possibility and its relation to the categories of *Being and Nothingness*. Speaking of the role of "situation," he observes:

> We consider above all that it matters little whether or not a man is endowed with an unconditional or metaphysical freedom. What counts is that he be defined by his social situation, by his belonging to one class or another . . . because he is defined by the ensemble of *interests* and *techniques* that form him such that there is no eternal man to be saved. *The only way to free men is to act on their situation.*[31]

Social situation is now all-important. Clearly, some situations are more conducive to concrete freedom than others. Their "constraints" are growing less "obscure" in Sartre's eyes. Introducing the concept of practical unity which will prove so important in the *Critique,* he writes: "The Assembly [*Rassemblement*] must perform an inverse labor to that of the Party. Cohesion, for us, must come from interest, from situation, from consciousness of this interest, and from concrete action in the situation, but not from the bureaucratic apparatus of the Party" (*Entretiens,* p. 105). Only in this way will it preserve the twin values of socialism and freedom which, as we noted, guide the practice of political existentialism.

His regard for the concept of objective possibility during this period comes most clearly into view in two series of articles for *Les Temps modernes* later published as books, namely, *What Is Literature?* and *The Communists and Peace.* The former, in addition to making the classical statement on committed literature, subscribes to a full-blown form of objective possibility: "[Since] the fundamental structures of our society are still oppressive," a mere ethic of intention will actually do harm. "Such is the present paradox of ethics: if I get absorbed in treating certain select persons as absolute ends . . . , I shall be led to pass over in silence the injustices of the age, the class struggle, colonialism, anti-Semitism, etc., and finally I shall be led to profit from oppression in order to do good." The pattern we observed in chapter 4 appears again: such oppressive structures make us objectively responsible for the harm they entail, even if our intentions are pure. (Recall his criticism of the colonialist "system.") "The good that I try to do" in such an oppressive situation, Sartre predicts, "will turn into radical evil" (*Situations,* 2: 296–97).[32] It is a case of objective relations which vitiate our best intentions and which, in any case, must be judged by other criteria.

One thinks immediately of Lukács's criterion of the historical totality. Sartre, indeed, begins to speak in such holistic terms. In his manifesto for the RDR he had sensed that other criteria besides the agent's intention must be found: "I too believe that the real meaning [*sens*] of an action, grouping, party, or assembly is its objective signification." But he challenges: "Who will decide its objectivity?"[33] The sign of another broadening of his conceptual scheme, he insists that whoever decides must believe in History (now written with a Hegelian capital "H"), that is, "in a development of the historical form whose meaning can be understood and whose *necessity* can be conceived, and on which one can act to produce certain hoped-for political and social phenomena in accord with that very development."[34] He is beginning to sound like Lukács, but without the Party.

The highwater mark in Sartre's relations with the French Communist party is undoubtedly the second series of articles, *The Communists and Peace* (1952). The "obscure constraints" of facticity have now hardened into the historical necessity which Lukács defends. Sartre begins to speak of an objective contradiction arising for the worker between the need to survive and the need to be human: "The contradiction is not only *in* him, it is imposed on him; mass production requires that he be contradictory" (CP, 53). Indeed, Sartre now judges the fortunes of the workers' movement *sub specie totalitatis:* "The historical whole determines our powers at any given moment; it prescribes their limits in our field of action and our *real* future; it conditions our attitude toward the possible and the impossible, the real and the imaginary, what is and what should be, space and time." He continues, now in full possession of the concept of objective possibility, "it is history which shows some the exits and makes others cool their heels before closed doors" (CP, 80).

We are on openly Marxist terrain: "Of course, the system of production is for a class the necessary condition of its ability to exist." This keeps class from being "an arbitrary grouping of individuals." But, he warns, "this condition is not *sufficient: praxis* is necessary" (CP, 99). It is his special use of the Marxist concept of praxis, as we shall see, that gives Sartrean Marxism its peculiarly existentialist flavor. On the one hand, he subscribes to the broad outline of Marxist social theory: "For my part, I maintain that the development of capital, taken in its generality, accounts for the aspects common to all workers' movements." Yet on the other, he will retain an inviolable place for praxis (and hence for existential-moral responsibility): "These in-principle considerations will never of themselves explain the particular traits of the class struggle in France or England between two given dates. A concrete fact is the singular expression of universal relations; but it can be explained in its singularity only by singular reasons" (CP, 134–35). The picture of Sartre's social theory, its method and ontological commitments, is becoming fully recognizable in *The Communists and Peace*. In *Search for a Method* and the *Critique* it will be completely systematized. So even at the peak of his cooperation with the French Communist party, it is evident, as he himself attests, that he agrees with the party "on precise and limited subjects, reasoning from *my* principles and not *theirs*" (CP, 68). Not the words of an enthusiastic convert; but what else could one expect from a presence-to-self, not a self?

Search for a Method and After

Sartre's espousal of theoretical Marxism, I have been arguing, consists in his adopting a concept of objective possibility and exchanging a philosophy of consciousness for one of praxis. Reserving analysis of the latter for the next chapter, I have focused on Sartre's growing awareness that objective factors actually condition our choices and that they must figure in any adequate theory of concrete freedom-responsibility.

He articulates this insight into social conditioning as he attempts to develop a methodology for the human sciences (*les sciences humaines*):

> To say what a man "is" is also to say what he can be—and vice versa. The material conditions of his existence circum-scribe the field of his possibilities (his work is too hard, he is too tired to show any interest in union or political activity). Thus the field of possibles is the goal toward which the agent surpasses his objective situation. And this field in turn depends strictly on the social, historical reality. . . . The field of possibles [should be seen] as a strongly structured region which depends upon all of History and which includes its own con-tradictions. (SM, 93)

Mention of "contradictions" in the field of possibilities is a typically Marxist *modus loquendi*, which Sartre adopts in his later writings. His present point is that the understanding of the individual requires an awareness of these objective possibilities. Built on the material conditions are what Sartre calls the "social possible." A further precision of objective possibility, this denotes "the real and permanent future which the collectivity forever maintains and transforms." An example is the greater number of physicians required by a society becoming industrialized. He argues that "the most individual possible is only the internalization and enrichment of the social possible" (SM, 95). As he explains in the *Critique*, the structure of relations between individuals is undetermined, i.e., it remains "abstract" in the Hegelian sense, until "the ensemble of material circumstances" on which it is established has been defined (CDR, 255), another instance of holistic thinking.

Thus far, Sartre would seem committed to the crassest form of historical materialism, where the arrow of "causal" influence points in one direction only, from material conditions to the social possible and thence to individual possibility as an "internalization and enrichment" of the latter. So he counters this reading by insisting that, if "the truth of a man is the nature of his work and . . . his wages, . . . this truth defines him just insofar as he constantly goes beyond it in his practical activity" (SM, 93). Sartre is not abandoning his lifelong project to comprehend the singular in favor of objective possibility. Rather, he is seeking to further his project by discovering social necessities. For "it is choice," he continues to insist, "which must be interrogated if one wants to explain [acts] in their detail, to reveal their singularity" (SM, 152). We must always keep in mind this "existentialist" balance to the increasingly objective factors whose necessities yield the History that Sartre has come to accept.

I have set my discussion of objective possibility in the context of freedom and necessity. Objective possibility is conceived either as a limit to freedom or as a path, depending on whether freedom is seen as the overcoming of obstacles (coefficient of adversity) or as the recognition of necessities (Marxist-Hegelian freedom). Some form of necessity is required, so it seems, if Sartre is to construct a science of History. But his constant challenge is to reconcile this necessity with a freedom which will bear the kind of moral ascriptions that the existentialist favors. In the *Critique* he introduces necessity (objective impossibility of the contradictory occurring) under several rubrics.

Before undertaking my brief typology of necessity in the *Critique*, I should caution that, due to the interrelatedness of the concepts, any analysis of a single topic from that work risks omitting considerations that modify the original analysis in important ways. For the *Critique* is not only a study in dialectic, it is a dialectical study as well. Hence we must begin *in medias res,* accepting brief, working definitions of certain crucial terms at this initial stage and leaving many concepts to be fully defined later.

Material Conditions. The first category under which necessity and objective possibility enter the *Critique* is that of material conditions (CDR, 606). This is roughly equivalent to Marx's "forces and relations of production" in historical materialism.[35] Sartre confirms his adoption of a quasi Marxist anthropology in the *Critique* by defining "man" as "a practical organism living with a multiplicity of similar organisms in a field of scarcity" (CDR, 735). This "situates" man more deeply in the world of work and social struggle than did *Being and Nothingness.* The basic interpersonal relations, formerly characterized as conflictive, are now seen as positive or negative, as cooperative or combative, depending on "previous circumstances and . . . the material conditions which determine the practical field" (CDR, 735). Scarcity renders us competitors for what goods there are and qualifies human history as one long struggle for limited resources.[36] But by historicizing conflict, Sartre now allows the possibility that cooperation may obtain in a society of material abundance. A ray of Marxist hope thus enters what may have seemed to be the dark world of existential despair.

Of equal importance for his understanding of social reality and the movement of history are the objective contradictions that obtain among these material conditions. Sartre assures us that he has no intention of dissolving them in a kind of dialectical idealism. Indeed, he considers such contradictions to be "the motors of the Historical process," but only when they have been "interiorized"—again the existentialist counterbalance (see CDR, 712).[37]

Exigency. This commonly used term in the *Critique* denotes any material circumstance which, as transcended by praxis, "imposes a certain content on the future towards which it is transcended. It restricts possibilities and provides a certain instrumentality which will characterize the final result" (CDR, 235). Of course, "exigency" does not produce the future; that requires human praxis. But it restricts the effective choices which lie open to that praxis. "Exigency" serves the function in Sartre's social system that "necessity" and "probability" play in those of Lukács and Weber respectively; it respects freedom while making predictive knowledge possible.

Thus the factory worker who procures an abortion because she cannot financially support a child is, in Sartre's words, "carrying out the sentence which has already been passed on her" by her "objective situation" (CDR, 235). Later he will refer to "the inert exigency of the object," e.g., production schedules, transportation requirements, and so forth, which "becomes a mortgage on the future of the new worker, a limitation of his possibilities to which he must submit" (CDR, 544–45).[38]

From the viewpoint of collective responsibility we shall observe numerous "exigencies" such as racism, class interest, the demands of the business (the elder von Gerlach), and the like, which generate solidarity as they convey responsibility. In each case an objective necessity is supported by individual praxes. But it is with the concept of exigency that Sartre translates Marx's dictum: man is the product of his own product.

When qualified by scarcity, exigencies become violent. Thus in the competitive market of the coal industry, for example, Sartre sees the mine owner's violence toward his workers as necessary: "this praxis is precisely that of a being of violence, which means that his free response to the exigencies of the situation can be realized only in the form of oppression" (CDR, 739). The same is true for the colonialist system: "For the child of the colonialist, violence was present in the situation itself, and was a social force which produced him" (CDR, 718). To the extent that concrete freedom is the expansion of the field of objective possibility, it will consist in liberation from these exigencies.

Role assignment. Concomitant with material conditions and exigencies are the limitations set on individuals by the division of labor and social stratification. Describing the situation of individuals born into a particular socioeconomic class, Sartre notes: "What is 'assigned' to them is a type of work, and a material condition and a standard of living tied to this activity; it is a fundamental *attitude,* as well as a determinate provision of material and intellectual tools; it is a strictly limited field of possibilities" (CDR, 232). When linked to oppressive practices and attitudes, these roles convey the kind of pervasive responsibility which Sartre ascribed to his compatriots in *Anti-Semite and Jew:* "It is our words and our gestures— *all* our words and *all* our gestures—our anti-Semitism, but equally our condescending liberalism—that have poisoned him" (AJ, 135). We find here and in similar passages not just outbursts of rhetorical flourish (though doubtless they are present) but expressions of sensitivity to the complex social conditioning to which we are subject.[39]

Three subspecies of role-assignment figure prominently in Sartre's later work. Two have been mentioned and will appear throughout the remaining chapters. The first is that of *class-being* as a structure of exigencies and interests, of actions and attitudes. In Sartre's analysis this involves a limitation of outlook and of opportunity. In the case of the proletarian, it forms "a limit to his practical comprehension" of who he is and of what he can be (CDR, 699).[40]

The next yields *institutional man,* the individual identified with the military, the firm, or civic and professional obligations, and so forth. An elaboration of the image of the perfect waiter, made famous in *Being and Nothingness,* this form incorporates features of institutional being which I shall discuss in chapter 8.

The final form of role assignment is that of *family conditioning.* A sign of Sartre's increasingly nuanced attitude toward the unconscious, it dominates the first two volumes of his Flaubert study. He writes that "the prehistoric past returns to the child like a Destiny. It is the source of permanent impossibilities which subsequent determinations . . . would be incapable of explaining." In fact, so important is this period in Sartre's eyes that "without [treating] early childhood [*la petite enfance*] it is not too much to say that biography builds on sand" (IF, 1:55). So his regressive analysis of Flaubert's youthful writings; for example, leads us "back to the objective structures of the Flaubert family" (IF, 1:330). There Sartre finds another form of objective possibility, another source of intelligibility: "The contradiction isn't first of all in him but in the family structures. There's a collective Flaubert pride but also a Flaubert inquietude which merely translates the objective conflicts of the age: agrarians and bourgeois, romantics and Voltarians" (IF, 1:503). As he observes elsewhere, structuralism in general and these "objective structures" in particular are an affair of the practico-inert.[41]

I have subjected "objective possibility"to a rather lengthy analysis because its discovery and employment mark the turning point in Sartre's social philosophy. Armed with this concept, though he seldom uses the term itself, he can speak of a single meaning (*sens*) of history, of various forms of institutionalized oppression, and of freedom as requiring radical expansion of the field of possibilities. He possesses a theoretical instrument for incorporating existential "situation" into historical materialism. Once he develops his own understanding of praxis and of what he terms the "mediating third," he will be in a position to introduce the ethical and humanistic insights of existential "for-itself" into a system of history as well. By appeal to the exigencies of the practico-inert, he hopes to wed freedom to necessity in a union that will render history intelligible without depriving it of its moral character.

Dialectical Reason

Although its full elaboration occurs only in *Search for a Method* and in the *Critique,* dialectical reason like objective possibility is adumbrated in

Sartre's earlier works, especially in *Being and Nothingness.*[42] The "nihilating" dynamic of consciousness, introduced in *The Psychology of Imagination,* along with its world-constituting, -totalizing, and -surpassing features, and its overall ethical case, reveals a Fichtean conception of consciousness, hospitable to dialectical relationships, in the midst of an ostensibly phenomenological study.[43] The "implicit dialectic" of *Being and Nothingness* is worked out chiefly through the ways in which human reality "is what it is not and is not what it is."[44] So my earlier remarks, especially about human reality as presence-to-self, should be read in this dialectical light. The circle of reflection-reflecting merely articulates a prior and more basic "inner distance" that is the preflective dialectic of for-itself as consciousness (of) self.

But the dialectic of *Being and Nothingness* is without synthesis. It is what Klaus Hartmann terms "a dialectic of pairs."[45] As such, it is more Kierkegaardian than Hegelian, intensifying rather than resolving options. Sartre's subsequent adoption of a more Hegelian dialectic rescues his thought from the impasse into which the dyads of *Being and Nothingness* have led it. Reserving discussion of its basic elements for the next chapter, I shall concentrate on the general features of Sartre's new dialectic.

Like Hegelian history, dialectical reason is both a process of objects "in the world" and the movement of our knowledge of them.[46] It resembles the classical Greek logos in being a principle of knowledge because it is a principle of being; it requires no potentially defective representations. But unlike the logos, dialectical reason is processful and timebound as are the knowledge and reality that it unites. For ease of clarification, let us consider six characteristics of dialectical reason, focusing on its epistemic dimension but allowing an ontological equivalent at every turn.

Totalization

Heir to the "spirit of synthesis" discussed earlier, dialectical thinking differs from atomistic, analytical reason (from the logics of Aristotle and Kant, for example) precisely by assuming the viewpoint of the whole and by reading atomic individuals as "abstract" parts.[47] As we observed in Sartre's criticism of the Jew's assimilationist friend, synthetic thought does not submerge the individual in the whole. It underscores uniqueness, but specifically in its contribution to and dependence on other individuals and the whole. It is analytic reason, with its abstract, timeless essences, Sartre believes, that would sacrifice the Jew to the man.

His distrust of what Merleau-Ponty calls "totalitarian thought" leads Sartre to shun many terms traditionally employed by methodological holists in the social sciences.[48] Thus he repeatedly denies a Durkheimian collective consciousness, claims that the group is not a "hyperorganism," and insists that only individual praxis is constitutive of social reality. Such disclaimers seen in the light of his absolute commitment to individual responsibility have led Raymond Aron to list Sartre among the methodological individualists.[49] But in fact, as our study of the nature and genesis of the group will confirm, Sartre's contribution in this regard is to offer a via media between holism and individualism, both methodological and ontological, which he terms "dialectical nominalism" (CDR, 37).

At this juncture I merely wish to indicate that dialectical nominalism finds its chief expression in Sartre's concept of praxis (purposive human activity in its material environment) as *totalizing*.[50] Totalization is a practical synthesizing activity that transforms a multiplicity of parts into an emerging whole which serves as the goal (*sens,* direction) of the on-going activity. Because the union is practical, it is perhaps better to speak of means-end rather than of part-whole. In any case, the focus is on totaliz*ing* and not on totality. The agent cannot totalize himself because the very condition of totalization—transcendence (*dépassement*) by consciousness now transferred to praxis—precludes his being an object for himself. In *Being and Nothingness* human reality is at most a "detotalized totality" (BN, 165). He will later observe that the simple group in process of forming is, from the methodological viewpoint, "the most simple form of totalization" (CDR, 407). In fact, the group like the existentialist individual "*is not,*" Sartre warns, rather "it constantly totalizes itself" (CDR, 407). We shall appreciate the full implication of this dynamic principle only in the following chapters. But we should realize from the outset that the very totalizing praxis which makes the group possible precludes full integration of any member: "a totalizing praxis cannot totalize itself as a totalized element" (CDR, 373).

Totalization enjoys an epistemic function in Sartre's thought. He calls it "the basic intelligibility of dialectical reason" and ascribes a "translucidity" and an "apodicticity" to it that makes it the ground experience of dialectical reason (CDR, 44). He appeals to totalization to constitute a practical field in which traditional dialectical principles such as the principle of double negation obtain.[51] But he makes clear that these principles and the totalizing action that underlie them are accessible only to a knowledge that is itself totalizing. Sartre calls this awareness "comprehension."

Comprehension

"To comprehend," which means "to include" as well as "to understand," aptly denotes the mode of awareness proper to the synthetic spirit. Analytic reason yields intellection, the abstract grasp of static forms, qualities, and causal sequences, proper to empirical science, mathematics, and, apparently, phenomenology.[52] "Comprehension," Sartre's adaptation of the *Verstehen* of German social theory, "is simply the translucidity of praxis to itself" (CDR, 74). It plays the same foundational role in Sartre's later thought that in his earlier work prereflective consciousness had played. Yet he now allows for a kind of opacity and hence possible mystification, delusion, and the like, in this inmost recess of the practical agent. I shall pursue this aspect of practical consciousness when I discuss ideology.[53] But it is important to remark this softening of his earlier rationalism; for it moves in tandem with his growing sense of objective possibility and dialectical exchange.

Relevant to his theory of collective responsibility, Sartre expands "comprehension" to denote the implicit, practical awareness which the members of a collective have of the meaning (*sens*) of their common actions. The participants in a lynch mob, for example, or those in a resistance group, have a common sense of "what they are about." This is the basis of that bad faith which Sartre finds rampant in the collectives to which he ascribes moral responsibility.

Finally, as I noted in a previous chapter, he often uses "comprehension" in a sense closer to that of *Verstehende Soziologie*. Because an agent comprehends his action in the two senses just discussed, he can understand the praxis of other social units even in distant and foreign cultures.The source of this epistemic optimism is Sartre's assertion that "the dialectical rationality of common praxis does not transcend the rationality of individual praxis" (CDR, 538). I shall assess his defense of this claim when I examine the epistemological primacy of praxis in the next chapter. His thesis, in brief, is that we can read the intentions of other agents, can comprehend their comprehension, if only they leave enough traces for the hermeneutic. Comprehension, like the praxis it rests on, is always totalizing; it will grasp other praxes in terms of what remains to be done in a concrete situation.[54]

Negation

Earlier in his career Sartre had criticized Descartes' failure "to conceive negativity as productive,"[55] advice which he scrupulously followed in constructing his own existential anthropology. Constitutive, internal negation flourishes in the *Critique* as well. But as consciousness materializes into organic praxis, so the negative appears first as lack and then as need. Sartre still insists that "it is through man that negation comes to man and to matter" (CDR, 83). But mention of matter in this regard is new and significant. The initial negation is *lack,* heir to value as nonbeing in *Being and Nothingness; need* emerges as the corresponding negation of this negation. Because these negations occur within an ultimately totalizing context—"there is no negation unless the future totalization is continually present as the detotalized totality of the ensemble in question" (CDR, 85)—this double negation constitutes a dialectical affirmation, a practical, synthetic integration of the elements as parts. Thus human work, which serves as original praxis for Sartre, is entirely dialectical and exists "only as a totalization and a transcended contradiction" (CDR, 89). Sartre credits Marx with demonstrating that proletarian praxis is a negation of negation (see CDR, 157).

New to Sartre's Marxist phase are the objective contradictions and counterfinalities which extend negation to the realm of matter, the so-called "practico-inert." Objective contradictions are those standard Marxian negations which obtain, for example, between the forces and relations of production at a certain point in socioeconomic development; when the technology, for example, is already "socialist" while the property system remains capitalistic. Counterfinality, on the other hand, is experienced when, in achieving one's project, one realizes results contrary to those intended. As examples of such dialectical reversals, Sartre cites the military ambush and the Spanish gold policy under Philip II, where hoarding led to loss of value through inflation. Sartre's brilliant discussion of "bewitched quantity" (CDR, 173), a sophisticated gloss on Marx's pages on commodity fetishism from *Capital,* underlines the fact that matter can become "inverted praxis," turning action into antipraxis (see CDR, 166).

Applying negation to objective possibility, we can see that Sartre's "materialist" dialectic traces a dynamic relation between "action as the negation of matter (in its present organization and on the basis of a future re-organization), and matter . . . as the negation of action" (CDR, 159). This problematic negative "activity" of matter is the basis of those "objective, negative exigencies" discussed earlier whereby "machines . . . create men," i.e., in which man, in Marx's words, becomes the product of his own product (CDR, 159).

Mediation

Sartre's move from a Kierkegaardian to a Hegelian-Marxist dialectic consists primarily in his discovery of mediating factors in experience and in the world that separate and unite individuals. I have argued that the absence of such factors or their limitation to the "gaze" of the Third seriously hampered the development of Sartre's social theory. He now insists that "the crucial discovery of dialectical investigation [*expérience*] is that man is 'mediated' by things to the same extent as things are 'mediated' by men" (CDR, 79). The laying bare of the forms of social mediation will constitute a major portion of the reconstruction of Sartre's theory of collective responsibility in chapter 6.

Appeal to mediation enables him to employ the concepts "abstract" and "concrete" in the Hegelian sense of "undetermined" (unmediated) and "determined" (mediated) respectively.[56] Thus the atomic individual is an abstraction, as are the social structures with which the first volume of the *Critique* concludes. There are degrees of mediation and hence of concreteness. The fully concrete—the singular universal, as he now begins to say[57]—is the agent in his completely articulated sociohistorical context. It was Sartre's aim in undertaking his exhaustive study of Flaubert to arrive at this singular universal, namely, Flaubert as the only person who could say "I am Madame Bovary." Whether Sartre regarded the singular universal merely as a regulative idea this side of the end of history remains unclear.

Temporalization

In the only address Sartre ever delivered to the French Philosophical Society (1947), he speaks of the need to "reintegrate temporality into the categories."[58] His explicitly dialectical philosophy does just that. He claims that "dialectic as a movement of reality collapses if time is not dialectic; that is, if we refuse to recognize a certain action of the future as such. . . . Time, as a concrete quality of history, is made by men on the basis of their original temporalization" (SM, 92n). This "action of the future as such" refers to the purposeful totalization which is human praxis. In fact, Sartre points out that totalization *is* temporalization (see CDR, 53). It advances in a spiral movement: the past is continuously reinterpreted in the light of the future as intended but unrealized totality. Since the context is dialectical, the past is not simply denied. For there are "irreversible" events like the closing of the national workshops and the consequent bloody riots and massacres of June 1848 that have permanently colored the class struggle in France (see IF, 3:342). Such events are subsumed in the "memories" of both the bourgeoisie and the proletariat. This temporal spiral is effective even at the individual level, as Sartre's lengthy analysis of Flaubert's "personalization" amply demonstrates (see IF, 1:649ff.). Such "diachronic" totalization, as Sartre sometimes calls it, is relevant both to establishing class identity and to assessing responsibility among the generations.[59]

The Logic of Praxis

"Dialectic and praxis are one and the same," writes Sartre (CDR, 802). Because of this identification—another of those "great inexact equations" that he favors[60]—dialectical reason is neither a feature of nature, which

Sartre takes to be antidialectical, nor is it disinterested, theoretical, and "objective" as analytical reason purports to be. In this regard, dialectical reason is more congenial with the methodology of Lukács than with that of Weber. It builds upon the "committed" thinking of the existentialist Sartre.

As the logic of praxis, dialectical reason subsumes analytic reason as the concrete realizes the abstract for Hegel. Whereas analytic reason utilizes abstract *concepts* in its analysis of a "detemporalized" reality, dialectical reason employs the *notion* (Hegel's *Begriff*), which Sartre defines as "a synthetic effort to produce an idea which develops by contradictions and successive overcomings and which is thus homogeneous with the development of things."[61] It is "notion" which reintegrates temporality into the categories: "A concept is a definition in exteriority which is likewise atemporal; a notion, to my mind, is a definition in interiority and includes in itself not only the time supposed by the object whose notion it is but also its own time as [an act of] knowledge. In other words, [notion] is a thought which introduces time along with it" (*Situations,* 10:95). This is, of course, exceedingly Hegelian. But Sartre retains enough of his Cartesian conviction to seek some "apodictic" dialectical experiences that can yield the meaning (*sens*) not only of my praxis but also of "our" praxis and of history itself as "totalization without a totalizer" (CDR, 817). Again, Sartre's epistemic optimism surfaces: the "fundamental identity" which he affirms "between an individual life and human history," that is, "the 'reciprocity' of their perspectives" is translated in *The Family Idiot* into the language of totalization; for example, "a man . . . totalizes his age to the precise degree that he is totalized by it" (IF, 3:426).

He never reconciles the "epistemology of vision" which he inherits from Descartes and Husserl with his more recent "epistemology of praxis" implicit in the theory of dialectical reason.[62] Combined, they enable Sartre to employ striking phenomenological descriptions of dialectical necessities and reversals as grounding experiences of the larger totalization of totalizations which is human history. These lend the otherwise ponderous *Critique* refreshing moments of charm. But they leave unanswered the question of their interrelation. He locates analytic reason on a level subordinate to that of dialectical reason (in the practico-inert), and I claimed that the phenomenological grasp of essences (the famous *Wesensschau*) belongs there too. But that leaves the "apodictic" evidence adduced by the several dialectical experiences which he describes in the *Critique* quite problematic: to the extent that they are apodictic, they seem to lack the open-endedness of the dialectical process and, conversely, to the degree that this ongoing process is respected, something less than apodicticity is the norm. In other words, the structures of dialectical reason are not themselves dialectical. But, of course, Sartre would retort that such structures are as "abstract" as is the atomic individual of the empiricist.

As I have already warned, there is something paradoxical about "analyzing" dialectical reason. My previous remarks have pointed to the root of the paradox. Levi-Strauss goes further in *The Savage Mind* where he criticizes Sartre's use of analytic reason in the *Critique* to discuss a "new" rationality. His point is that there are not two reasons, as Sartre contends, but only two uses of one reason, and that the analytic is the more basic.[63] In response, Sartre offers a summary description of dialectical reason with which I shall conclude my remarks on that topic: "dialectical thought is first of all the examination of a reality insofar as it belongs to a whole, to the extent that it negates that whole, and to the degree that that whole includes [*comprend*], conditions, and negates this reality . . . —all in a single movement" (*Situations*, 9:76). He adds that such "definitions" are necessarily lengthy (his own runs over twenty lines!) because it is a matter of the dialectical use of analytical terms. Whatever its justification, Sartre's description synthesizes the six features of dialectical reason which we have been considering: totalization, comprehension, negation, mediation, temporalization, and the "logic" of praxis.

These reflections on objective possibility and dialectical reason have fully immersed us in the social realm. The latter is Sartre's key to social intelligibility, but it also furthers his moral concerns.[64] The genius of these totalizations, counterfinalities, and dialectical advances, as I have noted before, is that they retain a crucial place for individual praxis and thus for existential-moral responsibility, while giving full play to those exigencies and dialectical necessities which enable one to understand the meaning of history. In answer to Garaudy, the past and the objective conditions for social existence enter positively (as negated negations) into the totalizing projects of individuals-in-society. And, in response to Merleau-Ponty, Sartre is now fostering a philosophy not of consciousness but of praxis. Yet his existentialist commitments remain to temper the necessitating claims of objective possibility. The introduction of dialectical reason enables him to escape the horns of the analytic either/or on which his earlier attempts at social theory were impaled. It is no longer a question of either boundless freedom or mechanical necessity. Freedom-in-situation is an ongoing phenomenon coterminous with totalizing praxis. It is his dialectical nominalism, as we shall see, that saves him from Hegelian "organicism" when he speaks of the constituted dialectic (the group) in which "freedom and necessity are now one" (CDR, 341). So let us continue to pursue *in extenso* the social ontology which permits Sartre to make that claim.

six

Sartre's Social Ontology
The Problem of Mediations

Jean-Paul Sartre is the philosopher of mediations par excellence.
Louis Althusser, *Lire le capital*

The subtitle of *Being and Nothingness* is "An Essay on Phenomenological
Ontology." The subtitle of the *Critique of Dialectical Reason* could be
"An Essay on Social Ontology," for it deals with the nature and function
of the basic kinds of social being. We have discovered the limits imposed
on Sartre's earlier social thought by his failure to acknowledge genuine
triadic relationships. What he terms the "Third" at that stage, I have
argued, is really the existential Other writ large. Although this Third
reappears in the *Critique,* the dismal claim which it previously warranted,
namely, that the basic relation among human beings is not *Mitsein* but
conflict, is now contextualized both ontologically and historically. The
ontological context is that of practico-inert mediation; the historical, one
of material scarcity, whether natural or induced, which makes man a wolf
to man.

One of the cardinal premises of Sartre's new praxis philosophy is that
"reciprocal ternary relations are the basis of *all* relations between men,
whatever form they may subsequently take" (CDR, 111). The nature of
these reciprocities, whether negative (struggle) or positive (cooperation),
depends on the mediation of the practico-inert or of praxis respectively
(see CDR, 113). Likewise, the social wholes upon which Sartre's social
ontology is grounded express either or both of these mediating factors.
So let us consider in depth these radical forms of social mediation. They
are best appreciated as constituents of the perennial dialectic of sameness
and otherness.[1]

Dialectic of the Other: The Practico-inert

The complex term "practico-inert" introduces aspects of being-in-itself
into the realm of action. Sartre describes it as "simply the activity of
others in so far as it is sustained and diverted by inorganic inertia" (CDR,
556). Not raw nature, but nature as modified by prior praxis is the mediating factor. This nonnegotiable primacy of individual praxis must be

93

kept in mind throughout this discussion of the *practico*-inert, for it guards the core of Sartrean humanism and moral responsibility from those "necessities" that regulate the social sphere. As Sartre enunciates his position: "I am in complete agreement [with Marxist determinists] that the social facts have their own structures and laws which dominate individuals, but I only see in this the reply of worked matter to the agents who work it" (BEM, 55). Leaving "the agents who work it" for the next section, I am interested now in this "reply" of worked matter. I shall consider it in three stages, first treating the general features of practico-inert mediation, focusing next on several examples of practico-inert unity germane to collective responsibility, and finally reflecting on a particular form of practico-inert mediation that defines the concrete class struggle, namely, the dialectic of interest/destiny.

Nature and Function of the Practico-inert

Basic sociality. Sartre allows for two fundamental kinds of social reality, that of the active group constituting the *common field* and that of effectively separated though ostensibly united individuals forming what he terms the *practico-inert field.* Since he conceives the group as arising through an essential negation of the practico-inert, he characterizes the practico-inert ensemble as "the matrix of groups and their grave" (CDR, 635). The practico-inert constitutes "fundamental sociality" (CDR, 318). All social forms to the extent that they are social have a basis in the practico-inert, that is, in the relations among agents mediated by such "worked matter" as natural languages, rituals of exchange, or physical artifacts. Sartre points out that "it is at the practico-inert level that sociality is produced in men by things as a bond of materiality which transcends and alters simple human relations" (CDR, 304). That bond of materiality, the practico-inert ensemble, is called the *collective;* the "thing" which forges it, the *collective object;* and the relations altered thereby, *serial.* Before considering each of these aspects of the practico-inert, let us begin with one of Sartre's most famous examples of basic sociality.

He asks us to consider a crowd queuing at a bus stop. The bus, a collective object, has stamped the crowd with a certain unity: personal differences are momentarily overlooked for the sake of a common need, transportation along this route at this time. But the commonality is really false; scarcity of places renders each a rival of the other and the very serial order of the queue is the sign of numerical equivalence; no rules or functions are assigned to anyone in terms of the "whole."* The bus queue is paradigmatic of what Sartre calls serial relations among individuals who are both united and separated by the collective object. Elsewhere in the *Critique* he offers similar analyses of the TV-viewing public, the customers of public utilities, and such collectives as public opinion, the free market, and the Great Fear of 1789. Thus Sartrean sociality at base consists of serial relations among atomic individuals gathered into collectives by material objects and operating in a practico-inert field.

The practico-inert in its mediating function bears a disvalue sign for Sartre, much as the "one" (*l'on*) does in *Being and Nothingness* and the *plebs* for Kierkegaard. If it is the basic form of sociality, it is likewise the initial source of personal and social alienation.[2] Indeed, otherness or *alterity* is the essential feature of practico-inert mediation. Whether it be the "they say" of public opinion, the "us and them" of racism, or the bureaucratic "system," the infallible sign of practico-inert mediation is the otherness it generates and maintains. This defining characteristic will recur throughout this chapter. It justifies speaking of serial relations as constituting a "dialectic of the other" even though, strictly speaking, the practico-inert is an *anti*dialectical concept for Sartre.[3]

Seriality. "The formal, universal structure of alterity," Sartre writes, "produces the *rationale of the series [la Raison de la serie]*" (CDR, 264; trans. emended). I have already noted Sartre's difficulty with the scandalous Other. No doubt the series inherits features of alienation from Sartre's earlier work, namely, the individual's being objectified and rendered interchangeable by the Other. To the extent that these relations are concrete, that is, triadic, this implies the presence of an "alienating Third," as we may now call the Third of *Being and Nothingness*. But as the social model becomes one of praxis, not looking/looked-at, otherness becomes a function of practico-inert mediation. The agent is "robbed" of his actions not only by the Other's power to attach foreign meanings or by a counterpraxis of some sort, but by the sheer power of the practico-inert forces set in motion or sustained by the agent's own undertaking. I shall examine such "processes" in a moment.

"There are serial behavior, serial feelings and serial thoughts," Sartre remarks. "A series is a mode of being for individuals both in relation to one another and in relation to their common being, and this mode of being transforms all their structures" (CDR, 266). That transformation entails, of course, "alterity," whose avatars include separation, social impotence, numerical equivalence, pseudoreciprocity, unity in exteriority like a seal on wax, and, above all, what Sartre terms "passive activity." He indicates the interrelatedness of these characteristics, when, for example, he claims that "impotence, as a force of alterity, is *primarily* unity in its negative form, *primarily* action in the form of passivity, and *primarily* finality in the form of counter-finality" (CDR, 310; emphasis his). He sees these inversions of unity, action, and finality as instances where individual praxis

95

"loses itself" to the advantage of "the maleficent actions of worked matter" (CDR, 310n). Even action itself seems out of our hands, as though it were an alien power sweeping us along. This awareness, simultaneously of necessity and of powerlessness, is the experiential basis for the concept of the practico-inert. In fact, Sartre claims that "powerlessness experienced [subie] is the bond [mastic] of seriality" (CDR-F, 325; missing on p. 277 of English translation).

Passive activity. This is the "action" proper to serialized individuals. It bears the mark of otherness. We find it in the other-directed individuals of social psychology, in the inauthentic person of classical existentialism, and in the object as distinct from the subject of history in Marxian analyses. Sartre views it as an abdication of praxis in favor of inertial "occurrences." In the language of existentialism, passive activity is basically flight from freedom-responsibility. A favorite metaphor of Sartre's to express this activity is "contagion." Thus the Great Fear that gripped the French countryside in 1789 was a matter of the Other who knew someone else who had heard, seen, . . . , an Other who was plotting, etc. The rumormonger is unwilling, perhaps even unable, to act in full responsibility for his actions. His is the echoing of others' acts. Politically, such passive activity is congenial to dictatorships. Epistemically, it favors belief or what Sartre calls "the Other in me" (IF, 1: 166) over evidence and knowledge.[4]

Process. This term denotes the impersonal sequence of events proper to the practico-inert field.[5] "The social field," Sartre observes, "is full of acts with no author" (SM, 163–64). We have witnessed the necessity and internal logic of the colonialist system. "In this [practico-inert] field," Sartre now explains, "everyone's action disappears, and is replaced by monstrous forces which, in the inertia of the organic and of exteriority, retain some power of action and unification combined with a false interiority" (CDR, 319). Those "monstrous forces" are the necessities and counterfinalities of the various systems or apparatuses or collectives to which individuals subject themselves or find themselves subject.

Sartre lists three "modalities of human action": individual praxis; common, constituted praxis; and praxis-process. They are, he insists, "in themselves distinct from the practico-inert process and . . . are its foundation" (CDR, 789). His point seems to be, pace Engels, that all negation—the foundational dialectical act—originates in human action and that whatever "action" we may ascribe to the practico-inert is really a deflection of praxis. Yet this need not imply that the latter's contribution is negligible. The angle of deflection, to pursue the metaphor, can be decisive, as our examination of objective possibility has revealed.

Of major significance for collective responsibility is Sartre's thesis that one and the same sociohistorical development can be viewed simultaneously as praxis (e.g., oppression) and as process (e.g., exploitation) and that the latter conditions the former at every turn (CDR, 789). When so viewed, these transformations of praxis appear as "a series of necessities of which [praxis] is *both the mystified victim and the fundamental support*" (CDR, 789; emphasis added). We encounter here the theoretical underpinning of his earlier assertion that the colonist is both victim and executioner under the colonialist system. This status of "mystified victim and fundamental support" characterizes all forms of what we may now call *serial responsibility* at this first level of sociality. Whenever Sartre employs this formula, we may assume that he has serial responsibility in mind. Were process a force independent of all praxis and we but pawns of some cosmic determinism, our "responsibility" would be purely causal, scarcely exceeding that of other "natural" processes. But as Sartre insists, human freedom (and, we can now add, existential moral responsibility) depends on the irreducibility of culture to nature (see SM, 152). The lower limit to this reducibility is the practico-inert.

The phenomenon of process reminds us that the practico-inert field is the "reign of necessity"; in other words, "the domain . . . in which inorganic materiality envelops human multiplicity and transforms the producer into its product" (CDR, 339). Yet with an eye toward the liberating unity of group praxis, Sartre claims that necessity "is the only possible relation between practical organisms and their milieu and, through the milieu, between them, in so far as they have achieved a new practical unity" (CDR, 339–40).

Note how Sartre has linked practico-inert "necessity" with Marx's famous critique of capitalist economics, namely, that it renders man a product of his own product. This affords Sartre numerous opportunities for acute descriptions of the servitude which ties both agent and patient to a system that makes some beneficiaries and everyone victims. Thus von Gerlach père, despite protests of innocence, is perceived by author and audience alike to be in bad faith: he is both mystified victim and basic support of the economic process, the enterprise that bears his name; he is the paradigmatic serial individual.

The collective. Sartre emphasizes that "the collective is not simply the form of being of certain social realities . . . but . . . is also the *being of sociality itself* at the level of the practico-inert field"(CDR, 304; emphasis mine). It is a kind of reduced model of that field and of all the passive activities exercised there. Its basis is a false reciprocity, as Sartre puts it, between practical agent and worked matter. This matter, the collective object, "stamps" a practical though exterior unity on serialized individuals. He defines "collective" as "the two-way relation between a material, inorganic, worked object and a multiplicity which finds its unity of exteriority in it" (CDR, 269). Rather than true, mediated reciprocity, the relations among individuals in the collective are serial. Indeed, because the relation between a "worked object" such as the bank note, the racist idea, or the oncoming bus and a multiplicity of individuals is two-way, we can focus on either term of the relationship. Sartre does this at the risk of some confusion when he uses "collective" to denote sometimes the inorganic object and sometimes the totalized plurality.

His reason for discussing such banal examples of serial unity as the TV-viewing public or the users of city transport is to gain access to a more far-reaching collective, the socioeconomic class (see CDR, 252). When we study class-being later in this chapter, it will help to recall that its basic social form is practico-inert, notwithstanding numerous group unities that pervade it, and that its proper unity is that of the collective mediated by interest or destiny as forms of collective object.

The collective object. Sartre characterizes this as "an index of separation" (CDR, 288). The false reciprocity, "Other-unity" (*unité-autre*), as he calls it, that these objects effect serves to keep serial individuals apart under the pretext of unifying them. The songs on the "Top 20," for example, are a sign of the desire of the other to like what the others like. Sartre calls this indirect, lateral human relationship *recurrence*. He claims, "for us the reality of the collective object rests on recurrence" (SM, 78). He adopts a term from mathematics to underscore the necessity with which a property passes among serialized individuals. Collective objects, he argues, "originate in social recurrence." The price in a "free market," for example, depends among other things upon what each thinks other buyers and sellers are willing to accept. Thus the price imposes itself on me because it imposes itself on my neighbor and so on indefinitely. "In general," he concludes, "it imposes itself on everyone as a stable collective reality only in so far as it is the totalization of a series" (CDR, 288). And a series is totalized recurrently.

Recurrence, flight, "Other-unity," and the like indicate that collective objects are "signs of our alienation" and barriers to a "true inter-subjective community." Sartre leaves unanswered the question whether socialism will put an end to all forms of alienation (CDR, 307n). I shall assess his views on the conditions and likelihood of final disalienation in my concluding chapter.

Examples of Practico-inert Unity

The discussion of the forms and function of the practico-inert in general clarifies several instances of serial unity, some of which we have encountered before.

The *Jew,* the *settler,* the *petit bourgeois.* These terms figure prominently in Sartre's popular ascriptions of responsibility. We can now see that they denote serial unities (see CDR, 267). The Jew's status for non-Jews in a hostile society, for example, when "interiorized as his responsibility in relation to other Jews," represents "the perpetual being-outside-themselves-in-the-other of the members of this practico-inert grouping" (CDR, 268). So we possess a social ontology on which to ground Sartre's claim that "the Jew" is a creation of the anti-Semite.

The milieu. One could consider this term generic, for Sartre does speak of "a new type of milieu, the milieu of freedom" that obtains with the advent of the group (CDR, 408). However, most of the time it denotes a collective and, as such, an "other-unity of a quasi-plurality of human relations." The milieu is perceived from within as "a homogeneous container and as a permanent (practico-inert) linking force." The laws of the market place, to take one example of milieu, seem to those subject to them as if they were "already inscribed in Being" and their individual transactions as a mere "inessential actualization of a practico-inert structure" (CDR, 279). Sartre warns sociologists and historians to look beyond such superficial self-perception of the participants to the forms of serial otherness which they articulate. "The *true structures* of the milieu," he insists, "those which produce its real force in the practico-inert field, are in fact structures of alterity" (CDR, 280). Sartre would remove all ambiguity were he to use regularly instead of only occasionally the complete expression "milieu of recurrence" to denote this collective (see CDR, 292).[6]

Racism. Although a form of the "milieu of recurrence" like the free market or public opinion, racism is sufficiently central to Sartre's ascriptions of collective responsibility to merit separate mention. It is one of his contributions to social theory to have located racism in the practico-inert. It gains in intelligibility if we enlist such concepts as "seriality," "otherness," "passive activity," and "powerlessness" in its comprehension. In particular, racism should be seen as Other-thought (*Pensée-Autre*), the kind of "thought without a thinker" that Sartre associates with the alienated state of serialized individuals. This "serial idea" is the medium

99

through which the majority of Sartre's ascriptions of collective responsibility are communicated. Racist humanism, as we have seen, is "the
settler in us all."

Language. Already in his prime existentialist years Sartre is aware of
language as a potent instrument of oppression.[7] In the *Critique* he systematizes this insight by locating language in the practico-inert. He translates de Saussure's *langue/parole* distinction into his own practico-inert/
praxis scheme. But unlike the structuralists, he predictably places the
emphasis on praxis-parole.[8]

To the extent that it is practico-inert, language like everything else in
a context of material scarcity fosters serial relations. This is most obvious
in the case of what Sartre terms the "verbal milieu." We are all familiar
with prejudicial talk. The civil-rights and feminist movements have heightened our awareness in this regard: "The native is lazy, dishonest, and
dirty; . . . he's an eternal child quite incapable of controlling himself; . . .
the native is properly understood only by the colonialist, etc." (CDR,
301).[9] Such expressions constitute the "material exigencies" of language.
If one thinks of the native, the foreigner, the female in such societies,
these are the words (and corresponding serial ideas) at one's disposal.
Sartre appreciates the verbal milieu created by sexist or racist language;
but his particular insight is to have situated it within the passive activity
and unity-in-exteriority of serial individuals mediated by the practico-
inert.

It is not too soon to underline the fact that it is not the practico-inert
as such that is alienating. After all, even in a disalienated community
people would have to communicate! It is the practico-inert as modified
by *scarcity* which turns us into competitors and "Others" to one another.
Sartre is saying that scarcity thrusts material mediation to the fore, where
it becomes decisive and distortive. In a "truly human society," on the
contrary, the practico-inert would remain in the background, preparing
the stage for free praxis to mediate other free praxes; no longer need our
work (or our words) be stolen from us. This positive social vision will
come to fuller clarity in succeeding chapters.

Socioeconomic class. Sartre states quite unequivocally that "on the ontological plane . . . class-being is practico-inert" (CDR, 686). He sees
class fundamentally as "inert collective being" and as "the inorganic
common materiality of all the members of a given ensemble" (CDR, 251).
Indeed, his entire discussion of the practico-inert is aimed at affording us
a more adequate grasp of socioeconomic class so that we might compre-

100

hend that intersection of class-being and group and individual praxis which is the truly concrete reality and the locus of history.[10]

The richness of Sartre's understanding of socioeconomic class will emerge if we view this complex reality as the instantiation of several forms of practico-inert unity. Thus it can be seen as a milieu of recurrence. This viewpoint reveals that "unity in impotence" that obtains, for example, among workers at the birth of a trade-union movement or with settlers who must "hold the line" even though personal preference counsels giving in to their own native workers.

Viewed as a collective, class becomes "a material thing made out of men in so far as it constitutes itself as a negation of man and as a serial impossibility of negating this negation. This impossibility," Sartre continues, "makes class a factual necessity: it is unchangeable destiny" (CDR, 312). The full significance of this claim must await discussion of the interest/destiny dialectic later in the chapter. At the moment it suffices to note that the proletariat, for example, "in so far as it is both Destiny and Negation of Destiny [via emancipating groups] constitutes in its very form a changing and contradictory reality" (CDR, 316).

Finally, practico-inert unity is conferred on class members by what Sartre calls *objective class spirit* defined as "milieu for the circulation of significations." He is referring to that "comprehension" which I spoke of earlier whereby each class member understands the meaning of actions or events in terms of class interest. Sartre calls this "other comprehension" in which class being affects one's very way of seeing the world.[11] One contemplates a painting or a plot of land, for example, as a bourgeois—a commonplace in the sociology of knowledge, but one enhanced by Sartre's analysis of the practico-inert. "The result," he continues, "is not communication and *never* can be: there is nothing to communicate, since the same comprehension is present in everyone. Rather, every class event has a *circular, shifting permeability* for everyone, and every class 'mode' has a solubility in the class substance" (CDR, 776–77). I shall appeal to this "permeability" in the next chapter when I consider the epistemic conditions for collective responsibility.

The foregoing examples of practico-inert unity reveal the power of Sartre's social ontology to clarify terms employed in his popular ascriptions of responsibility to collectives. Practico-inert mediation is essential to a certain kind of collective responsibility that I have called "serial." And this mediation reaches concrete articulation in the passive activity of the members of the socioeconomic class. But the dialectic of the Other, which is the hallmark of practico-inert mediation, assumes the guise of the interest-destiny antithesis within the class struggle. Since Sartre considers this struggle to be the concrete motor of history as we know it (see

CDR, 787), I shall conclude my discussion of practico-inert mediation with some reflections on the interest-destiny relation.

The Dialectic of Interest/Destiny

I have been insisting that Sartre has "humanized" every aspect of the world—even time, space, and now the "impersonal" laws of economics. It was a common thesis in the Enlightenment that between blind passion and cold reason stood *interest,* the true motor of human acts.[12] The classical British economists appealed to this concept in their theory that by the unhampered pursuit of individual interest, which would be guided as if by some "invisible hand," the common interest of all would best be served. Man is by nature selfish; but, as Hobbes had pointed out, he is capable of a calculated selfishness. The spirit of competition is proper to man's timeless nature and should be allowed full rein. This view is ingredient in the weltanschauung of liberal capitalism. It even influenced Marx, except that where Adam Smith and others perceived the guiding hand, he saw a clenched fist: struggle and class warfare, not friendly competition, are the rule in the social history of modern times.

Of greater significance is the fact that Marx historicized this view of interest. Far from being an unchangeable feature of human nature, the spirit of economic competition is seen as a product of the capitalist system which it serves. Marx thus held out hope that, with a change in the mode of production, man's selfish, acquisitive nature might be altered as well. He subscribed to what Sheldon Wolin terms a "regenerative" political philosophy.[13]

Sartre adopts this Marxist view, but here as elsewhere gives it an ontological grounding in the practico-inert that Marx never conceived of.[14] He understands "interest" as a species of exigency and hence of the practico-inert. Interest is defined as "being-outside-oneself-in-a-thing in so far as it conditions praxis as a categorical imperative" (CDR, 197).[15] By identifying interest with exigency, Sartre is likewise appealing to his own solution to the freedom-necessity question discussed in the previous chapter.

Thus bourgeois property, for example, can be read simply as an extension and reification of the self in the manner described phenomenologically in *Being and Nothingness* under the rubric "Doing and Having" (see BN, 575). In a move typical of the relation between this book and the *Critique,* Sartre considers this earlier view of property relations to be an abstraction that ignores the socioeconomic and historical aspects of a particular owner in a specific society at a certain stage of development. Now the owner can be seen as identified with the property system and as ready to sacrifice others and perhaps himself in its defense.

Interest is a social phenomenon for Sartre; the abstract, atomic individual would have needs but no interests. Need becomes interest when it involves a collective object, e.g., the firm, with which an individual so identifies that he acts throughout the entire practico-inert field to foster this object at the expense of other individuals and objects, like an organism feeding off its environment. It is in these terms that he understands the need of French industrialists to introduce English machinery in the 1830s (see CDR, 199ff.). A typically Marxian inversion is underway whereby the agent becomes the instrument of his instrument, sacrificing all to its successful operation.[16]

But interest is a unifying factor, conferring the "identity as otherness" proper to its practico-inert status. Thus the unity of the ownership class is precisely private property,[17] a collective object and, to cite a specific example, it is the machines in this plant. Property constitutes the unity-in-exteriority of the bourgeoisie, at once its strength and its vulnerability. Sartre seems to take as a basic principle that the interest of the bourgeoisie is the destiny of the proletariat (see CDR, 206).

Destiny is a future inscribed in the practico-inert. Sartre describes it as "an irresistible movement [that] draws or impels the ensemble toward a prefigurative future which realizes itself through it" (CDR, 551). The future is external to the ensemble and the means of achieving it is passive activity or process of some kind. "In so far as praxis is process," Sartre observes, "goals lose their teleological character. Without ceasing to be genuine goals, they become destinies" (CDR, 663). Such is the relationship of the proletarian to the machine, for example. Far from the worker's objectifying himself in the machine, as does the owner, Sartre argues, "the machine objectifies itself in him." He must adjust his life to the demands of the machine: labor under extreme physical conditions, change night into day, and the like. Sartre insists, "there are *several* workers' interests, but only *one* working-class interest," liberation from a system that imposes the interest of the few as the destiny of the many (CDR, 210).

Since it is practico-inert mediation through the capitalist relations of production which gives rise to interest/destiny, liberation will consist in neutralizing this mediation by socializing these productive relations—the standard Marxist remedy. At present, interest/destiny always coexist; they mark the limits of the practico-inert field, the active man, inert in his product, becomes the only way of preventing his interest from becoming destiny, or of transforming his destiny into interest" (CDR, 219).

To the degree that the individual defines himself outside in "bewitched matter," in machines or Dow Jones averages, to that extent his battle against destiny is not free human affirmation, but merely a serving of his

103

interests (see CDR, 219). Only an end to material scarcity and so to the alienating mediation of the practico-inert will usher in Sartre's ideal of revolutionary humanism, "freedoms in possession of their own destinies" (MR, 245). A fleeting glimpse of this disalienated condition is achieved in the praxis of the group, to which we now turn. But it is a passing phenomenon as long as material scarcity continues to contort human relationships on a wider scale. Until the advent of a socialism of abundance, human history will continue to spin out a dialectic of the Other: "If, as Marx has often said, everything is *other* in capitalistic society, this is primarily because atomization, which is both the origin and the result of the process, makes social man an Other than himself, conditioned by Others in so far as they are Other than themselves" (CDR, 309).

Dialectic of the Same: Praxis

I said that one way of reading the difference between the early and the later Sartre was as the contrast between consciousness (for-itself) and praxis. "My early work," he admits in an interview in 1969, "was a rationalist philosophy of consciousness" (BEM, 41). We have watched the role of material environment (objective possibility) grow as Sartre's focus shifts from consciousness to praxis, a technical term in Marxist writing.[18] The Marxist connotations of the term are reinforced by the fact that Sartre takes work as the model of praxis (see CDR, 90 and 124). In fact, he argues: "The essential discovery of Marxism is that labor . . . is the real foundation of the organization of social relations. This discovery *can no longer* be questioned" (CDR, 152n.; emphasis his).

"Praxis" is purposive human activity in its material environment.[19] We have seen how praxis inherits the intentionality and self-transparency of the for-itself. Praxis, like consciousness, is ontologically free, for it is the unifying and reorganizing transcendence (*dépassement*) of existing circumstances toward the practical field (see CDR, 310n). But Sartre has come to realize that this transcendence is dialectical; that is, that it is simultaneously negation, conservation, and spiraling advance. In other words, it is totalizing.

Since Sartre claims that "totalization is always an attempt to dissolve the other in the same" (CDR, 705), one might be led to believe that praxis is absent wherever the practico-inert predominates. But this is not the case. Praxis is all-pervasive in Sartre's social thought. I have indicated this by insisting on the *practico*-inert. But the matter requires closer scrutiny. As a prelude to demonstrating the primacy of praxis in Sartre's social philosophy, I shall examine three forms of praxis that he is careful to distinguish in the *Critique:* individual, constituting praxis, common praxis (of the constituted group), and *serial praxis*. I emphasize the last because it is overlooked in most discussions of the practico-inert.

"Serial praxis" simply refers to "the praxis of an individual in so far as he is a member of the series and to the praxis of the series as a whole or as totalized via individuals" (CDR, 266; F, 316). How is serial praxis related to passive activity? It grounds such activity in a basic existential choice and thereby retains the promise of possible deliverance in the future. Indeed, without such grounding, Sartre's pleas that serial individuals change the "system" would be in vain! Passive activity is not originative; it is an ontological deformation of praxis because of practico-inert mediation. Taking panic as an example of passive activity, Sartre points out:

> The basic difference between serial activity, which—though counter-finalized and passive—does have its *teleological reason,* and group praxis . . . is not the freedom of individual praxis, since contagious panic, as much as a deliberate attack, realizes itself through everyone's praxis; it is that in the first case, freedom posits itself only to reveal its alienation in the passive activity of impotence. (CDR, 397)

Having just analyzed the mechanism of deformation which praxis undergoes through the mediation of the practico-inert, I shall focus on that praxis itself.

In the *Critique,* Sartre develops and applies what I shall call *the principle of the primacy of praxis.* Stated generally, it asserts that "praxis alone . . . is, *in its dialectical freedom,* the real and permanent foundation (in human history up to the present) of all the inhuman sentences which men have passed on men through worked matter" (CDR, 332; emphasis his). Since this is the specifically existentialist principle of Sartre's Marxist existentialism, its full significance must be weighed. Praxis enjoys a threefold primacy in Sartre's social and political thought: epistemic and methodological, ontological, and ethical.

The Epistemic and Methodological Primacy of Praxis. In one of his expansive interjections in the *Critique,* Sartre announces that praxis is "the measure of man and the foundation of truth" (CDR, 801). As the measure of man, it serves as the standard for a new humanism. As the foundation of truth, it forms the basis of what may be termed Sartre's "praxis epistemology." Elsewhere I have argued at length that two distinct though overlapping epistemologies can be found in the Sartrean corpus, the one a Husserlian epistemology of vision and the other an epistemology of

105

praxis. They give rise to mutually conflicting theories of evidence, truth, and knowledge.[20]

My present concern is to indicate how the self-awareness of individual praxis grounds the intelligibility of group praxis and, specifically, how practical comprehension enables each agent—even the outsider—to comprehend the practical unity of the group. At issue is not only the question of methodology in the social sciences but especially the matter of the *cognitive* component of collective responsibility. What I wish to call "collective bad faith" will make sense only if I can account for the series' and the group's practical awareness of the meaning (*sens*) of their praxis or passive activity.

The epistemic primacy of praxis turns on Sartre's thesis that praxis is fully comprehensible to itself, a claim made on behalf of the prereflective cogito in his earlier work. He speaks of the "translucidity of individual praxis" as opposed to the opacity of the practico-inert which, in contrast, he implies is the "intelligible limit of intelligibility" (CDR, 94). As with the concrete historical dialectic revealed through group praxis, he warns:

> The impossibility (for a union of individuals) of transcending organic action as a strictly individual model is the basic condition of historical rationality, that is to say, that constituted dialectical reason (as the living intelligibility of all common praxis) must always be related to its ever present but always veiled foundation, constituent rationality. (CDR, 678)

No doubt, practico-inert structures, essences, and the like are intelligible without immediate reference to praxis.[21] But they yield the abstract, conceptual knowledge proper to analytical reason. In the concrete social realm, that of series, groups, and institutions in interaction, the intelligibility is *dialectical* and the dialectic is constituted by individual, totalizing praxes. "Praxis," Sartre writes, "as the action of a multiplicity, is far from being an opacity in dialectical rationality. On the contrary, dialectical rationality implies the basic priority of constituted praxis over Being and even over hexis, simply because in itself this rationality is nothing but the praxis of the multiplicity in so far as it is maintained and produced by free organic praxis" (CDR, 789). Thus, the intelligibility of group praxis, though "not in itself a mere amplification of the praxis of an individual . . . , depends on the intelligibility of individual praxis, in so far as individual praxis is lost and then rediscovered in the practico-inert field" (CDR, 409–10).

That loss and rediscovery he traces in a wide variety of examples taken from sociology, anthropology, history, and biography. Thus he appeals implicitly to the primacy of praxis when he criticizes the holistic sociology of Kurt Lewin and Abram Kardiner's concept of "basic personality (see SM, 66–77), when he "completes" Lévi-Strauss's theory of the structures of kinship in primitive societies by appeal to a more fundamental dialectic of interiorization/exteriorization of scarcity and external danger (see CDR, 479ff.), when he uncovers the self-perception of the Girondists (SM, 44–47) or "reads" the intention of the Parisian crowd storming the Bastille (CDR, 379ff.), or as he interprets the meaning of another individual's acts (Flaubert's, for example, as he despises the rosette of the Legion of Honor, then covets it and, after Sedan, refuses to wear it; see IF, 3:566ff.)—even when such meanings escape the knowledge, though not the comprehension, of the agents themselves.[22]

In the earlier discussion of "comprehension" as "the translucidity of praxis to itself," I observed how this implicit self-awareness was the basis for his adoption of the *Verstehen* of interpretive sociology. His defense of this thesis, however, is little more than a phenomenological "pointing-to" coupled with an appeal to the coherence which it introduces into a historical sequence or an individual life and the support it lends to the cherished values of freedom and responsibility. In the final analysis, Sartre's "argument," here as at so many junctures, rests on a kind of obviousness (in effect, an intuition) that many would dismiss as uncritical common sense. The fact that it leads to so many noncommonsensical conclusions is doubtless what offends his critics most. Yet there is a cohesiveness to his position that demands it be read in full. Thus for the sake of fairness I shall reserve extended criticism for the concluding chapter.

The epistemic primacy of praxis figures in the way Sartre conjoins social intelligibility with those existential psychoanalyses at which he excels. In his extensive study of Flaubert, he joins the praxis principle with the concept of totalization to arrive at a major methodological thesis: "Man . . . totalizes his age to the very extent that he is totalized by it" (IF, 3:426). To totalize, he explains, is "to grasp the world from the front in a practical unveiling" (*Situations*, 8:441). In other words, it is teleological. Thus, the comprehension of an agent's own totalizing comprehension (his pro-ject), Sartre believes, reveals the meaning-direction of his age, and conversely. He applies this thesis extensively to interpret the reciprocity that obtained between Flaubert and his times. Thus the young writer's "choice" of "Neurotic art" (*l'Art Névrose*, a complex of attitudes that stressed detachment, solitude, derealization, failure [*l'échec*], misanthropy and nihilism) reflected the impossible demands of Louis Philippe's society upon artists to become, or at least to act like, neurotics (imaginary men) in order to write (see IF, 3:65–66). The French under Louis-Philippe were developing a self-image that was positivist and utilitarian, as personified in Flaubert's father (see IF, 3:662). Sartre sees the son's "choice" of the life of an invalid and author in his personal crisis of 1844 both as an anti-utilitarian reaction and as a prophetic anticipation of France's own option for imaginary glory in the person of Napoleon III as it flees the dark side of its image revealed by the massacres of 1848. In fact, Sartre believes that this is the deep reason for Flaubert's popularity during the Second Empire: the unreal is addressing the unreal.[23] What we are witnessing is the way that objective spirit (possibility) limits a person's effective options and how those de facto choices both contribute to this spirit and illumine the self-image of the age.

This synthesis of existentialist psychoanalysis and historical materialism that Sartre calls the *progressive-regressive* movement is built upon the methodological primacy of individual praxis.[24] Without an existentialist hermeneutic of the signs of an original choice (the regressive movement), we would have to rest content with the "general particularities"—abstractions such as "the Soviet bureaucracy" or "the petite bourgeoisie" that masquerade as concrete individuals for Marxist economism (see SM, 24 and 43). On the other hand, without the dialectical interplay of objective possibility and totalizing praxis (the progressive movement), we would lose sight of history for biography. Yet in both cases the epistemic terminus (a quo in the latter case, ad quem in the former) is individual praxis.

The Ontological Primacy of Praxis. Well into the *Critique,* Sartre writes: "It has been obvious from the beginning of our dialectical investigation that the original foundation of unity, of action, and of finality is individual praxis as the unifying and reorganizing transcendence of existing circumstances towards the practical field" (CDR, 310n). This analysis of the practico-inert, including the discussion of serial praxis, has revealed the ubiquity of praxis in Sartre's system. But praxis is foundational as well.

Thus the class struggle, which for some orthodox Marxists is an impersonal interplay of conflicting forces, draws its reality from praxis. The unity of two struggling classes is a fact of antagonistic reciprocity, Sartre argues, and "this contradictory unity of each in the Other is generated [*suscitée*] by praxis and by praxis alone" (CDR, 794; F, 735). Sartre's "existentializing" of the Marxian dialectic consists primarily in appeal to the ontological primacy of praxis:

> In short, if the mode of production is the infrastructure of every society in human history, this is because labor—as a free, concrete operation which becomes alienated in the collective and which already produces itself as a transcendence of an earlier alienation to this collective—is the infrastructure of the prac-

tico-inert (and of the mode of production), not only in the sense of diachronic totalization . . . , but also synchronically since all the contradictions of the practico-inert and especially those of economic process are necessarily constituted by the constant re-alienation of the worker in his labor. (CDR, 713)

There are only individuals and real relations among them, Sartre claims in *Search for a Method* (76). Now it is clear that these individuals are "sovereign praxes" and that their relations are practical.[25]

It is essential to Sartre's social ontology that praxis be fundamental to all "impersonal" processes: "The practico-inert can be treated *as a process* . . . , but this process in so far as it is *already* passive action, presupposes the entire praxis . . . , which it reabsorbs and transforms in the object, while still being based on its real, abstract pullulation" (CDR, 713). Consequently, the "system" of colonialism as a practico-inert process with a life and a logic of its own, "is nothing but oppression as a historical praxis realizing itself, determining itself and controlling itself in the milieu of passive activity" (CDR, 729). Witness Merleau-Ponty's observation that Sartre favors the anarchists' emphasis on oppression over exploitation.[26] I shall consider the ethical significance of grounding institutional exploitation in oppressive praxis in the next section. But at this point it suffices to note that praxis is ontologically primary even for passive activity and in the realm of the practico-inert generally.

The basic motive for forming groups is to liberate serialized praxes from the alienating mediation of the practico-inert, supplanting it by the practical mediation of the praxes themselves. The group-in-fusion arises through the spontaneity of individual praxes. Each interiorizes the multiplicity of other praxes, making them "the same" (*le même*) in practice without resorting to an abstract idea (the sameness of a universal) on the one hand or to mere nominalistic stipulation on the other. Later in the chapter I shall analyze the type of social wholes that praxis mediates—the fused group, the pledged group, the organized group—as well as their devolution into practico-inert mediation as the institution. But from the viewpoint of ontological primacy, we must appreciate Sartre's claim that "praxis is the only real unity of the fused groups: it is praxis which creates this group, and which maintains it and introduces its first internal changes into it" (CDR, 418).

The unity of the group-in-fusion turns on what I shall call the "mediating Third" (as distinct from the "alienating Third" introduced in *Being and Nothingness*). But this is also a form of praxis. In fact, the whole "inner life" of the group is a revolving circle of practical relations whereby each praxis "interiorizes" the multiplicity of the rest: neither I nor you, but

109

we are a hundred strong. The specific unity of the group, Sartre argues, is "a synthetic relation which unites men for and by an action, and not those vague interpenetrations which an idealist sociology sometimes tries to resuscitate in some form or another" (CDR, 390). The ontological primacy of praxis thus saves Sartre from Hegelian "hyperorganisms" and even, he sometimes insists, from Durkheimian "collective consciousness." Only with the cessation of external danger and the advent of self-imposed inertia through a social pledge of some sort does the focus of praxis within the group get blurred. Yet even here praxis remains primary, for this inertia is originally *self*-imposed.

Ethical Primacy of Praxis. I have insisted from the start that Sartre is fundamentally a moralist. All the categories of the human world as he describes it conspire to give the inauthentic person a bad conscience and to call the oppressed to freedom. So we can expect that the epistemic and the ontological primacies of praxis culminate in its ethical primacy, the root of existentialist-moral responsibility and the touchstone for Sartre as a committed philosopher. There is a particularly moral flavor to his insistence that "it is men whom we judge and not physical forces" (SM, 47).

Reserving Sartre's portrait of the industrial capitalist for extended description in chapter 8, let us observe this ethical primacy in the case of the neocolonialist. As we have seen, colonialism is a system, a practico-inert process, which necessitates occasional overt violence such as repressing rebellions and which entails a racist ideology (*pensée-autre*) to justify such acts. In terms now familiar to us, the natives are serialized and their serial impotence is harnessed to the colonialist enterprise. As with any practico-inert process, there is serial alienation at all levels. The settler cannot succumb to "excessive" humanitarian feelings toward his native workers, or he may perish at their hands. A modus vivendi is established, a *hexis*, which governs the lives of settler and native alike. But this *hexis*, Sartre observes, "[is] no more than a diachronic mediation between two cycles of praxis" (CDR, 719). His point is that responsibility is not lessened by the exigencies of the system, for "this new serial *hexis* cannot exist unless everyone realizes and adopts it as *other* in his everyday praxis" (CDR, 720; emphasis his). The inert exigency now experienced "is the object of an oppressive praxis and . . . was the objective (now achieved and transcended) of past oppression" (CDR, 722). In other words, at the base of impersonal necessities lie personal praxis and responsibility.

Take the example of very low wages, a key to the economic success of colonialism. It is usually assumed that they are beyond the control of the individual plantation owner. But Sartre's analysis in the *Critique* is aimed at establishing that "the process on the basis of which [low wages] were settled was a necessity of the practico-inert only in so far as an oppressive praxis had deliberately produced a situation which made the process necessary" (CDR, 723). In Sartre's social archaeology, a level of serial hexis (habit) is sandwiched between two levels of praxis: the one that establishes it and the other which maintains it.

Similar analyses can be made of racism and institutionalized violence. Thus, the original violence with which the colony was established is reabsorbed by the "inertia-violence" of the institution. It is symbolized and fostered by the presence of the army in various "trouble spots" throughout the colony. Strategic displays of force when overt violence erupts merely serve to remind the populace of the pervasive violence that has become a way of life. And running through this process like an ethical mandate of some kind is the racist idea that Sartre sometimes calls "process-thought" (CDR, 721). As I noted in the discussion of practico-inert mediation, it is oppressive praxis that constitutes this verbal milieu which helps reduce the native to the subhuman status that warrants his "natural" servitude. "If violence *becomes* a praxis of oppression," Sartre warns, "this is because it always was one" (CDR, 732; emphasis his).

Whether it be the isolated settler keeping the native "in his place," the local commandant quelling a riot, or the board of directors setting the profit margin for a mining operation, "the praxis of oppression . . . complements the process of exploitation and merges into it" (CDR, 721). The common *interest* of the settlers as vested in continuance of the exploitative system is simply the other side of "oppression as a historical praxis realizing itself, determining itself, and controlling itself in the milieu of passive activity" (CDR, 729). In other words, the "meanness" is not entirely in the system.

It should now be clear that the principle of the primacy of praxis affords Sartre's social theory an intelligibility, a concreteness, and an ethical significance integral to his project of existentializing Marxism. It supports his contentions that analytic reason, with its acceptance of history as a brute fact (though it deals quite readily with "histories"), is inadequate for this project, that the "class struggle," though immersed in seriality, is not merely the product of practico-inert forces, and that exploitation must be inseparable from oppression. This is the reason behind his extended discussion of colonialism: "To show, by reference to a simple example, the possible importance of substituting History for economic and sociological interpretations, or generally for all determinisms" (CDR, 733).

I have characterized relations mediated by praxis as exhibiting a "dialectic of the same." Although I have appealed to this thesis at this juncture in order to underscore the overcoming of otherness as the raison d'être of the group, it will be examined in its entirety in the next section of this chapter. My reconstruction of Sartre's social ontology is progressing from the "abstract" to the concrete. Simple practico-inert and pure praxis mediations are ideal types. The concrete is a mixture of groups constituting themselves as the ongoing negation of collectives and of collectives absorbing moribund groups or perduring as part of the basic, albeit negated, structure on which living groups arise. "We can identify at the extremes," Sartre concedes, "groups in which passivity tends to disappear entirely . . . and collectives which have almost entirely reabsorbed their group" (CDR, 254). But the "tends" and the "almost" merely underline the ideal typical status of these terms. In combating Marxist "economism" and positivistic accounts of history, Sartre has no intention of defending the other extreme. "If [the class struggle] is praxis through and through," he cautions, "the entire human universe vanishes into a Hegelian idealism" (CDR, 734). Concrete historical reality, in effect, is a dialectic of the other and the same. This being the case, there is something Faustian about Sartre's vision of total disalienation: "The worker will be saved from his destiny only if the human multiplicity as a whole is permanently changed into a group praxis" (CDR, 309).

Dialectic of the Other/Same: Social Wholes

The exposition and argument in this chapter have imitated Sartre's quasi-Hegelian moves in the *Critique* from the abstract to the more fully determined. Concretization is a matter of establishing those factors that mediate identity and action in history. Sartre has offered us two such factors at a generic level, praxis and the practico-inert, giving rise to social relations of sameness and otherness respectively. But historical reality, as we know, is an interplay of these factors in concrete multiplicities, the concrete being "the line of intersection of the group and the serial" (CDR, 554n). More specifically, Sartre distinguishes three concrete types of multiplicity generated by these mediations, the collective, the combat group in various stages of formation, and the group-institution or "sovereign," as he calls it: "each . . . is the mediation and the totalizing signification of the other two" (CDR, 794). Although I have discussed serial unities in the context of practico-inert mediation and have briefly considered the group-in-fusion as an example of praxis mediation, I have not treated these social wholes in their concrete interaction nor have I mentioned the third member of this trio, the institution, at all. So after a closer study of the collective in the light of what we now know about Sartre's social ontology, I shall turn to a detailed analysis of the ontology of the group itself, giving specific consideration to one of Sartre's major contributions to social theory, the concept of the mediating Third, and concluding with an examination of that relapse of the group into seriality, the institution. This will complete our study of Sartre's social ontology in preparation for a full reconstruction of his theory of collective responsibility in chapter 7.

The Collective (*le collectif*)

We know that seriality with its characteristic otherness is the basic type of sociality. Whatever social wholes may form stand either as expressions of or in opposition to practico-inert seriality. Sartre claims that "in every non-serial praxis, a serial praxis will be found as the practico-inert structure of the praxis in so far as it is social" (CDR, 266). At first blush this seems to imply that seriality is never overcome entirely and that the ideal of universal praxis mediation is just that. Although Sartre never deals with this objection, it could be answered by pointing out the real but innocuous presence of the practico-inert in a "socialism of abundance" where the product no longer produces the man, but the man the product. This would be akin to the Marxists' vision of the policeman reduced to traffic cop in the classless society. The point is that the practico-inert does remain, if only to flavor those groups that arose in opposition to it, like "the tang of the cask they came in," in John Locke's pungent metaphor.

Sartre designates two basic forms of seriality in the *Critique,* the collective[27] and the institution. The collective is the paradigm of unity in exteriority. The collective object, whether machine tool or opinion poll, does not merely symbolize our exterior unity—it constitutes it (see CDR, 264). Interpersonal relations at this stage are not those of true, positive reciprocity: imitation or contagion, not cooperation, is the rule; interchangeability and numerical equivalence, not uniqueness. This is what Sartre in *The Communists and Peace* calls the "mass," namely, "a collective whole which reacts like a thing, like a material milieu where the stimuli are propagated mechanically" (CP, 207).[28] In Marxist terms, the collective forms the object, not the subject, of history. The task of the party militant, Sartre writes in that Bolshevist period of his thought, is to agitate "the masses-object in order to transform them into proletariat-subject" (CP, 207). We know that in the *Critique* it is the class-collective that Sartre wishes to understand[29] and that he explains the historical class struggle by a dialectic of interest/destiny in a practico-inert field of scarcity.

The Group

Sartre takes the group as the second degree of sociality. Although not necessarily later in time than the series, the aim of the group is the dis-

COLLECTIVE RESPONSIBILITY: THE EMERGENCE OF A THEORY

solution of seriality. Since Sartre equates seriality with unfreedom, that is, with passive activity, the appearance of the group can be considered "the sudden resurrection of freedom" (CDR, 401). It is a distinctive feature of Sartre's Marxist existentialism, and one which some read as a radical conversion from his earlier thought, that the individual is free only in the group. By now we should see this not as a conversion but as a corollary both to Sartre's commitment to concrete thinking and to his early concept of freedom-in-situation. And if "freedom" continues to be coterminous with "responsibility" for Sartre—and there is no reason to doubt that it does—we may conclude that full responsibility is likewise achieved only in the group. But then we must determine whether group responsibility differs significantly from individual responsibility, and that requires the present analysis of the ontology of the group.

Sartre's prime ontological thesis and the keystone of his theory in this regard is an echo of Marx's assertion that "there are only men and *real* relations between men" (SM, 76; emphasis mine). This thesis will recur like a leitmotif throughout the remainder of this study. At this stage it implies that "the group is not a metaphysical reality, but a definite practical relation of men to an objective and to each other" (CDR, 404n). Unfortunately, Sartre never provides an ontology of relations and so we cannot be sure what he means by contrasting practical relations with metaphysical reality. Presumably, he is claiming that the group is not a substance or "superorganism," a position that he reiterates often in the *Critique*. But relations are, of course, metaphysical realities—a point upon which I shall have occasion to insist later in this study.

The group-in-fusion (*le groupe en fusion*) is that nascent social whole which forms spontaneously as a plurality of heretofore serial individuals respond simultaneously to a perceived danger and to the likelihood of collective reaction to their stance. Here is that knowing-through-doing (comprehension) coterminous with praxis of which I have been speaking. In this case it is dissolving serial alterity and passive activity.

Sartre's example of the group-in-fusion is the crowd in the Quartier Saint Antoine, July 14, 1789, in serial flight before the royal troops. Suddenly (in Sartre's reconstruction), as if by prior agreement, someone shouts "Stop!" and the "command" (*le mot d'ordre*)[30] is echoed by scores of people who reverse direction even as they change their perception of the scene. What was construed as flight now is read as mobilization for counterattack. It is a practical awareness that "we" are acting—at first a small band, but soon swelling to large proportions, each member of which is buoyed up by the realization that "we are a hundred strong" (see CDR, 351ff.).

114

The point of this phenomenological description is that a practical change in direction-attitude constitutes both the group *and* the joining of it (a claim similar to that of the social contractarians). Prior to this original move, there was no group to join. At this crucial moment each becomes co-sovereign as the organizer of a common praxis. Sartre calls this constitutive action the interiorization of multiplicity. It denotes that crucial praxis whereby each takes the rest as "the same" and adopts what was the "elsewhere" of serial flight as the "here" of common concern. Each emerges as the common individual, the practical negation of serial individuality.

Although necessary for the emergence of the group, it is not sufficient that there be common need, common objectives, or even common praxis. What Sartre has in mind with the concept, "group-in-fusion," is a community. And for that, he argues, each must *feel* individual need as common need and project himself, "in the internal unification of a common integration, towards objectives which it produces as common" (CDR, 350). I take this last clause to mean that "interiorization of multiplicity" requires each to act *as* common individual much as Rousseau required that each person vote as citizen, judging in terms of the general will and not the will of all.

What has emerged is reciprocity mediated by praxis, the ideal social relation for Sartre. Although inchoate at this stage, the group exhibits Sartre's fourfold condition for true reciprocity: (1) that the Other be a means to the exact degree that I am a means myself, i.e., that he be the means toward a transcendent goal and not *my* means; (2) that I recognize the Other as praxis, i.e., as totalization *en cours,* at the same time as I integrate him into my totalizing project; (3) that I recognize his movement toward his own ends in the very movement by which I project myself toward mine; and (4) that I discover myself as an object and instrument of his ends by the same act which makes him an object and instrument of mine (CDR, 112–13; F, 192). This reciprocity is practical, as is the unity of the group, and mediated not by a practico-inert collective object but by praxis itself: everyone's doing, or willingness to do, "the same." This specific form of practical mediation, which distinguishes the group from the collective, Sartre terms the "mediating Third" (*le tiers médiateur*).[31] Because his social philosophy turns on it, I shall discuss the mediating Third in detail shortly.

The group, from the ontological viewpoint, is thus a revolving set of praxes, each reciprocally related to the others via the praxis of anyone, the common individual, treated as "the same," in a project that is interiorized as "ours": a single act with a plural subject (see CDR, 506). What results is a "synthetic enrichment" of individual praxis, what social phi-

115

losophers call a *societal fact* with properties of its own such as right, duty, function, and power (see CDR, 510).

But is responsibility one of these group properties? Sartre does not say so explicitly. The analogy between "freedom," "praxis," and "responsibility" which we have been witnessing suggests that group responsibility accompanies group praxis. A closer analysis of the mechanism of group praxis, especially an examination of the mediating Third, will reveal both the possibilities and the limits of this use of "responsibility."

The group fuses in the face of an external threat perceived as common. With the passing of that danger, another threat returns, the possible loss of this hard-won freedom through collapse into serial impotence once more. To avoid this and to achieve a certain permanence, the members introduce a form of "self-imposed inertia," the oath or pledge. Each promises the other under pain of death not to exercise that power of betrayal which, as organic praxis, is ontologically his.[32] Because of this stability, Sartre characterizes the pledged group as "the origin of humanity" (CDR, 436). This is the group's stage of reflective self-awareness: "It is through the pledge that the group posits itself for itself" (CDR, 436n). The group had formed at a *pre*reflective level. The inner union now established depends on relations of "fraternity-terror," a kind of self-induced fear that replaces the diminishing external threat.[33]

So the "inner life" of the group is an interplay of opposites: immanence-transcendence, quasi-subject and quasi-object, and above all, that sameness-otherness which yields "free alterity." What keeps these characteristics in dynamic union is the mediating Third. It renders possible ascriptions of collective predicates to individuals-in-relation. We must now look at this key concept in Sartre's social theory, since it opens the door to the existentialist categories of freedom, responsibility, and the primacy of praxis to the realm of what Sartre calls "socialities," the proper subject matter of the social sciences.

The Mediating Third

Proclaiming the manifesto of the Revolutionary People's Assembly, Sartre declares: "Our goal, our common purpose, is the integration of the free individual in a society conceived as the unity of the free activities of individuals" (EP, 40). That integration is achieved conceptually only with the introduction of the mediating Third in the *Critique*.

It is dialectical reason with its stress on the concrete as the mediated that requires the mediation of a Third. Sartre refers to the ternary relation ontologically as "a free inter-individual reality" and as "an immediate human relation" (CDR, 367).[34] Simply stated, where the practico-inert mediates, the human relations are serial; where praxis mediates, the relations are free. Sartre need not violate his thesis that there are only men and real relations between men, for the reality of the group-in-fusion *is* the relations constituted by the praxis of the Third. Let us consider this mediation in its several aspects.

The Third is first of all a praxis. Sartre describes it "in its original structure" as "the practical power of unifying any multiplicity within his own field of action, that is to say, of totalizing it through a transcendence toward his own ends" (CDR, 368). This is precisely how Sartre will later define "sovereignty" (see CDR, 578). This totalizing praxis serves as constitutive dialectic for the constituted dialectic of the group.

By the practical interiorization of multiplicity, sheer numerical dispersion is perceived as (and transformed into) power. Each approaches the group-in-fusion "as constituent and constituted power." Power, in effect, is the first common quality that the nascent group possesses: "We are a hundred strong." The Third "receives the power he gives, and he sees the other third party approaching him as *his* power" (CDR, 376).

If power is the first, many other "common qualities" emerge with the being-in-the-group of the individual—"adopted inertia, function, . . . rights and duties, structure, violence and fraternity." The member "actualizes all these reciprocal relations as his new being, his sociality" (CDR, 510). Accordingly, a new field of dialectical investigation opens up, the constituted dialectic, where these properties of the group as a form of "interindividual reality" are considered.

Now each is a member qua Third. But every other is likewise member as Third, i.e., as mediated by the group. As Sartre remarks: "The members of the group are third parties, which means that each of them totalizes the reciprocities of others. And the relation of one third party to another has nothing to do with alterity: since the group is the practical milieu of this relation, it must be a human relation . . . which we shall call *mediated reciprocity*" (CDR, 374; emphasis mine). This free reciprocity is the effect of a twofold mediation, that of the group between Thirds, and that of each Third between the group and the other Thirds. Let us examine each.

The mediation of the group cannot be that of some organic whole. To maintain the nonsubstantial character of the group's unity and mediation, Sartre introduces two technical terms, "the same" and "ubiquity." Their function is to account for that practical unity which reflects multiplicity as transformed from impotence to power.

I have already discussed "the same" as an alternative to organic identity among individuals and to mere extrinsic denomination of the serialized individuals. The point of Sartre's "dialectical nominalism" at this, its most decisive, stage is to respect, indeed to underline, the individual's contribution to a collective undertaking. The interiorization of multiplicity, which yields the common individual, is not a theoretical abstraction from individuating features but a praxis, a practical accommodation of one's project to *our* project. "The third party," Sartre argues, "is my objectivity interiorized" (CDR, 377). It is not an alienated objectivity; rather, it is the quasi-object/quasi-subject of reciprocity mediated by the group. As Sartre notes: "The transformation of free action into common free action by the free praxis of the group is absolutely intelligible. . . . [There is] nothing mysterious here, just my own freedom recognizing itself as common action in and through my individual action" (CDR, 378). It is precisely in these terms that he understands community as "a transition from the Other to the Same" (CDR, 612).

"Ubiquity" refers to that "circularity" proper to the group. Recall that the circularity of flight or recurrence characterizes the series: each is "other" to the rest and the source of action is "elsewhere" to denote interest and concern; again, this is the "human" space of existential thought. "My praxis," he writes, "is in itself the praxis of the group totalized here by me in so far as every other myself totalizes it in another here, which is the same, in the course of its development of its free ubiquity." This translates into the fact that each is doing what I would do were I over there. Every "over there" becomes "here" to the group member. Sartre draws a major ontological conclusion from this analysis: "Here there appears the first we [reading *nous* in the subjective, not the objective, case as in the English translation] which is practical but not substantial, as the free ubiquity of the me as an interiorized multiplicity" (CDR, 394). Clearly, the We has surfaced in Sartre's social ontology as far more than the mere "psychological *Erlebnis*" of *Being and Nothingness*. This synthetic enrichment enables my organic praxis to produce in reciprocity a common result, where "common action" means simply "everywhere, the same."

But I am also mediated by the other Thirds as totalizing sovereigns. Sartre writes, "I am integrated into the common action when the common praxis of the third party posits itself as regulatory" (CDR, 379). But the "regulation" is not obeyed, properly speaking. As we saw above, the "word" (*le mot d'ordre*) circulates, it does not command. Sartre calls the individual's being-in-the-group, insofar as it is mediated by the common praxis of a regulating Third, his "bond of interiority" with the group (CDR, 381).

This all-important interiorization whereby each becomes "ours," i.e., the same, everywhere, translates into *responsibility*. It is obviously an ontological phenomenon, being a function of praxis, and not merely psychological. But for that same reason it bears an ethical weight as well. It is easy to redescribe the foregoing analysis of interiorization in terms of responsibility. Thus, the genesis of the group can be seen as "interiorization of responsibility" such that "my" responsibility becomes "ours." And just as the other group qualities are synthetic enrichments of individual praxis, so what we may now call *group responsibility* is likewise enriched by "sameness" and "ubiquity," for example. Sartre implies such a reading when he notes that the *mot d'ordre* brings it about that each discovers his own praxis in the circulating "word" of the regulating Third. Subsequent questioning of participants in some spontaneous demonstration would reveal their common belief that "they are *all* responsible" (CDR, 397).

The Institution

When the group imposes a kind of inertia on itself by pledging mutual fidelity under pain of death, each member in effect makes a wager: "I depend on everyone, but through freedom as practical recognition I am guaranteed against this dependence" (CDR, 404). As we have come to see, my freedom-in-situation simply *is* this practical recognition by other freedoms. What Sartre terms "institution" is the loss of this wager, the voidance of this guarantee. Whatever the historical or personal conditions that occasion this shift, the pledged and organized group tends to harden into hierarchical strata; self-preservation of the organization becomes the overriding concern; the Third, mediator of group freedom, crystallizes into an insuperable Other; and some emerge as "more equal than others," in Orwell's telling phrase. This is easily recognized as a reintroduction of serial otherness into interpersonal relations. Sartre explains it under three aspects: sovereignty, authority, and bureaucracy.

Sovereignty. An indication of what Georges Gurvitch calls Sartre's "camouflaged antistatism" is found in his definition of "sovereignty."[35] Sartre defines it precisely as he had defined "mediating Third" earlier: "The absolute, practical power of the dialectical organism, that is to say, purely and simply its praxis as a developing synthesis of any given multiplicity in its practical field, whether inanimate objects, living things, or men" (CDR, 578). The concept of sovereignty is descriptive and original for Sartre. As Sartrean man *is* freedom, so he *is* sovereign: "There is no such thing as diffuse sovereignty: the organic individual is sovereign in the abstract isolation of his work" (CDR, 636). He becomes *co*-sovereign in the group.[36] The limit to sovereignty, as to freedom, is simply another sovereignty-freedom.

But what was cooperation in the fusing group and wary brotherhood (fraternity-terror) in the sworn group becomes a system of rights and duties in the organized group and outright reign of terror in the early days of the institution (see CDR, 593). In the language of existentialism, "freedom . . . becomes afraid of itself" (CDR, 586). Briefly put, each construes himself "through the Other and through all, as an inorganic tool by means of which action is realized" (CDR, 599). Sartre terms this "vicarious freedom" and it characterizes "the institutional individual" (CDR, 591), who is serialized by the virtual otherness of hierarchical relations and by the corresponding "passive activity" demanded by the institutionalized sovereign. The birth of the institution out of the group is in effect "the systematic self-domestication of man by man" (CDR, 606), where each gives himself to the cause which is "greater than all of them." The fact is that "there is only one freedom for all the members of the [institutionalized] group: that of the sovereign" (CDR, 621). His individual freedom is likewise the common freedom of the institutionalized members. This nonreciprocal sovereignty of the leader of the institution is what Sartre means by "authority."

Authority. Authority finds its complete expression only in the institution. Sartre subscribes to what we may call a "command theory" of authority. This amounts to the claim that authority, like belief, is the *Other* in us. It is the power to transform the practical field, including other men as instruments of this nonreciprocal power. Where the otherness of the collective is horizontal, each being united from without via a collective object, that of the institution is vertical, each united to the others by a kind of interiority, the command-obedience relation. It is this ambiguous internal unity that is appealed to by exhortations to company loyalty and to doing one's duty. "The institutional system as an exteriority of inertia necessarily refers to *authority* as its reinteriorization; and *authority,* as a power over all powers and over all third parties through these powers, is itself established by the system as an institutional guarantee of institutions" (CDR, 607). So authority is both the product and the guarantee of institutions. In terms of the dialectic of exteriority/interiority, authority is the "reinteriorization" of the institution.

Unlike sovereignty, authority is thus derivative. It is a unilateral development of the group's quasi-sovereignty, a short-circuiting of the mutuality of the Third. The power of life and death (fraternity-terror), which is a basic determination of sociality for Sartre, loses its reciprocity and becomes centered in one—the leader. As the unilateral supplants the reciprocal, coercion (command-obedience) supersedes self-imposed inertia (*le mot d'ordre*): "This permanent, living structure of coercion is a necessary determination of sovereignty as authority" (CDR, 608). Sartre continues:

> From the moment in which a regulatory third party . . . be-
> comes a pledged holder of the power of regulation as organized
> function, and when this third party receives and concentrates
> the internal violence of the group as a power to impose his
> regulation, everyone's shifting quasi-sovereignty is immobi-
> lized and becomes *authority* as a specific relation of one in-
> dividual to all. (CDR, 608)

Since, in Sartre's mind, authority relations are basically coercive, they
leave individuals no choice but obedience. This obedience of the institutionalized individual is "something like an acceptance" of sovereign
authority. But, being the "interiorization of the impossibility of resisting
it" (CDR, 630), such obedience confers on the sovereign at best a "serial,
pseudo-legitimacy" (CDR, 637). This is why Sartre can claim that "obedience legitimates the sovereignty of the exploiters in the eyes of the
exploited" (CDR, 617). Its illegitimacy, on the other hand, is revealed
only by acts of disobedience, and ultimately nothing but revolution, Sartre
insists, can uncover the raw power relations that obtain between the
classes.

Bureaucracy. A further but seemingly inevitable crystallization of institutionalized group praxis is the bureaucracy. Sartre sees it as the reaction
of seriality on the sovereign. It is constituted by a triple relation: "other-
direction of the inferior multiplicity; mistrust and serializing (and serialized) terror at the level of the peers; and the annihilation of organisms in
obedience to the superior organism" (CDR, 658). This relation of what I
have called "vertical otherness" implies what Sartre calls "the mineralization of man at every level, except the highest" (CDR, 658). In order
to underscore the particularly anti-Communist implication of this thesis,
Sartre points out that the cult of personality as well as bureaucracy itself
is more easily avoided in capitalism than in socialist societies because of
the countervailing influence of class tension in the former.

Here too serial impotence is the material out of which bureaucracy is
fashioned. Sartre offers a glimpse of his own social vision when he recommends that the socialist world decentralize and democratize: "and this
last term should be taken to mean that the sovereign must gradually
abandon its monopoly of the group (the question arises at the level of
workers' committees)" (CDR, 661). As long as this participatory move
is not undertaken, the group will crystalize by a quasi-automatic process
that Sartre in a parody of the group describes as each becoming "an
excluded Third" (*tiers exclu*), leaving merely a practico-inert instrument
in the hands of the sovereign. As it is, the institutionalized group's efficacy
lies not in its praxis but in its sheer materiality; in the numbers that it can

turn out for a mass rally. In other words, its efficacy lies in its "becoming-process." But, Sartre warns, "in so far as a praxis is process, goals lose their teleological character. Without ceasing to be genuine goals, they become destinies" (CDR, 663).

And so it appears that the spiral of Sartre's social dialectic has completed another revolution. The group seeking to escape the practico-inert relations of interest/destiny, imposed from without, ends by inflicting a destiny on itself when it casts its lot with the sovereign Other. Of course, these "abstract" social wholes—collective, group, and institution—interact in the concrete. Each mediates and gives meaning to the other two. But their intelligible interrelation, I have argued, is that of the basic dialectic of sameness and otherness which I have been depicting.

By way of concluding this protracted analysis of Sartre's social ontology as a dialectic of other (practico-inert) and same (praxis), let us examine these opposing rationales as they contrast at each juncture. As I noted at the outset, Sartre's is a philosophy of social *mediation*. Praxis and the practico-inert pervade every facet of social life as he understands it. The following sets of contraries summarize the polar opposition that forms the backbone of his social ontology, while revealing his failure to mediate the mediations themselves.

Otherness	*Sameness*
practico-inert (process)	praxis
series	group
solitude	community
absence (elsewhere)	presence (ubiquity)
passive activity	active passivity[37]
serial individual	common individual
impotence	power
reign of necessity	reign of freedom
unity of flight (recurrence)	common project
collective object	common objective
exteriority	interiority
pseudoreciprocity (authority)	positive, mediated reciprocity
alienation (horizontal/vertical)	disalienation
objectifying Third	mediating Third
interchangeability	uniqueness enhanced
practico-inert field	common field
interest/destiny	practical autonomy

Sartre embarked on his political odyssey proclaiming that he would "fight for the freedom of the person *and* for the socialist revolution."[38] The foregoing dialectic reveals why, after a decade of laboring for such a conjunction, he referred in somewhat chastened fashion to "the strange circular conflict, where all synthesis is impossible, which is the untranscendable contradiction of History: the opposition and identity of the individual and the common" (CDR, 559).

seven

The Conditions and Range of Collective Responsibility The Theory Reconstructed

We are all assassins.
Situations, 5:68

I have argued that Sartre employs an implicit theory of collective responsibility in his popular writings and that this theory attains reflective grounding only in the *Critique.* Yet even there the theory exists only in its elements; though it pervades the volume, Sartre gives us no ex professo treatment of the topic. What is called for is a rational reconstruction of this theory in accord with the social ontology of the *Critique.* In undertaking this task, one must keep in mind that the relation between these elements is dialectical and that their adequate comprehension presumes a grasp of their interrelatedness. To speak of individual features is to abstract from the concrete reality, which is dynamic and historical. Yet abstract we must. So with this caveat, let us first assay the conditions that, Sartre believes, warrant our saying "we (they) are responsible," then chart the extent of the theory's applicability, and finally reconsider Sartre's three basic social ensembles—collective, group, and institution—under the aspect of responsibility.

Conditions for Collective Responsibility

"Responsibility," taken in its basic juridical sense, denotes answerability "to another for something."[1] As such, it need not carry a moral connotation, and in an accommodated sense it can denote simply an impersonal, causal relationship as, for example, when we say that the heavy rains are responsible for our late spring this year.

Collective responsibility is the kind of answerability incumbent either on social wholes or on individuals by virtue of membership in such ensembles. Thus, we say that the Department of Philosophy at this university is responsible for the education of its students and that I, as a member of the department, share that responsibility.[2] It is reference to the social whole that makes this responsibility collective, much as it is reference to

124

the banking system that transforms the simple exchange of paper into the cashing of a check.[3] If the chair at a departmental meeting exhorts: "Colleagues, we must improve relations with other departments on campus!" he doesn't mean that I must improve relations, that professor X must do so, and so forth. Much less does he mean that some substance called "we" must do so. What he has in mind is that all of us together, qua members, that is, as mediated by that social whole called "the Department of Philosophy," have certain responsibilities which are not ours taken singly. If we would understand collective responsibility as a social fact, that is, in essential reference to the social ensemble, our attention must focus on those various factors which mediate collective responsibility. The point of this chapter, then, is to indicate how the basic kinds of social mediation constitute the fundamental forms of collective responsibility.

The conditions for ascribing responsibilities to collectives, in Sartre's thought, are of two kinds, ontological and what we may broadly term moral.

Ontologically, of course, we must begin with the primacy of individual praxis. This is the root and source of all Sartrean responsibility. Concrete, individual organisms working out a living in their material and social environment constitute the ontological touchstone for Sartre's theory. As we have seen, individual praxis alone is constitutive of social wholes. Yet the Enlightenment myth of a Robinson Crusoe is just that; individuals are always constituting social wholes and finding themselves enmeshed in the same by others. Praxis is outgoing and relational.

One might object that there is nothing new here, that Sartre had claimed as much in his notoriously individualistic *Being and Nothingness* when he insisted that being-for-others was as basic a category for human reality as was the dichotomous for-itself or in-itself. But recall that there he reduces the We to "a purely psychological *Erlebnis.*" By denying collective agents even the ontological status accorded the us-object, Sartre at that stage seems committed to a form of ontological individualism.

By subsuming "consciousness" into "praxis" as the pivot of his social ontology and thereby breaking the looking-glass model of social relations, Sartre makes possible a third alternative regarding the ontological status of the We. The we-subject can be seen as a real, practical relation among organic individuals whose activities are "interiorized" by each considering the rest "the same" as himself in praxis and practical concern. No doubt the fusing and the organized groups are parasitical upon the praxes who constitute them. There is no "hyperorganism," no substance existing independently of these specific agents. The relation cannot obtain without the *relata*. And yet this does not mean that the relation is not real or that it cannot modify the relata in turn. Sartre admits such modification when he speaks of the group's "synthetic enrichment" of individual praxes, and he even appeals implicitly to Durkheim's famous example of social constraint when discussing the serial individual (see CDR, 301–4). Of course, a psychological factor is present in group synthesis as in serial dispersion. It is generated, for example, by the realization that "*we* are a force to be reckoned with." But this enrichment is a real, practical increase: "We are a *force* to be reckoned with; together we have a power which you and I lack by ourselves (or in serial impotence)."

Sartre calls his position "nominalism" in order to underscore the threefold primacy of praxis I discussed in the previous chapter. But his adoption of Marx's claim, "There are only men and *real* relations between men," sits ill with traditional nominalism's penchant for merely verbal relations (*flatūs vocis*). So he qualifies his brand as "dialectical" (CDR, 37), indicating its practical and mediating character. His is a dialectic of emergence and decline, the group surfacing at a certain point in historical praxis only to sink back into seriality under pressure from the practico-inert forces and from the sheer unreliability of human praxis. The concrete, as we saw, is "the line of intersection of the group and seriality" (CDR, 554n).

This feature of emergence must be emphasized as we consider collective responsibility. For it suggests that among the "group properties" of power, function, rights/duties, oath, and being-in-the-group that Sartre lists, group responsibility might be included as well. As I noted, he does speak of the "synthetic enrichment" of individual praxis by group membership and he allows that group properties are irreducible to the sum of individuals' acts taken singly.

In order to respect both the specificity of group existence and its "parasitical" nature, Sartre distinguishes two dialectics, the *constituent,* which denotes the individual praxis as ontologically primary, and the *constituted,* referring to the life of the group. This constituted dialectic is precisely that revolving interplay of mediation between the group and the Third and among the Thirds themselves that was discussed in chapter 6. Group responsibility, I shall argue, can be seen as a function of the constituted dialectic. To appreciate the distinctive contribution of Sartre's dialectical nominalism to the problem of collective responsibility, we must distinguish it from two standard alternatives in social ontology, ontological individualism and ontological holism.

Ontological individualism denies the specific reality of social wholes. It is a form of social atomism that claims so-called social facts are simply logical constructs, what F. A. Hayek reduces to mere "mental modes." Karl Popper holds that associations and institutions are "abstract models constructed to interpret certain selected abstract relations between individuals."[4] In other words, only facts about individuals are real and/or explanatory. Hayek allows that "words like 'government' or 'trade' or 'army' or 'knowledge' do not stand for single observable things but for structures of relationships which can be described only in terms of a schematic representation or 'theory' of the persistent system of relationships between the ever-changing elements." But he insists that "these 'wholes,' in other words, do not exist for us apart from the theory by which we constitute them." In other words, Hayek allows that these social wholes are theoretical entities but denies they are real relations.[5]

On the contrary, ontological holism insists on the ontological specificity of the social, on the irreducibility of social wholes to the sum of their parts. Thus Emile Durkheim in his famous *Rules of Sociological Method* stands in direct contradiction to Hayek and Popper when he writes: "The first and most fundamental rule is: *Consider social facts as things.*"[6] By "social fact" he means "every way of acting, fixed or not, capable of exercising on the individual an *external constraint;* or again, every way of acting which is general throughout a given society, while at the same time *existing in its own right independent* of its individual manifestations."[7] Sartre allows for the phenomenon of external constraint; such, perhaps, is the self-imposed inertia of the oath, and such certainly is the practico-inert exigency of the "system." But as for the feature of independent existence—that is a stronger claim than Sartre is willing to make. Nor does it seem implied by the phenomenon of constraint, as our study of the pledged group attests. Yet even in this respect Sartre would doubtless admit that the group and a fortiori the institution exist independent of any *particular* individuals; that while it requires members (praxes), the group does not demand these particular praxes to perdure.[8] It is Durkheim whom he seems to have in mind primarily when he rejects "hyperorganisms" in society.[9]

Sartre's dialectical nominalism is a via media between individualism and holism. The social wholes, whether mediated by praxis or by the practico-inert, are not mere extrinsic denominations, even though his discussion of the "external" unity of the collective might suggest this. Neither are they superorganisms, despite his suggestion that it must look as if this were the case (see CDR, 506–7). When he denies "ontological" or "metaphysical" status to the group, Sartre is simply excluding any hypostatization of such an entity. "In effect," he clarifies, "the group is not a metaphysical reality, but a definite practical relation of men to an objective and to each other" (CDR, 404n). But, of course, relations *are* metaphysical realities, and *real* relations are capable of mediating the identity, action, and responsibility of organic individuals. We shall better appreciate why this is true and how dialectical nominalism differs from

127

both holism and individualism if we examine once more the respective inner workings of the collective and the group, but now in terms of the holist-individualist controversy.

As an example of the collective, let us take the socioeconomic class, Sartre's chief concern in introducing this social category.[10] He seems to fly in the face of his "nominalism" by employing the concept of class substance. He takes it as roughly equivalent to "class-being," which he describes as "an *inert (untranscendable) relation* with [each one's] class comrades on the basis of certain structures. Destiny, general (and even particular) Interest, Exigency, Class Structures, Values as common limits, all necessarily direct our attention . . . *to a type of collective being* as the basis of all individual reality" (CDR, 250; first emphasis mine, second his). This collective being is the class. It is more "concrete" than the solitary individual. Its ontological basis is "the inorganic common materiality of all the members of a given ensemble"; for example, the machines that both symbolize and effect the workers' "destiny."[11]

Anticipating objections from ontological individualists, Sartre adds:

And it cannot be argued that this substance does not really exist, that there are only individuals threatened by a single destiny, victims of the same exigencies, possessing the same general interest, etc., for it is precisely *the ensemble of structures of the practico-inert field* that necessarily conditions the substantial unity of the being-outside-oneself of individuals, and conversely, this being-outside-oneself as a substantial and negative unity on the terrain of the Other conditions the structure of this field in its turn. (CDR, 251; emphasis mine)

These objective structures of the practico-inert field ground that "inert, untranscendable relation" among individuals that is class-being.

But, contra holism, he warns against "those gelatinous realities, somewhat vaguely haunted by a supra-individual consciousness, which . . . a discredited organicism" tried to foist upon us (CDR, 251). It is the practico-inert, the machine, the factory, the "system," and not praxis, which is the unifying factor in this domain. This is reflected, Sartre believes, in our ordinary language when we speak of someone's being born *into* the working class or having sprung *from* the proletariat. Class is conceived as an original, common inertia that, paradoxically, synthesizes multiplicities. But unlike the group, it does so via indistinction and interchangeability (signs of alienation, for Sartre), not through the "sameness" of practical concern (see CDR, 252).

Ontologically, the group's unity is its praxis and its objective, not its passive activity and collective object. Again, Sartre lets ordinary language

128

suggest the nature of group praxis as constituted dialectic. In sentences such as "the people of Paris have taken the Bastille" or "the team has won a match," he remarks, "the subject is plural (or unified but multiple) and the action is *singular,* seen either as a temporalization . . . or in its common result" (CDR, 506). He concedes that the matter would be far more simple if, corresponding to the "concrete, living temporalization of the group" through group praxis, there were some "living concrete group which temporalized and objectified itself." Though more difficult, the concepts of ubiquity and sameness account for the phenomenon of singular action by a plural subject without appeal to any such group substance. He illustrates dialectical nominalism at work when he explains:

> Ubiquity is the reciprocity of unity as, with a single movement, it excludes both the manifold and the identical [seriality and organic unity]. This double exclusion is perfectly conveyed by language with the first person plural, when it expresses the interiorization of the multiple: in the *we*, in fact, the multiple is not so much eliminated as disqualified; it is preserved in the form of ubiquity. (CDR, 535)

It is this delicate balance between the manifold and the identical that Sartre's dialectical nominalism achieves and that justifies his speaking of the We in more than merely psychological terms. For the crucial expression "interiorization of multiplicity" that gives rise to and sustains the group denotes more than a psychological metanoia. It is a praxis proper to the mediating Third and constitutive of the group and its dialectic. Failure to note this leads commentators like Raymond Aron to read a simple return to ontological individualism in such remarks as the following:

> In fact . . . the group . . . does not exist anywhere except *everywhere,* that is to say, it belongs to every individual praxis as an interiorized unity of multiplicity. And the ubiquity of the *heres* corresponds to the real practice of negating plurality. . . . There is a practical determination of everyone by everyone, by all and by oneself from the point of view of a common praxis. (CDR, 506)

In effect, this "real practice of negating plurality" is tantamount to accepting responsibility for the practice, thereby making it common, i.e., "ours."

So the ontological conditions for ascribing responsibility to social ensembles for Sartre are those real, practical relations that mediate individuality and praxis or passive activity. Ultimately, of course, they are grounded in praxis and the practico-inert. But at a more concrete level, they are mediated by the Third and the collective object respectively. Their effect is to enable each to say "we" or "they" in a manner that denotes more than merely verbal stipulation but less than organic identity.

Taking the term "moral" in its broad sense as referring to mind, character, and will, the moral conditions for ascribing responsibility to collectives are twofold, cognitive and volitional. In order to achieve the far-reaching responsibility that Sartre requires to justify his many popular and polemical ascriptions, these factors of awareness and control must extend well beyond their common forms of "reflective deliberation" and "choice."

Our excursion into existentialist anthropology revealed such an expansion of denotation that "consciousness" and "choice" emerged as coextensive for Sartre. Likewise, ontological "freedom-responsibility" was seen to be extensionally equivalent to "consciousness-choice." So it makes sense in the Sartrean context to speak of an all-pervasive moral responsibility, including prereflective moral responsibility.[12]

Moreover, because we are originally and pervasively responsible, that form of moral evasion which Sartre terms "bad faith" remains a constant possibility. Indeed, in *Being and Nothingness* he writes as if it were inevitable. As part of his discovery of objective possibility and shift to a praxis philosophy, he subsequently admits that bad faith is conditioned by one's socioeconomic situation. As we might expect, this socialization of bad faith is a function of the practico-inert. Let us consider the cognitive and conative conditions for collective moral responsibility under four headings: comprehension, ideology, objective spirit, and, culminating in a new social designator, collective bad faith. Although the first is most basic and already familiar to us, the last is most commonly employed, at least implicitly, in his popular ascriptions.

Comprehension. Integral to his philosophy of praxis is the collapse of the cognitive and the conative dimensions of human action into one. Thus the epistemic purport of the primacy of praxis principle is grounded in the fact that comprehension is the self-awareness of praxis; there is no unconscious praxis.

Appeal to implicit awareness has been a hallmark of Sartre's thought since *The Transcendence of the Ego*. At that early stage it was based on the concept of the prereflective. To this was added the Heideggerian notion of "preontological comprehension" in *Being and Nothingness*.[13] We have observed that term assume a social dimension approximating the *Verstehen* of German social theorists. It is to this comprehension that Sartre appeals in ferreting out the implicit awareness that, he believes, permeates a social ensemble.

In *The Family Idiot*, for example, he develops an argument first sketched in "Materialism and Revolution" to the effect that the worker is aware of the nonreciprocity in basic human relations that an exploitative socioeconomic system entails.

> Thus the most elementary praxis, insofar as it is actual and lived from within, already contains . . . in its living state [à l'état vivant] an implicit, intuitive and nonverbal knowledge [*savoir*], a certain direct and totalizing but wordless comprehension of contemporary man among men and in the world, as well as an immediate grasp of the inhumanity of man and of his subhumanity—the first seed of a *political* attitude of refusal. (IF, 3:45)

Sartre adds that "at this point, everything is present, but in an extremely compressed state which eludes verbal elaboration."

Now it is to this "compressed state" of awareness that he appeals when he claims that the metropolitan Frenchman "knew" as much about the cruelties of his government's colonialist policy as did the German whom the Frenchman condemns for ignoring the evils of the Nazi regime. The awareness is a doing, a praxis, which precedes and often eludes reflective articulation. It is not only practical but also evaluative. It is an awareness infected with desire, an attention that excludes as it includes and hence a "choice" in the sense discussed in chapter 1.[14] We must keep this in mind, lest we dismiss Sartre's approach to responsibility as merely cognitive. For the categories under consideration bear a conative reading in accord with the nature of Sartrean consciousness studied earlier. This aspect is simply heightened by Sartre's shift to "praxis."

Sartre distinguishes two forms of comprehension according as the praxis in question is free (as it occurs within the active group) or is serialized through practico-inert mediation. The group, Sartre argues quite plausibly, "has a silent knowledge of itself through each common individual . . . not available to those who do not share its objectives" (CDR, 501). This was the reason for his recommendation that the historian, himself a situated investigator, first of all "comprehend the comprehension of the regulatory third party" (CDR, 696). Such self-comprehension exists, he insists, even if it is a kind of false consciousness later to be unmasked. The challenge is to grasp the "objectives" in terms of which the common individual makes himself common. Since such awareness is constitutive of the group, it must be available to the members.

In the case of the series, the phenomenon of other-comprehension (*l'autre-compréhension*) comes into play. This is exemplified by the interpretation of an artwork or a social event *en bourgeois*. Here in particular the evaluative nature of Sartrean consciousness enters the scene. Bourgeois humanism, for example, as a practico-inert idea, affects the cognitive aspect of praxis. Specifically, its leveling of all values to the monetary and its implicit racism, discussed earlier, serve to engender the otherness (e.g., competition and inequality) that we expect from practico-inert mediation. "The result," Sartre contends, "is not communication and never can be" (CDR, 777). Obviously, in his mind, "communication" as distinct from "contagion" is a positive value, presuming praxis, practical unity, and freedom.

If sameness/otherness constitutes the master dialectic of Sartre's social ontology, reciprocity/nonreciprocity enjoys that distinction in his "moral" thought, including his epistemology. (See his "definition" of "truth" as "the elimination of all alterity" [CDR, 535].) I shall have much to say about this toward the end of this study, but it should be noted here how the value disjunct reciprocity/nonreciprocity underlies Sartre's analysis of social awareness.

Yet even in the noncommunication of other-comprehension there must remain the possibility of achieving more adequate awareness. Indeed, such possibility is grounded in the epistemic and the moral primacy of praxis. Finally, it is in this primacy that we must locate the "seed of a politics of refusal" spoken of above and, more generally, that "idea of freedom" which cuts through class distinctions entirely.[15] As I noted when I discussed the latter, Sartre's ethical strategy depends on a notion of nonreflective awareness that obtains at the level of what historical materialists call a society's economic substructure. As *pre*ideological, such an "intimation of freedom," as we might call it, is presumably available to proletarian and bourgeois alike. Thus the truncated ignorance known as bad faith can infect anyone whose knowledge at the reflective or "theoretico-practical" level does not conform to his prereflective or "practico-theoretical" knowledge.[16] Doubtless, the very idea of such a "substructural awareness" is heresy to the orthodox Marxist for whom economics determines consciousness, not vice versa, and it might even strike the revisionist as nonsensical. But something like this is required if Sartre is to reserve a place for individual moral responsibility in the flow of economic determinism. Accordingly, it affects Sartre's approach to the Marxist issue of ideology and false consciousness.

Ideology. Alasdair MacIntyre defines "ideology" rather neatly as "the self-image of the age."[17] In terminology to which we are now accustomed, Sartre describes ideologies as "false totalities" which are cut off from living, totalizing praxis and which arise proximately from the need to legitimate power (for the rulers) or impotence (for the ruled). Ultimately,

132

however, ideologies originate in that flight from freedom-responsibility that was termed "inauthenticity" in the golden days of existentialism.[18] Sartre agrees with MacIntyre that ideologies are reflective phenomena and he points out that they are either explicitly verbal or involve "a connected ensemble of determinations of discourse" (IF, 3:47). In uncovering this ensemble, one can lay bare the self-image of the age.

Sartre admits that the worker has his own ideology, usually implicit and nonverbalized, which enables him to endure his exploited condition. He accepts Marx's thesis that these are mainly inculcated by the dominant class "through its systematic exercise of power" (IF, 3:46). But it is the ideology of the ruling class that concerns him chiefly. He finds in scientism (the proto-positivistic intellectual habit of Louis Philippe's society), for example, not only the expression of the need of that class to legitimate its power (IF, 3:222) but more profoundly "the will to grasp the facts about man as *en-soi,* fully formed" (IF, 3:420). In effect, this is the denial of freedom-transcendence, characteristic both of the analytic spirit and of the bourgeois humanism discussed earlier. Significantly, such denial is the deep motive behind the racism of the anti-Semite as well.

Ideology, as inauthentic and "other" than its sustaining praxis, is a phenomenon of the practico-inert. The habits and systems of legitimation and flight remain long after practico-theoretical knowledge has begun to illumine other praxes. Sartre calls these "irreducible passivities in their ensemble"—whether written or otherwise preserved—" 'objective spirit' " (IF, 3:47).[19]

Objective spirit. Sartre does not blush to adopt this typically Hegelian concept, "provided the word 'spirit' is shorn of its spiritualistic associations" (CDR, 776). He accomplishes this by locating it in the realm of the practico-inert. Objective spirit is objectified praxis, totalized by present praxis. In other words, it is "culture as practico-inert" (IF, 3:44). As such, it stands over against lived experience. And yet, "it exists *in act* only via the activity of men and, more precisely, by that *of individuals*" (IF, 3:50)—again, the primacy of praxis.

Describing objective spirit in terms reminiscent of Franz von Gerlach's defense of his generation, Sartre writes: "Following generations will make of the present lived experience today a totality that is past, surpassed (dépassée), still virulent in certain respects, and one of which the present [agents], whether dispersed or united, *have an obscure presentiment*" (IF, 3:50; emphasis mine). It is this "obscure presentiment" that interests us because it is the vehicle for common awareness of properly class activities. Far from seeing objective spirit as a moment in the march of Hegelian *Geist* through history, Sartre gives it a properly cognitive interpretation: objective spirit is simply a "medium for the circulation of significations" (CDR, 776). As such, it fulfills a condition for collective responsibility as moral.

Thus, in the case of what he calls "objective *class* spirit," each member is aware of the meaning of individual actions in terms of class interest. Describing the French proletariat under the Nazi occupation, Sartre remarks: "Each member of every group discovered the objective class-spirit as the permeability of every common undertaking to comprehension" (CDR, 792). The workers "read" the meaning of individual acts in terms of solidarity against a common enemy. The comprehension was a praxis, of course, and not some detached surveillance. As he summarizes it: "everyone saw his class totality as an infinite temporalization, . . . as a genuine task and as a common freedom" (CDR, 792). This is the mutual awareness of the members of a combat group that Sartre tends to idealize.

And yet to the extent that this is a class spirit, it is tinged with the practico-inert. That is why in *The Family Idiot* Sartre reminds us: "When human intentions are addressed to us via worked matter, materiality renders them *other*. . . . Human reciprocity is broken by the mediation of the thing, and the curdled intention that calls upon us *as others* can have no other structure than that of obligation." He concludes that "objective Spirit . . . cannot address us, not even in literature, except as an *imperative*" (IF, 3:55).[20] And hence, the cognitive relations mediated by objective spirit are alienated.

This is most evident in Sartre's analysis of the nineteenth-century practice of bourgeois "respectability," which becomes the "inert limitation and guiding schema of [the capitalist's] comprehension. . . . This means that he comprehends all class practice—and therefore the entire passive activity of seriality—both in recurrent flight . . . and as a tactic of organized oppression" (CDR, 774). It is such serial practices, hexis-ideas, and general bourgeois culture as objective spirit that mediate this awareness as well as the responsibility that this comprehension entails. Such is the ground for Sartre's frequent contentions that "everyone knew."

Collective bad faith. When he first introduces the concept of bad faith in *Being and Nothingness*, Sartre speaks of a weltanschauung of bad faith. This includes a particular concept of truth and a specific type of evidence, nonpersuasive evidence (BN, 68). The roles of desire and "choice" are more obvious in the case of such "evidence." "One *puts oneself* in bad faith," he writes, "as one goes to sleep and one is in bad faith as one dreams" (BN, 68). The pervasiveness of comprehension conjoined to the concepts of ideology and especially of objective class spirit as practico-inert limit and guide to comprehension enables us to speak of collective bad faith as a natural extrapolation to social ensembles of that famous category from Sartrean existentialism.

We know that bad faith is grounded ontologically in human reality's nonself-coincidence. Thus it is able to "objectify" itself in its own eyes and "see" itself as it would have the other see it. But such a project is carried out in inner tension and is ultimately doomed to failure precisely because of the self-transparency of Sartrean consciousness. We have seen that a similar self-awareness obtains in the case of individual praxis and have suggested that it makes the category "bad faith" available to Sartre's philosophy of praxis.

There is a lengthy analysis of the Eichmann case in *The Family Idiot* that bears out our talk of collective bad faith. Sartre writes:

> Evil is of its very essence *intentional*. If men secrete it without intent, it must be because they are keeping themselves *in a state of permanent distraction* . . . so that the judgment of things on persons—what elsewhere I have called the practico-inert—is interiorized by them and hence intentionalized in the absence of any subject. Evil must befall them and [do so] precisely as the practical meaning [*sens*] of the established order, that is to say, of disorder maintained by violence. This infinite and deep meaning must . . . become the rule of their actions or, if you will, of human relations as long as *systematic distraction* produces a false consciousness in them—all the more easily sustained by bad faith because Evil as the meaning of a society is "unrealizable"—which presents alienation in disorder as a fascination with order and [interprets] the intention to treat people like things as the urgent duty to preserve the present structures of the community—even at the price of human sacrifices. (IF, 3:631–32; emphasis mine)

This is Sartre's rather complex way of glossing Hannah Arendt's famous "banality of evil" remark apropos the Eichmann affair.[21] His talk of "permanent" and "systematic" distraction suggests more than individualistic bad faith and his reference to an "intentionalized practico-inert" confirms this reading. Not that he has finally admitted the collective consciousness he so adamantly rejected from the outset. But the practico aspect of the "practico-inert" is being underscored in light of the intentionality of moral evil. For praxis as conscious must be intentional; Sartre never questioned that basic thesis. As such, it can infect with moral disvalue what would otherwise be the traditional physical evil of natural events.[22] The practico-inert is thus liable to moral assessment; "the meanness is in the system," for example, assumes a new meaning. And in the case of Eichmann, Sartre sees the evil in a bureaucracy that diverts the attention of its passively active members from the real evil of genocide to the pseudogood of maintaining an orderly process in the state.

What makes this bad faith collective? Precisely the internalization of collective structures, whether these be the hexis-idea of racism, for example, or the bureaucracy itself. As with other collective objects, these structures mediate individuals (unite and separate them) in serial impotence. But, of course, their serial praxis allows them to remain in such a state of impotence:[23] "evil must *befall* them"; it is nothing they do. As in Eichmann's case, it is merely a matter of following orders (command-obedience). It is the role of collective objects in the genesis and maintenance of bad faith that justifies its being called "collective." And all of the features of seriality come into play. Thus the bad faith is communicated by contagion (passive activity) and entails the belief, for example, that "someone else" perpetrated the atrocities "elsewhere."

The extended quotation just analyzed employs the term "false consciousness" so dear to Marxists.[24] What does Sartrean "bad faith" add to this social category? Precisely the feature of moral responsibility communicated to each agent qua passively active in the series or institution. I mentioned this specifically existentialist contribution to the discussion of collective responsibility when I first distinguished the existentialist-moral from the Marxist-causal senses of "responsibility." I am now prepared to examine this distinction in detail.

The Nature and Scope of Collective Responsibility

Given the ontological and moral conditions for ascribing responsibility to collectives or to individuals by virtue of their participation in social wholes, I must make two fundamental distinctions before undertaking an analysis of Sartre's basic social ensembles in terms of responsibility. For these distinctions cut through the division of series and group. The first regards the nature of collective responsibility and the second its scope.

Two basic modes of collective responsibility. In a famous passage from *Capital,* Marx argues that "capitalist production begets with the inexorability of a law of Nature its own negation."[25] This is an example both of "scientific socialism" in practice and of what I have called the Marxist-causal sense of "responsibility."

It presumes a determinist social theory that sees a certain inevitability, at least in the long-range outcome of social processes. Far from excluding determinism, responsibility in this sense seems to call for it. This, of course, is Hume's criticism of libertarian theories of responsibility, that they leave us in a wonderland where anything can happen and where no one should take credit for anything.[26]

In its drive to construct a scientific socialism, orthodox Marxism[27] has sought necessary connections between apparently disparate conditions in the economic and in the cultural spheres. Modeling themselves on the classical British economists with their iron laws, such Marxists see a causal link (albeit not of the crude, knee-jerk variety) between "the material conditions of society" and the ideological superstructure of that society. The individual, whatever his intentions, is objectively powerless to breach the limits of the possible set by his socioeconomic conditions.

If we take this as the orthodox version of the determinist thesis, we must admit that Marx's own position is ambiguous. On the one hand, he seems to favor determinism. He writes in his preface to the first edition of *Capital* that the evolution of the economic formation of society is "a process of natural history" and he disavows any intention of making "the individual responsible for relations whose creature he socially remains, however much he may subjectively raise himself above them."[28] His classical statement of the economic determinist thesis occurs in an earlier preface, this one to his *Critique of Political Economy,* where he defends the explanatory priority of productive forces in social analysis.[29] Yet in recent years it has become fashionable to modify Marx's reputation as a collectivist and economic determinist, stressing rather the "humanist" strain even in his later writings.[30]

Whatever the final judgments of Marxist exegetes, there is no doubt that Marxist-causal responsibility is a defining characteristic of orthodox Marxism. Whether nuanced or mechanically applied, the theory focuses on the structural and functional relations that obtain within a society quite independently of the intentions or acts of individual agents.

We know that Sartre employs this usage at times; for example, when he speaks of the "meanness" of the colonialist system (CP, 183). Good intentions are rendered nugatory by institutionalized exploitation. It is the very fact of being a settler that mediates one's responsibility with all settlers for the violence and exploitation entailed by the system.

But such responsibility is merely a description of an individual's status or function within the system itself. It is quite indifferent to what I have called the "moral" conditions for collective responsibility. Hence it is inadequate for ethical evaluation, where basic cognitive and conative conditions must be fulfilled.[31] Indeed, Sartre always believed Marxist "economism" to be incompatible with moral responsibility. This conviction reaches exaggerated proportions in his autocritique late in life when he characterizes his period of fellow-traveling as "political realism" where he judged in terms of efficacity and "suppressed ethics [*la morale*]."[32]

137

Sartre's analysis of practico-inert process is likewise a tacit appeal to this Marxist-causal usage. Consider, for example, his description of the "logic" and the practico-inert "exigencies" behind the development of the steel-coal complex in the nineteenth century:

> It is undoubtedly true that—as Engels says—slaves appear at the moment when the development of the techniques of agriculture makes them possible and necessary, that is to say, that an institution is a response to the practico-inert exigency of an already constituted field of passive activity. Nor can there be any doubt . . . that exploitation in its many historical forms is basically a *process* which corresponds . . . ultimately to the development of the mode of production. (CDR, 738; emphasis mine)

Of course, "exigency-response" is not precisely "stimulus-response," much less "cause-effect." As I have noted repeatedly, whatever the rigors of Marxist "economism," Sartre's practico-inert processes at their most formidable remain *practico*-inert. Again, it is a matter of preserving a structural intelligibility in history without dissolving the historian (or anyone else) in an acid of universal determinism.

But in what sense is Marxist-causal responsibility "collective"? In the sense that these productive forces are social, that they modify such collectives as "socioeconomic class," economic "system," and the like. Marx's "immanent laws of capitalist production itself,"[33] such as the inevitable pauperization of the middle class, refer to classes and not to individuals as such. They affect individuals only through the mediation of the social whole.

The second basic mode of collective responsibility is the existentialist-moral. Despite their commitment to various degrees of determinism, Marxists do not fail to level moral condemnations against their foes—a practice Sartre takes as evidence that they accept a kind of freedom, however inconsistently.[34] While admitting the limitations imposed on agents by objective possibility and specifically by the practico-inert "exigencies" of their individual and collective situations, Sartre insists on the responsibility of each agent for shaping his individual and collective future. This is the ethical primacy of the principle of praxis discussed in chapter 6. It finds typical expression in claims like the following: "Totally conditioned by his class, his salary, the nature of his work, conditioned in his very feelings and thoughts, it is he who freely gives to the proletariat a future of relentless humiliation or [one] of conquest and victory, according as he chooses to be resigned or revolutionary. And it's for this choice that he is responsible" (*Situations,* 2:27–28). No longer is the choice merely one of meaning. It is a praxis and, as such, shapes the future that it interprets.

Although Sartre does not use these terms, he had been bent on reconciling existentialist-moral and Marxist-causal responsibility ever since he entered mass politics in the mid 40s. He voices this concern to respect individual dignity while coming to grips with economic factors in the inaugural editorial for *Les Temps modernes:*

> Contemporary consciousness seems torn by an antinomy. Those who hold above all for the dignity of the human person, his freedom, his inalienable rights, by that very fact lean toward "the spirit of analysis," which conceives of persons outside of their real conditions of existence, which confers on them an immutable, abstract nature that isolates them and blinds them to their solidarity. Those who have forcefully understood that man is rooted in the collectivity and who wish to affirm the importance of economic, technical, and historical factors, rush toward the spirit of synthesis that, blind to persons, has eyes only for groups. This antinomy is observable, for example, in the widespread belief that socialism is the polar opposite of individual freedom. (*Situations,* 2:24–25)

Although he soon gave up the search for a "third force" between communist East and capitalist West, and although the spirit of synthesis triumphed in the form of dialectical reason, the later Sartre can scarcely be said to "have eyes only for groups." The primacy of praxis and the mediating Third save him from the excesses of collectivist thought. Moreover, that basic idea of freedom, grounded in ontological freedom as transcendence and cutting through the basis/superstructure distinction, preserves an irreducibly existentialist factor in the most "determining" conditions that Sartre can conceive of. It guarantees that even Marxist-causal responsibility be sustained by an underlying existentialist-moral responsibility precisely as oppressive praxis undergirds exploitative process. Indeed, his development of a Marxist existentialism can be read as an attempt at synthesizing these two modes of responsibility.

The temporal and structural axes of collective responsibility. Sartre's sense of the scope of responsibility in the social sphere is captured with accustomed paradox in the claim that "one doesn't do what one wants and yet one is responsible for what one is: that's the fact" (*Situations,* 2:26–27). The limits of collective responsibility as Sartre discusses them seem to be those of collective identity and of practico-inert process. This responsibility ranges across the group's praxis and the passive activity of the serialized individual. But practico-inert "exigencies" reveal that it

139

extends over the generations as well. A new aspect of Sartrean collective responsibility thus comes to light if we consider what may be called its synchronic and diachronic dimensions.

Under the rubric "synchronic" we can gather the basic social ensembles—series, group, and institution—focusing not on their inner workings but on their outer reaches. When we prescind from the temporal expanse of responsibility, we discover what might be called its "dispositional" aspect or, in Sartrean terms, "hexis responsibility."

Taking each ensemble in turn, we may say that the group's responsibility extends as far as its identity and its power. We have seen that power is a social fact, a specific modality of the group: "we are a *force* to be reckoned with." I pointed out that interiorization of multiplicity is in effect interiorization of responsibility; it is responsibility as ubiquity. But this responsibility extends not only to what we do but to what we can do as well; it extends across the entire practical field constituted by group praxis. This aspect of "ubiquity," left undeveloped by Sartre, is quite in accord with his ascriptions of responsibility to agents for what they "could have done." Of course, this thrusts him in the midst of the controversy over omissions and so-called negative responsibility. He does not meet this question head-on. But it seems clear that, given his concepts of the primacy of praxis and of the mediating Third, whatever arguments hold for the negative responsibility of individuals, would apply to the group as Sartre understands it.[35] The matter is clearer in the case of the series.

With the series, of course, the practico-inert comes into play. Serial responsibility extends as far as class identity and interest. Each serial individual is dispositionally responsible for undertakings that foster his class interest. In this case, responsibility extends across the practico-inert field. It includes the "exigencies" of socioeconomic systems and is born by such hexis-ideas as racism. Does it extend to racist acts and colonialist violence, for example, of which one is totally unaware? of which one heard only after the fact? Sartre says "yes" on enough occasions to indicate that this is a major feature of synchronic responsibility.

Describing the provincial bourgeois who has opposed the National Workshops and favored the government's bloody quelling of the workers' riots in 1848, for example, Sartre claims that this person will discover only by the next day's news from Paris that he is a murderer (see CDR, 761). Appealing to the concepts of verbal milieu, interest, and the like, Sartre explains how such epithets as Saint-Marc Girardin's "the proletarians are our barbarians" (CDR, 753–54) and the objective economic demands to keep the workers in serial impotence conspired to implicate the provincial bourgeois in the massacre of workers in the capital. Recall a similar argument linking the metropolitan Frenchmen in the Algerian crisis.[36]

Because the responsibility is serial and the action "passive," this is perhaps more clearly a form of dispositional ("hexis") responsibility. Its paradigm is the famous "slippery fellow" (*le rat visqueux*) of Sartre's early polemics: "The slippery fellow has not betrayed. But the Party is sure that he would have been able to if the occasion had arisen. In brief, the word designates this—unfortunately very widespread—category of individual in our society: *the culprit who has done nothing for which to be reproached*" (CP, 9n; emphasis mine). In a sense he is infected with serial responsibility for what he *is,* not for what he does. But as dispositional, it is responsibility for what he not only can but would do if. . . . Doubtless, the mediation of practico-inert factors like milieu and interest assures that existentialist-moral responsibility will apply even here. One is responsible, e.g., for allowing such an atmosphere of distrust and hatred to exist. But the point is that such responsibility encompasses the practico-inert field established by such collective instruments as public opinion, vested interests, and the like.

Finally, in the case of the institution, the paradigms of which are the army and the state (see CDR, 604 and 635ff.), identity and responsibility, though parceled out hierarchically, extend to the meaning (*sens*) of all institutional acts, including the disposition to act, which the mere presence of the institution proclaims. Thus the conscript in the barracks near the native quarter of a colonial city is aware that his very presence both signifies and effects the repressive violence on which colonialism is based. Sartre implies that, although each soldier might actively protest such connotations, play with the native children, or even resign his commission, only dismantling the system itself will relieve him of serial responsibility for the evils it entails (a moral we have come to expect).

The diachronic dimension of collective responsibility is particularly relevant in our age of energy conservation and ecological concern. Let us pursue Sartre's understanding of it, again in terms of these social ensembles.

If the primacy of praxis is the root and source of Sartrean responsibility, the fact that praxis is totalizing forms the basis of its diachronic dimension. Each member by interiorizing multiplicity, by effectively saying "we," assumes responsibility in a totalizing act for what "we" are doing, shall do, and *have done*. As the existentialist individual is his project and his facticity, so the Sartrean group is its objective and its situation. Responsibility for the present is adequately conveyed by the *mot d'ordre* and that for the future by the pledge. But what of the past? What is this member's relation to group actions that occurred before he ever joined? Sartre offers two reasons for assuming that he would hold the member responsible for these as well. First in terms of group identity, if I interiorize this multiplicity, I assume its overall project and that includes its temporal stretch through past to future. This seems implied by identifying with a practical ensemble. The group that I call "us" did such and such in the past. Only by a deliberate repudiation of its past activities on the part of the present member does it seem possible to lessen this responsibility. Yet even in this case, such responsibility (answerability) is not entirely removed. It lingers as the facticity with which each member must constantly come to terms as long as he continues in the group.

Second, such responsibility seems to follow from the mediating role of the group and of the Third. Since the group is the bearer of social features like power and function, it can arguably carry a certain historical character as well, based on the praxes of prior members who are now interiorized as "the same" as I: "That is what we did in those days." Again, the oath as quasi-sworn inertia could serve as bearer of past praxes for which we assume responsibility in pride or shame much as the practico-inert bears historical sedimentations.

In sum, one's joining the group is a totalizing act. As such, it implies assumption of responsibility for the group praxis as a totalization of prior praxes.[37]

Although the practico-inert figures centrally in synchronic responsibility, it is crucial to the diachronic as well. We have just seen its role in the pledge. But it comes more fully into play in the series. Not only is the practico-inert "the judgment of things upon persons," it also carries the judgment of past generations on subsequent ones. In the next chapter I shall trace such a judgment across three generations. For the present it suffices to explain the general features of diachronic responsibility as mediated by the practico-inert.

In *The Family Idiot* Sartre notes once more the bourgeois penchant for the structural and the synchronic. It adopts what Marcuse has termed a "one-dimensional" view of social reality in order to escape the pangs of guilt: "For each [bourgeois], . . . historicity reveals itself as man's unhappiness [*malheure*] and his deep guilt [*culpabilité*]" (IF, 3:429).[38] This same analytic tendency is blind to class solidarity. In fact, Sartre clearly sees class solidarity and "diachronic totalization" as going together. Their most obvious union occurs in what we may call "class memory," a hybrid of practico-inert "inscriptions" of past oppression, betrayal, and massacre, and of the appropriation of this legacy of hatred-guilt by totalizing praxis (or passive activity). Members of opposing classes, as they face each other across the barricade or the bargaining table, do so having internalized this heritage which defines them and the Other.

It is diachronic responsibility and class memory that give rise to *l'homme-événement,* the product of the massacres of June 1848: "the man of 1850 is no longer simply boss or simply worker; after June 1848, he is, *qua* boss, in solidarity with the massacrers and, *qua* worker, in solidarity with the massacred." A certain irreversible event has historicized each person, but this historical dimension eludes the static categories of analytic reason. "It is proper to dialectical reason," Sartre argues, "to understand *l'homme-événement* insofar as he both suffers history and produces it in one and the same movement" (IF, 3:342). These events are "inscribed" in the practico-inert class-being of both sides and constitute part of the fundamental situation out of which each defines itself.

These, then, are the structural (synchronic) and the temporal (diachronic) axes along which collective responsibility can be charted. Aware of the modes of such responsibility, the Marxist-causal and the existentialist-moral, we are finally ready to complete our reconstruction of Sartre's theory as exhibited in his basic social wholes.

The Inner Workings of the Social Ensemble from the Viewpoint of Collective Responsibility

Readers familiar with Heidegger's *Being and Time* will recall how the second half of that volume is a reprise of the first half from the viewpoint of temporality. That *Wiederholung,* far from trapping one in dull monotony, offers fresh and powerful insights into the previous analyses which, in turn, serve to illumine the newer conclusions. On a far less monumental scale, let us attempt a kind of reprise here as well. We are now familiar with the inner life of the Sartrean social ensembles from an ontological perspective. I shall conclude my reconstructive analysis of his theory by rereading these social wholes—series, group, and institution—under the aspect of responsibility. Respecting the decisiveness of praxis and practico-inert mediation, we again face two subspecies of collective responsibility, serial and group.

Serial responsibility: the *collectif*

As "the inert gathering with its structure of seriality is the basic type of sociality" (CDR, 348), serial responsibility seems to be the basic form of social responsibility. Due to its grounding in practico-inert mediation, its features will include impotence and otherness. The unity of the social whole will be external—the "unity of flight" from responsibility. But this

143

unity-in-otherness entails its own type of responsibility nonetheless. Serial responsibility within the collective is best understood insofar as it is mediated by a hexis-idea or by some properly collective object.

The hexis-idea of racism. We know that Sartre believes that colonialism as the common interest of the settlers both contributes to and builds upon this idea. I have remarked the "verbal milieu" in which this idea is sustained, those racist slurs that infect the speech of an entire society. What is transmitted by "contagion" is an atmosphere that welcomes racist acts. In Sartrean terms, a kind of verbal violence is symbolized and, worse, perpetrated by such talk. But responsibility is incurred by failure to combat an atmosphere which makes racist violence the acceptable form of action. The responsibility of all collective individuals is *real though serial* for the acts of injustice that arise "spontaneously" in such a milieu. We have seen him employ similar arguments regarding the implicit racism of the capitalist as well. In all such instances it is the milieu of otherness that Sartre underscores as the vehicle for a particular form of responsibility-in-otherness that I have called *serial.*

Here belong those practico-inert exigencies to act "like the others." In Sartre's scenario of the besieged plantation owner: "I try to realize the Other—that is to say, to make myself more deaf, ruthless, and negative to the claims of the native, than my plantation or my own interest actually requires—so that my attempt becomes, for some other who might be tempted to make a concession to the natives, the real presence of the Other, as a magical force of constraint." This is the kind of passive activity that makes us serially responsible. There is nothing unusual about all this. It is a typical case of serial responsibility wherein each is answerable for the injustices perpetrated by the "others, elsewhere."

The machine as collective object. We know that the collective object for Sartre is an index of separation and the sign of our alienation. The unity it effects is serial; so too is the responsibility it engenders. Take the example of the industrial proletariat.

The economic system of a society is a collective (see CDR, 306). The capitalist system of wage-labor and private property presumes a monetary equivalent of workers in the "labor market." This equivalence and interchangeability—what we know to be the standard marks of Sartrean alienation—are both symbolized and realized by the machine.[39] It mediates workers in otherness and they see in it capitalism as "Machine-Destiny" (CDR, 311). This is Sartre's explanation of why the Lyonais silk weavers during their revolt of 1830 destroyed the weaving machines. They were seeking liberation from this "destiny." But their zeal was misguided; new

144

models would replace both the damaged ones and eventually the weavers themselves. What should be dismantled, Sartre argues, following Marx, is the capitalist system itself. Its practico-inert mediation renders machine-destiny the inevitable unifier of the workers in serial impotence. This is his reading of Marx's phrase that we are the products of our own product: whether worker, who must adjust his life rhythm to that of the machine, or owner, who must keep a constant eye on the technical advances of the competition, each is responding to the exigencies of the machine. It becomes clear that "the powerlessness *of everyone* is the objective form of the inflexibility of the object" (CDR, 304).

Viewed in terms of responsibility, the series is the locus of those numerous cases where one blames "the system" for unpleasant situations. As we noted in another context, serial responsibility characterizes individuals as both victims and perpetrators of the harm in question. Because the colonialist and the capitalist systems are praxis-processes, they have a necessity of their own which, once set in motion, defies the power of the individual to control. But because it is *praxis*-process, the responsibility is existentialist-moral and hope of liberation from serial impotence ever remains. Again, to the extent that we do not act against it (chiefly by forming liberating groups), we are serially responsible for the meanness of the system.

We can now interpret Sartre's brilliant descriptions of collectives such as public opinion, the newspaper readership, the radio audience, free market, and the like as so many portraits of serial responsibility. Not only are these relations infected with impotence and otherness, they render us "passive" accomplices in whatever evils the respective collective inflicts-endures.

In terms of the modes and axes of responsibility distinguished earlier, serial responsibility mediated by the collective object or the hexis-idea in its concrete, i.e., fully determined, reality entails both modes and can be plotted along either the synchronic or diachronic axis. Since such has been done earlier in this chapter, it suffices to call attention to the fact that from the viewpoint of collective responsibility, the concrete reality is the intersection of each mode and both axes. Serial responsibility extends synchronically to the outermost reaches of class identity and interest, diachronically from past praxes "sedimented" in present processes to future projects (of serial flight), causally to the quasi-automatic workings of the "system," and morally to the serial praxis that sustains and appropriates such a situation by the passive activity that it endures in bad faith.

Throughout his discussion of responsibility, like an underlying rhythm that urges the argument along and gives it a unity that its single parts would otherwise lack, runs Sartre's moral imperative formulated in *Existentialism is a Humanism:* "freedom for all." It warrants his implicit use of arguments from negative responsibility, i.e., the claim that we are responsible for our omissions, because it assumes that each is called to maximize freedom under pain of practical inconsistency. Thus he combines this principle with tacit use of serial responsibility when he claims that the committed writer "is accomplice of the oppressor unless he is the natural ally of the oppressed. And this not only because he's a writer but because he's a man" (*Situations,* 2:51). The writer, he continues, "must see to it that no one can ignore the world *or call himself innocent of it*" (*Situations,* 2:74; emphasis mine). For this reason, the "literature of praxis" must teach the bourgeoisie and others "that they are at once victim and responsible for everything, both oppressors and oppressed . . . , and that one can never separate out what a person undergoes, what he accepts, and what he wishes" (*Situations,* 2:312). His, in effect, is a classic case of serial responsibility.

Group responsibility

I have suggested that the "interiorization of multiplicity" which constitutes both the group and the group member (common individual) be read as interiorization of responsibility as well: all for one and one for all. It follows that *we* assume responsibility for whatever the group does, has done, or will do, for, as I argued apropos diachronic responsibility, the group *is* what it does, has done, and aims to do. This is the ethical significance of the notions of sameness and ubiquity; we are accountable for every aspect of common praxis. When Sartre describes group praxis ("the subject is plural . . . and the action is singular" [CDR, 506]), he is indicating that the responsibility is mine *because* it is ours; it is mine qua group member, qua common individual, qua mediating Third. My continued association with the group and my contribution to its project *is* my active appropriation of this collective undertaking and vice versa. The group, ontologically, simply is this revolving set of practical relations—relations, we may now say, of responsibility.

Given the continued correlation between freedom and responsibility in Sartre's thought, we can conclude that the advent of the group as "the sudden resurrection of freedom" (CDR, 401) is likewise the sudden resurrection of responsibility. By means of the mediating Third "an interiority creates itself as a new type of milieu (a milieu of freedom)" (CDR, 408). For this same reason it is likewise a milieu of responsibility. As it reaches its climax in the group-in-fusion, "responsibility" comes to mean "answerability *to* everyone *for* everyone *as* the same." The inner space that the group opens to its members is thus the space of freedom-responsibility where alienating objectification and numerical equivalence are held at bay; in effect, the very model of Sartrean freedom-responsibility.

One of the criticisms leveled against collective responsibility is that if everyone is responsible no one is responsible. But if we continue to accept parity of argument between freedom and responsibility, this is not true of the group. Speaking of the sovereignty proper to praxis alone but which emerges in the group, Sartre writes: "Sovereignty is limited by its very reciprocity; everyone is sovereign: but it should not be inferred that no one is," for, in effect, each group member is "quasi-sovereign" (CDR, 579). So, too, each member can be considered co-responsible for the common praxis. To say that "we" did x, is not to deny that I did it, for example, but is merely to specify the effect and the manner of my doing.[40]

As the group forms into the pledged ensemble and divides into organized functions and tasks, responsibility is shared accordingly. We have observed how the pledge can be read as a commitment to appropriate future as well as past actions of the group. "Terror" is the negative violence that guarantees this appropriation. Similarly, as the rights and duties, merely implicit at first, become articulated in the organized group, responsibility entails acceptance of "responsibilities"—a nuance unrequired at the more fluid stage of the fusing group.

Regarding the modes and axes of collective responsibility, one of the leading features of group responsibility and, doubtless, the reason why Sartre's favors it is that here alone the existentialist-moral sense of responsibility triumphs. The Marxist-causal uses of "responsibility" would accordingly be subordinated, though not eliminated, precisely as would be the practico-inert itself. Likewise, diachronic responsibility is accepted in order to be overcome (the past) or realized (the objective). In the present stage of world history, the concrete is the confluence of serial and group responsibility. I reserve thoughts about Sartre's vision of the total end of practico-inert mediation for the concluding chapter.

Serial Responsibility: The Institution

As the group is a kind of raft in a sea of seriality, so mediated reciprocity—true freedom and total responsibility for Sartre—easily slips into the nonreciprocity of command-obedience and institutional "sovereignty." Voicing his social ideal as it surfaced in his later works, Sartre proclaims: "The true relation among men is reciprocity, which excludes commands properly speaking" (IF, 3:48).[41] But we know that the essence of the institution is authority understood precisely as the nonreciprocal relation of command-obedience. How does this affect responsibility?

Obviously, whatever responsibility obtains among institutionalized individuals will be serial. With the advent of the institution, Sartre notes, "everyone construes himself, through the Other and through all, as an inorganic tool by means of which an action is realized" (CDR, 599). This is the responsibility of the Eichmanns who merely "obeyed orders" or simply "did their duty." With keen metaphorical eye Sartre calls this process of construal the "mineralization of man" (CDR, 658). Of course, such passive activity does not escape responsibility, it merely exchanges one form for another. In the institution as in the collective, the individual is at once victim and accomplice of serial activities. Although Sartre sometimes talks as if responsibility is diminished at the lower rungs of the institutional ladder, he is adamant in insisting that all confer a pseudo "legitimacy" on the institution by their passive activity of obedience.

Institutionalized responsibility is carried to the extreme in the bureaucracy. As we saw in chapter 6, Sartre's characterization of bureaucratic relations is one of virtual alienation; they are shot through with serial otherness. The responsibility of the functionary is instrumental; it is that of the human tool:

> The model for the institutional group is *the forged tool*. And everyone is implicated as such in institutionality. But on the other hand this is also because they are its victims *even before they are born*. The previous generation already defines their institutional future, as their external, mechanical destiny . . . even before they are born. "Obligations"—military, civic, professional, etc.—constitute in advance an untranscendability deep inside everyone who is born into the group. . . . Being born into the group is a pledge . . . to realize the institution." (CDR, 606)

Here is a clear instance of diachronic responsibility within the institution. No one escapes responsibility for the effects of that gigantic instrument that each has allowed himself to become. The responsibility is serial, but the complicity is real.

Responsibility within this milieu of other-direction is exemplified by what Sartre describes as the "induced pogrom" of anti-Semitic governments: "Every act of violence was irreversible, not only because it destroyed human lives, but because it made everyone *an other-directed criminal,* adopting the leaders' crimes in so far as he had committed them *elsewhere* and as other in an other" (CDR, 653; emphasis mine). Unlike the dispositional responsibility of the provincial bourgeois, though such is not excluded here, institutional responsibility involves manipulation of serial impotence by the "authorities." As Sartre explains it: "Acceptance of the sovereign's acts of violence, as a hexis in the milieu of other-direction, may always, through the transcendent action of the directing group, be converted into a pogrom as the passive activity of a directed seriality" (CDR, 653). In technical language to which we should now be accustomed, Sartre is referring to the responsibility of those who have allowed themselves to fall into such a state of manipulability that "spontaneous" outbursts of fire-bombing, looting, and so forth can be instigated by action groups almost at will. But Sartre's point is that such "spontaneous" and "disconnected" eruptions merely "make everyone into *the other who is responsible* for the maximum violence committed *by an other*." His conclusion is a concise summary of this discussion of serial responsibility:

> At the level at which "collective responsibility" is serial responsibility, its acceptance or rejection by a given other are simply two contradictory expressions (in discourse) of one and the same fact. And this serial responsibility—as the projection of a precise, totalizing policy in the milieu of alterity—increases the power of the sovereign group to precisely the extent that it deepens everyone's impotence while sustaining the misleading scheme of the totalizing ceremony." (CDR, 654)

Despite the trappings of political freedom, such as elections and national plebiscites ("totalizing ceremonies"), Sartre is saying, the serialized individual is responsible for the violence that his leaders choose to exercise against the Other, whether at home or abroad. Tacit appeal to serial responsibility underlies Sartre's castigation of the Americans in Viet Nam and the French in Algeria.

And so this reconstruction of Sartrean theory of collective responsibility is complete. Complex and far-reaching, formulated in concepts that are technical but precise, yet stated in language that rocks between the subtly insightful and the wildly exaggerated, this theory is typically Sartrean in spirit, exhibiting an absolute commitment to the cause of human freedom, but fully in accord with his existential Marxism. (The consistency of that project itself will be assessed in Part III.) It should serve the cause of clarity as well as the aims of subsequent critical evaluation if I were to summarize Sartre's rich and variegated theory with a scheme. And so I offer the scheme shown in Figure 1.

Again, because the context is dialectical, the distinctions indicated in the figure are abstract. Concrete reality is neither the purely active group nor the entirely passive series but a mixture of both at the intersection of each of these lines of analysis. Responsibility, in other words, is a multifaceted reality for Sartre as is the human praxis that grounds it. Accordingly, one and the same "organic praxis," as he puts it, will support

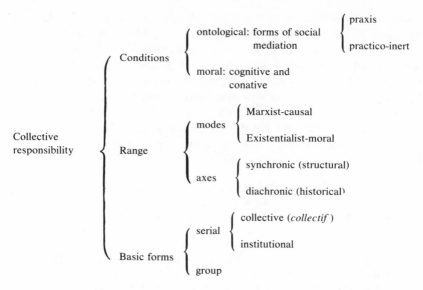

Figure 1. Sartre's Theory of Collective Responsibility

several forms of responsibility under as many descriptions. We know that the same social reality, for example, can be described either as exploitative process or as oppressive praxis. But I have been emphasizing that it is the unequivocal *primacy of individual praxis* throughout these combinations and permutations that marks both Sartre's unyielding humanist commitment and his specifically existentialist contribution to the theory.

eight

Responsibility and the
Industrial Capitalist

The French proletariat is a historical reality whose singularity was made manifest in recent years by a certain attitude; I do not go looking for the key to this attitude in the universal movement of societies, but in the movement of French society; that is to say, in the history of France.

The Communists and Peace

The contour of argument in Part II, recall, extends from practice to theory and back. We have witnessed Sartre's frequent and seemingly hyperbolic ascriptions of collective responsibility in the polemical literature of the postwar years (chapter 4). On the assumption that these ascriptions stem from a full-blown social ontology and ethic *in fieri*, I laid bare the foundations and reconstructed the framework of Sartre's systematic social philosophy with an eye toward the theory of collective responsibility (chapters 5–7). Let us return to practice once more as I fill in the theoretical framework by applying it to a nineteenth-century French industrial capitalist family. Such a "thought experiment" should reveal the interpretive power as well as some of the limitations of Sartre's theory. As points of contrast, one might keep in mind how the same material would be treated by the extremes of Marxist political economy, on the one hand, and of "analytical" sociological surveys, on the other. I shall proceed in two stages, beginning with a descriptive analysis of the bourgeoisie as a class, always in terms of class responsibility, and concluding with a portrait of three generations of a French industrial family.

The Bourgeoisie

We now possess the means for understanding class identity and responsibility, namely, the practico-inert in general and, specifically, objective spirit, passive activity, milieu, exigency, ideology, interest, and the rest. Applied to that admitted abstraction, the bourgeoisie, these concepts will provide the intelligible context for a phenomenological description of three generations of French industrialists. Sartre distinguishes the bourgeoisie

151

by four marks: analytic spirit, comprehension of specific class interest, refusal of the proletariat, and a particular value system, "humanism."

The Analytic Spirit

"At a certain level of abstraction," Sartre writes in the *Critique,* "class conflict expresses itself as a conflict of rationalities" (CDR, 802). What is at stake is the very recognition of class existence and class struggle. In the inaugural issue of *Les Temps modernes,* Sartre explains: "One makes oneself bourgeois by once and for all choosing a certain analytic vision of the world which one tries to impose on all men and which excludes the perception of collective realities" (*Situations,* 2:19). This does not mean that Sartre opposes positive science as some reactionary plot. It does mean that he recognizes the latter's limitations, especially its obliviousness to the class struggle. He regards its value-free status as fraudulent, for it entails an implicit commitment to the socioeconomic status quo and its atomism blinds it to diachronic responsibility for the injustices of previous generations.

But, of course, in Sartre's world one is not simply "born" bourgeois; one chooses to be so. And Sartre considers the "choice" of analytic reason that of "an instrument of distraction." In effect, analytic reason, like every human product, must be "totalized" in the historical struggle for the emancipation of humankind in accord with Sartre's moral imperative and universal freedom conditional.[1] To fail to undertake such totalizing praxis is morally reprehensible because of our "vague comprehension" of the meaning of such "ignorance"; in other words, this is the first of several ways in which the bourgeoisie is said to be in *collective bad faith.*[2]

At the outset I noted Sartre's "existentialist" intent to "humanize" every dimension of the real. The very choice of reason—analytic as opposed to dialectical—is a human act for which responsibility must be assumed. The overridingness of the moral dimension demands that we submit even "value-free" scientific inquiry to the criterion of social emancipation. In this, Sartrean existentialism affirms the Marxist unity of theory and practice.

Comprehension of Class Interest

We have witnessed Sartre expand the notion of comprehension to include not only the self-awareness of praxis and the *Verstehen* of interpretive sociology, but also that "dawning of reflection," as yet unverbalized, which entails "an obscure grasp of the *sens* of a process beyond its [conceptual] significations" (IF, 2:1544). The discussion of objective class spirit as the "milieu for the circulation of meanings," indicated the way in which praxes and processes are understood from the perspective of class interest.

Such comprehension is operative in the examples treated earlier where one must "set an example," must judge in terms of the effect on class interest "if everybody" did what one is contemplating, and the like. In this respect the boss resembles the colonialist in dealing with his workers. The constraint felt by the boss under fire from his workers is a combination of practical awareness and decision, an interiorized prohibition against giving in. Its source of unification is private property as class interest—the collective object in which each has his unity-as-other (*unité-autre*) outside himself.

Interest becomes exigency in the realm of practical comprehension. Speaking of the bourgeoisie becoming aware of itself as a class, Sartre observes: "The class is just Other-Being and . . . the praxis of every Other, through the limitations it assumes and claims to adopt, displays it and realizes it for him as the *signification-exigency* of whatever he undertakes and as a *norm* by which to judge what every Other does. Moreover, class as the limitation and norm of every praxis, itself becomes the solidified intelligibility of every economic and social action, in the form of total praxis." From this he concludes that "every capitalist has his individual, practical *comprehension of every operation* (his own and those of the Other) on the basis of oppression as historicity (past-future) and of exploitation as a process" (CDR, 770; emphasis mine). Again, this grounds Sartre's accusation of moral responsibility: "They all knew what was going on."

Thus we can speak of genuine class (passive) activity carried out by each bourgeois in practical awareness of the demands and constraints imposed by class interest.

Reverting to his existentialist social model—when it is a question of class consciousness—Sartre insists that it is the *eyes* of the proletariat that first seal the bourgeoisie with the unity of class action. The employer sees himself through his workers as an object of hatred or distrust, not as a particular person but as a common individual. The history of class conflict intervenes to consolidate bourgeois identity in the workers' eyes. "Thus every *other* bourgeois," Sartre concludes, "through his object-being for the other class [sees] himself as co-responsible member of a concrete group which [is] none other than his class" (CDR, 758). Comprehension, in other words, like the gaze (*le regard*), includes awareness of how one is comprehended by the Other.

We have seen that class interest, for the bourgeoisie, is private property in the technical, Marxist sense.[3] But from the viewpoint of the other class, for whom private property is "destiny" in the Sartrean sense, Sartre argues that the meaning of bourgeois class activity is the *refusal* of the proletariat. By stressing refusal of the worker rather than defense of property, Sartre once more is "existentializing" an otherwise objectivist (Marxist-causal) analysis of interclass relations. Let us consider this specifically Sartrean trait.

Refusal of the Proletariat

Sartre revives his existentialist social ontology of looking/looked-at, translated into a politics of mutual refusal, once his attention turns to power relationships within society. We know that he interprets the workers' "implicit, intuitive nonverbal knowledge" of their collective situation as "the seed of a politics of refusal."[4] But their action is a reaction to that original refusal by the bourgeoisie that established the proletariat as such. Like everything else in Sartre's ontology, this refusal is a kind of chosen necessity.

Refusal is a necessity inscribed in the capitalist system. "The hypothesis of a progressive bourgeoisie is in itself absurd, at least as far as the 19th century is concerned," Sartre observes. "[Twentieth-century] neo-paternalism presupposes a certain level of industrial development; it was not conceivable in the nineteenth century and, in the scarcity which was so brutally revealed during crises (poverty in 1845–48, poverty and war in 1870–71), the bourgeoisie produced itself as having either to kill or to disappear" (CDR, 797). This Marxist-causal analysis again reveals the meanness in the system.

But refusal is *chosen* necessity, as we might expect. Sartre sees the first phase of industrialization in England as "a praxis of systematic oppression." He elaborates: "It is perfectly erroneous to interpret English cruelty as indifference, blindness or contempt: it was in fact quite deliberate." Reiterating in this context a now standard theme, he insists: "From its origins and installation, the process of exploitation is a practice of alienated and serialized oppression" (CDR, 743).[5]

The chief strategy in this politics of refusal from the bourgeois viewpoint is to keep the proletariat in a state of serial impotence. This is Sartre's plausible interpretation of management's traditional opposition to workers' associations. The model of passive activity, other-conditioning, and serial manipulation is the free work-contract in which labor is given no choice but to sign or starve.[6]

In periods of economic expansion, this politics is latent, buried in the nonverbal "comprehension" of both classes. But it becomes overt in moments of social strife, revealing to each side the true nature of their relationship. This is a common thesis in Sartre's thought, repeated in the

Critique and in *The Family Idiot,* but expressed most forcefully in *The Communists and Peace:*

> History advances in disguise: when it takes off its mask, it marks the actors and the witnesses for all time. We have never recovered from the two "moments of truth" which France experienced in the nineteenth century, and our bourgeoisie is playing a losing game today because it saw its own true face in 1848 and in 1871. . . . Suddenly, the bourgeois was defining himself by his refusals: in arrogating the right to prescribe limits to his species [bourgeois humanism], he had set his own limits; if the excluded were to make themselves the measure of man, the bourgeois would perceive his humanity in others as an enemy force. (CP, 148–49)

This is a gloss on the epigraph for this chapter; the specificity of social relations, beyond their economic conditioning, derives from the contingencies of a society's history. Exhibiting his diachronic understanding of "responsibility," Sartre believes that the massacres of 1848 and 1871 have indelibly colored relations between the French proletariat and bourgeoisie as long as these classes continue to exist. "Each proletariat [and, by parity of reasoning, each national bourgeoisie] derives its constituted violence (what might be called its violence-character) not only from the real conditions of production and from the structures proper to the worker, but also from its own history" (CDR, 797n). In assuming responsibility for these events—by assuming his class-being—the individual bourgeois, *l'homme-événement,* becomes *l'homme-refus* as well.

The strategy of maintaining the proletariat in serial impotence is carried out by a policy of socioeconomic Malthusianism. This consists in a deliberate decision to preserve inefficient, family firms, often located away from growing industrial centers, as a way of keeping the number of workers low and of discouraging their concentration in potential centers of power. Sartre sees this as a feature that distinguishes French industrial capitalism from its Anglo-American counterpart in the nineteenth century.[7] Rather than import new machines from abroad, which would increase productivity—to the benefit of the workers but at the price of a dangerously large urban proletariat—nineteenth-century French capitalists, Sartre claims, preferred to purchase obsolete or secondhand equipment. He terms this "voluntary obsolescence" technologically and "induced scarcity" from the economic viewpoint. He sees it as the application of a sustained policy of refusal of the proletariat, but one with a peculiarly Gallic twist.

In terms reminiscent of his pages on sadomasochism written fifteen years earlier, he summarizes:

> Capitalists in this period assumed that it was necessary for others to be poor; and to assume the poverty of others is to acquiesce in producing it, and thus to transcend the assumed necessity by a free adoption of its laws and its themes; it is to justify this free transformation of necessity into oppression in terms of a class Manichaeism which designates the oppressed as anti-humans who *deserve their oppression,* and thus to condemn them to it. Lastly, it is to make this necessity-freedom even more intolerable for the oppressed, in that it presents itself as a *condemnation* of the exploited (a free human sentence) *by things* (the "inexorable" laws of liberal economics). (CDR, 798)

This is the irreconcilable interest/destiny dichotomy which Sartre, with Marx, believes will keep the bourgeoisie and the proletariat ever on collision course. It is a necessity-freedom made concrete by Malthusian practices and "justified" both by appeal to "iron laws" of economics and to a "class Manichaeism" to which we now turn.

Bourgeois Humanism

In a sense, this value-image of man as he ought to be has haunted Sartre's social theory from the start. We have encountered it in *Anti-Semite and Jew* and in the other bridge essays, especially *Existentialism Is a Humanism* and *The Communists and Peace.* It is obviously of greater interest to the newly politicized Sartre than are the economic relations that Marx took as definitive of the bourgeoisie. This anti-humanism, as it might best be termed, is connected with the politics of refusal by means of what he calls class racism: "One important fact of nineteenth-century history is that the workers experienced the absolute intransigence of the employers. They wished (initially) *to reach a mutual understanding as men;* and they gradually realized that this was impossible, *because to the employers, they were not men*" (CDR, 798). This is the key to the irrationality in class relations during the second and third quarters of the last century. One class assumes it is dealing with another species; hence the swing from condescending paternalism in some cases to harsh accusations of ingratitude in others, as the better classes deal with their inferiors.

The components of this antihumanism are basically four. The first element is the concept of a *timeless human nature* as expressed in the "Declaration of the Rights of Man and of the Citizen." Sartre sees this declaration, defined to support the bourgeois claim to equality with the

156

nobility, as a vehicle to exclude the proletarian who has little property to protect and who values collective effort over individual achievement.

Accompanying this is a *competitive spirit* inculcated by bourgeois education. Sartre describes the young Flaubert's schooling in this fashion: "Since man—that is to say, the bourgeois—is defined under Louis-Philippe as a competitor, the 'humanities' must be structured competitively" (IF, 2:1121). Refusal enters in when the "natural elite" self-selects, leaving the others, primarily workers and, later, guest-workers, in a somewhat less than human (less than bourgeois) state.

The third component is *bourgeois freedom,* which is not merely the Hobbesian "freedom from," so often associated with it, but a far more sinister concept, in Sartre's interpretation: "A close look reveals that our liberties were conceived by the bourgeoisie for the bourgeoisie, and the worker could never enjoy them short of becoming a bourgeois himself. Our liberties make sense only in a regime of private property and they are precautions which the owner of goods takes against the arbitrary action of the group" (CP, 122).[8] Having linked freedom to social atomism and private property, Sartre underscores the dimension of refusal in bourgeois freedom by joining it to misanthropy. Referring to the freedom of the employer to dismiss half of his staff, of the general to decide a murderous offensive, and of the judge to choose leniency or severity, Sartre concludes: "*True* bourgeois freedom, positive freedom, is a power of man over man" (CP, 122; emphasis his). By implication, socialist freedom would entail no such power.

The final component of bourgeois antihumanism is more a hexis than a praxis, the nineteenth-century practice of "respectability" (*la distinction*). Sartre defines "hexis" as "the ensemble of daily practices which are born from its [the class's] situation and from its enterprise and which give it, before every verbal explication, a certain image of itself, which is lived rather than represented." This bourgeois hexis from 1850 on, Sartre believes, "can be summarized in one word: *respectability*" (IF, 3:245). The bourgeois of the period can scarcely distinguish himself by nature from the workers, since he had used "equality" to cut the nobles down to size. "He must thus set himself apart by dissembling his body, by suppressing its needs, by denying Nature in his own person." Sartre concludes this arresting interpretation of the phenomenon: "In short, the class of exploiters refuses to share materiality with the exploited: respectability creates vulgarity, as the law, according to Paul, creates sin" (IF, 2:1450). I shall trace the vagaries of this hexis in my portrait of a bourgeois family.

Assessing the effect of bourgeois humanism over the last century, Sartre remarks: "As a concept [it] crumbles and disappears; as a practical inertia, it is a passive activity of exclusion and rejection." It is a "serial ideology," a redundancy for Sartre, and, as such, is "solidified ideological violence" (CDR, 752–53).

Exhibiting his own spirit of synthesis as well as a sense of cultural determinism, whose consistency he never seems to have weighed, Sartre observes: "Society makes the decision before our birth: it defines in advance our capacities and our obligations; in short, it places us. It *ties* us to others: in sum, the most insignificant of our gestures and the most unobtrusive trait of our characters are in fact synthetic acts which, in particular circumstances, effect the unity of the bourgeois class: each of our behavior patterns manifests our belonging to such and such a family or professional group; each contributes to integrating us in it further" (CP, 122). These multidirectional ties are likewise the vehicles of responsibility. How they carry this burden *in concreto,* Sartre's portrait of a typical upper-bourgeois family will show us.

A Capitalist Triptych

> The men had built Sainte-Cecile-de-la-Mer. In 1882, they had founded the Federation of Shipowners and Merchants of Bouville "to group in one powerful entity all men of good will, to cooperate in national recovery and to hold in check the parties of disorder. . . ." . . . Stopping at no sacrifice to assist the improvement of the best elements in the working class, they created, on their own initiative, various centers for technical and professional study which prospered under their lofty protection. They broke the famous shipping strike of 1898 and gave their sons to their country in 1914.
>
> —Roquentin viewing portraits of the Bouville elite.[9]

On three different occasions Sartre undertook a specific "type analysis" of three generations of a French capitalist family in the mid and late nineteenth century.[10] As we have come to expect, his aim each time is to ascribe existentialist-moral responsibility to the typed individuals qua bourgeois by unmasking oppressive praxis and collective bad faith beneath the institutions, mores, and established practices of the capitalist system in its accumulative, consolidating, and defensive phases. Although pockets of group responsibility are admitted—so-called pressure groups formed to whip the bourgeoisie into line—the collective responsibility portrayed here is primarily serial: the capitalist as such is both victim and executor of an exploitative system.

I am aware that Sartre sees the specificity of the French proletariat and bourgeoisie in the history of France itself. Marxist economism fails to account for this, just as a comprehension of the human individual eludes it, and for the same reason: in its rage for the "scientific," such Marxism collapses individual praxis into impersonal process or statistical generalization. By calling us back to the human agent, existentialism not only preserves a significant role for biography but likewise restores to us our history as *human*.

The First Generation

The family likenesses which we are about to examine exhibit a growing awareness on their subjects' part of who they are; that is, of class consciousness and of the radical refusal of the workers that their class-being requires. We shall observe this awareness solidify and temporalize by certain historic events which, we have seen, serve to modify subsequent interclass relations in an irreversible way. The chief such event for this first generation of capitalists is the revolt of 1848.[11]

Sartre sees the closing of the National Workshops, which triggered the riots, as the result of general bourgeois prejudice and pressure. The experiment in socialization could not succeed, it was held, because "the proletariat is lazy; it has no sense of responsibility." The propertied class brought its weight to bear on the National Assembly to halt the experiment and, once the workers were in the streets, it used "the forces of order" to cut them down. These actions of the assembly and the military were read by the proletariat for what they were: class actions. Accordingly, their hatred of the bourgeoisie made of each capitalist the common individual in the workers' eyes—the bearer of the opprobrium for the action of his class. In typically Sartrean fashion, this common responsibility conferred by the hatred of the workers is interiorized by the individual capitalist who accepts this judgment of the radically other as "common, transcended responsibility (as past, preserved inert determination) . . . in a historic praxis of repression" (CDR, 758).

The uprising of the Parisian proletariat occasioned a panic, propagated in seriality, on the part of the national bourgeoisie. The provincial capitalist was (figuratively) in flight. The national guards had been mobilized and were converging on the capital. In this context of serial alterity, those guards who did not go to Paris were elsewhere, fighting as Others. This serial activity "produced practices of violence in everyone, normally verbal ones. The guards who stayed home produced here, as Others, the (im)moral equivalent of what their confreres and counterparts, as Others, effected in the capital: "a clash followed by a massacre" (CDR, 760). Sartre employs the concept of unity in alterity as the basis for this collective passive activity.

We can expect Sartre to link this serial activity with a genuine oppressive praxis to which existential-moral responsibility can be attached. The provincial capitalist, he argues, is tied to oppressive praxis in a threefold way. The government troops are defending the general interest of capitalism, private property and the system of rights and duties which supports it. To the extent that their action defines the capitalist by a passive system of the type "right/duty," it confers on him, says Sartre, the status of "common individual" (but, again, not in the proper sense as in the group, for seriality is really strengthened and not dissolved by the massacre).

The panicky circulation of the Other makes *him* one of the murderers:

> Not that he approved of the massacres or even knew about them: the news from Paris may not have reached him—but because *he carried them out.* He did not go to Paris, but this omission was accidental (a matter of distance, difficulties of communication, personal reasons); but he was there as Other: here, he was afraid; *there,* in the person of some other, he was proud in his bourgeois courage. This identity in alterity, which was described above, nevertheless continues through events of which he is still unaware: tomorrow he will learn that he has killed a man. (CDR, 761)

What Sartre is describing here is that variety of serial responsibility which I have called dispositional. When set in the context of unity in alterity (both in the eyes of the other class and in those of each bourgeois himself) it makes of each one that other in the fleeting series of "others" who have acted elsewhere and in another. Recall Sartre's reference in this context to "that passive mark which [the serial agent] receives in his Being-Other" as "precisely what one had tried in vain to define by the name of collective responsibility" (CDR, 761). The "passive mark" he speaks of is that identity in otherness which is a central feature of his general theory of class-being. If its immediate source is in the gaze of the other class and its interiorization by the class members themselves, its ultimate origin is found in that unity of interest, private property, which forms the practico-inert basis of class-being itself.

It must be admitted that Sartre is vague as to whether this kind of serial activity is to be considered oppressive praxis in itself or whether it is linked with oppressive praxis (he promises the latter but delivers what looks suspiciously like the former). In any event, the result is the same, the justification for ascriptions of responsibility in the existentialist-moral sense.[12]

The final link of the first generation capitalist with oppressive praxis consists in his relation to those pressure and action groups which manipulate him as a serial being. "He *executes their long-term policy* by the act of panic which he performs over there as Other and by the organized oppression which he recommends here in his factory" (CDR, 761). This policy, according to Sartre, rigorously defines the status of the bourgeoisie. The individual capitalist receives that status to the degree that, insofar as Other, he is its means or passive agent. This is an instance of other-conditioned responsibility. For the pressure groups condition class seriality and this conditioning becomes the very meaning of the repression exercised in Paris. Each capitalist's action in the panic following news of the uprising is passive mediation between the oppressive action in Paris (an action which as conditioned seriality is both common and other) and its effects.

Above all, the pressure groups[13] intervene to prevent compromise of any sort (a function analogous to that of the party in Leninism). In effect, they make the position of the bourgeoisie radically negative. "In short, the groups determined the intransigence of the French bourgeoisie: they claimed that capitalist economics required that the proletariat should be left entirely at the mercy of economic laws and that no attempts to attenuate their harshness should even be considered" (CDR, 765). As we have seen, Sartre regards these and other groups as the true movers of history. In the present case, they convert the bourgeoisie from the simple practico-inert process of exploitation to a common and systematic praxis of oppression via economic, social, and political control of the executive apparatus of the Assembly, by provocation of the exploited class, and by manipulation of serial panic within the bourgeoisie itself.

Whether the provincial capitalist is aware of this manipulation (this other-conditioning) or not is irrelevant.

> In any case, in so far as he becomes the instrument of the group's praxis, that is to say, in so far as he *in fact* fought the workers demanding bread in Paris, or condemned them in what he has said, thus making himself one of the *murderers;* to the extent that he, as an Other, has spread the calumnies invented in Paris about the cruelty of the rebels, or in so far as he has already *accepted* and *repeated* everywhere the idea, often whispered about before 1848, but suddenly trumpeted by Falloux from the Assembly rostrum, at least a week before the insurrection: "The workers are *lazy*. The workshops have failed because they could not succeed, owing to the *sloth* of the workers." In short, in so far as he spread this new attribute of the anti-human, free to perpetrate Evil, as widely as he could, he glimpsed (or clearly saw, depending on his intelligence and his economic and political position in his province) the praxis

161

of the groups as his class *practical-being,* and he discovered—as the obverse of his activities and as their class meaning, as a seal of their inert alterity—the radical negation of the proletariat as a radical necessity if his free activity as a manufacturer was to continue and if he was to enrich bourgeois society with his products, in the framework of the capitalism of accumulation. (CDR, 765–66)

Everything is there—the full panoply of serial mediation that Sartre has developed in his social ontology: passive activity, verbal milieu, comprehension of class interest, chosen necessity to refuse the proletariat, antihumanism, and the rest. Of course, the root of class responsibility depicted here is the Marxist axiom of the ineluctably antithetical interests of capital and labor. But rather than describe this situation with the cool eye of a "scientific socialist," Sartre, employing the "comprehension" integral to his praxis epistemology, refers to the *awareness* which each class member has of the significance of the events in Paris for his class interest. Like the anti-Semite and the settler, he "knows," and in knowing, he becomes an other-conditioned criminal in the existentialist-moral sense.

Such, then, is the portrait which Sartre paints of the father. He is basically a "good," hard-working man who knows that God helps only those who help themselves. The bloody uprisings of 1848 were an unfortunate episode in his eyes, but one cannot be weak-willed, if the company is to survive. And now he has the uneasy feeling that things will never again be quite the same. Sartre captures this malaise when he observes that "after 1848 . . . employers were a curious historical product of the massacres for which they were collectively responsible without actually having committed them. . . . [Each] was *the* bourgeois in so far as this is defined as *the* victor of June (and *the* coward and *the* murderer)" (CDR, 767).

The Second Generation

The sons have inherited the oppressive structures of their fathers' society, especially the historical impossibility for either class to erase the massacres. But since the individual does not completely coincide with his class-being, each son has the possibility for what Sartre calls a "reflexive recoil"[14] with regard to that being by which he interiorizes his social legacy. This interiorization is twofold, involving a synthesis of contemporary class and interclass relations (synchronic totalization) with these same relations in their temporalized, i.e., historical, perspective (diachronic totalization). Thus what were three distinct and irreducible stages of reality for the father—oppression/exploitation, mortal interclass combat, and negative radicalism—become for the son mutually complementary indices of the meaning of social praxis. As the son reads history, he will comprehend it in terms of the absolute necessity for the bourgeoisie never to give in.

> Thus when the massacres were interiorized, they took on a synthetic signification which they did not have for the generation which committed them; the pressure-groups which had been formed spontaneously in the time of the fathers became, in the reflection of the sons, a practice demanded by the situation. Absolute refusal to retreat, as a use-truth [vérité d'usage] revealed by the action of the fathers, was adopted by the sons as a double inert limit, that is to say, as an impossibility and as a pledge. (CDR, 769)

Sartre views this reflective comprehension as a case of solitary operations which are temporalized via the reaction of each heir with his factory. The context is always one of seriality. So when his practical thought returns to him via the mass media, it is always as *pensée-autre,* "as alienated in the infinite flight of recurrence." And the pledge, as assumed impossibility of retreating, is really what Sartre calls "quasi-pledged inertia"—no oath at all, not even implicit, since the class lacks the unity proper to the group. "The pledge isn't given to anyone, but the quasi-pledged structure is apparent in the fact that individual freedom, interiorizing its collective limitation, appears—as in the case of pledged faith—to be the source of its own negative inertia" (CDR, 769).

A certain integration is effected by this reflexive recoil on the part of individual bourgeois and by their interiorization of collective limit: the bourgeoisie has become conscious of itself as a class. Class now becomes limit and norm of each praxis so that every economic and social action assumes an intelligibility for every member of the class in terms of the irreversibility of a common past and of the "use-truth" of the previous generation. Again in technical language, Sartre underscores the specificity of this generation's collective responsibility in terms of its newfound class consciousness:

> This means that every capitalist has his individual, practical comprehension (his own and those of the Other) on the basis of oppression as historicity (past-future) and of exploitation as a process (the present and a prediction of later presents). Thus, whatever the other manufacturer does, he knows it immediately, because *the Other also* acts on the basis of an untranscendable refusal to surrender: He *does him justice,* and if, in its individuality, the action of the Other realises the oppressive praxis which History requires, he will recognize it—*it will be his own over there.* (CDR, 770)

So it is with the second generation of capitalists that a genuine class consciousness comes to the fore and with it responsibility for all "class actions" no matter where they are performed. Among the oppressive class actions which Sartre ascribes to this generation is that of respectability, analyzed briefly earlier in this chapter. Sartre insists that radical opposition between the classes (the need to repress or be repressed) exercised a transcendent function vis-à-vis every social act of the class members. It is the "beyond" of each particular practice, providing its overall meaning (signification-exigence) and that meaning, Sartre takes pains to point out, is oppression of the worker as an anti-man. In the present case, for example, the austerity of the father was a necessary means toward building the family fortune; while that of the son, assumed without economic necessity, "is a *virtue* but, at the same time, it is taken up and reactualized as a nature-against-nature, as a family *hexis* transformed into *praxis*" (CDR, 773). Because the meaning of this practice is oppressive and since each act is "*an individual creation, a free practice*" (CDR, 773), the responsibility ascribed to each class member will be existentialist-moral.[15]

Thus the sons differ from their fathers by the fact that what was merely pragmatic "use-truth" for the latter is reinteriorized by the heirs as free limit to their freedom and as class action. They are liable to every sort of manipulation by pressure groups as long as this is understood as furthering class interest. The heir, by interiorizing the praxis of such groups, becomes coresponsible for their consequences without thereby losing his serial status (see CDR, 780–81). Sartre sees a clear example of this reinteriorization by the sons of what was merely other-conditioning for the fathers in the Malthusian policy of the French bourgeoisie adopted toward the turn of the century. But this characterizes the next generation.

The Third Generation

At the turn of the century class hatred between bourgeoisie and proletariat was at a new level of intensity. This generation of heirs was united by two memorable massacres, 1848 and 1871, which had colored class relations indelibly red. Aware that its interests entailed the radical negation of the working class, the national bourgeoisie adopted a policy of Malthusianism which would increase profits without augmenting the number of workers and swelling the urban proletariat (already at a dangerously high figure, as the Paris Commune brought graphically to the bourgeois mind). Sartre calls this the "French" solution to the problems of the second industrial revolution because it was deliberately chosen in preference to mass production with its increase of the national living standard but at the price of an enlarged working population.[16] The latter was the

Anglo-American solution and, Sartre insists, it was the one produced by the practico-inert capitalist process itself if not interfered with. In other words, like their fathers' practice of respectability, "Malthusianism is an oppressive and radical response based on refusal: the French capitalists refuse the free development of the process in order to save their class" (CDR, 782; F, 726). Sartre is claiming that the French bourgeoisie, in fact, is more intent on preserving its supremacy in the nation than it is concerned with its economic progress, if the latter entails concessions and benefits for the working poor.

Thus the radical and oppressive negation of the other class appears to the grandsons as it had to the previous generations as the inert limit and deep significance of every change. In the present case, the limit is imposed on industrialization and *eo ipso* on the industrial proletariat which survives solely on the sale of its labor. As with respectability, Sartre insists once more that the policy of Malthusianism is tied to oppressive praxis (and hence responsibility) by a threefold refusal. The ruling class intends to exercise a rigorous control over births in the working class.[17] When a woman from that class procures an abortion, according to Sartre, she is merely interiorizing the contrived impossibility for a worker's family to support an extra child. As we have noted, Sartre believes that this could have been avoided by letting the economic process run its course toward mass production. Choice of the Malthusian alternative with its perpetual risk of unemployment for the worker is "*an oppressive use of the right of life and death*" over the proletariat. As we have come to expect with Sartre, he explains this rather hyperbolic claim with the valid and pointed observation that "this oppression is complemented . . . by the attitude of the dominant classes to working class mortality: as we know, every society selects its dead" (CDR, 783). He points out that this is determined at the level of the upper classes, namely, the sovereign and the class seriality, in terms of budget allotments, working conditions, public health, etc. "This means that the French employers—in the historical perspective of a bloody struggle, which was never forgotten, and which might be resurrected at any time—proceeded, after the troubles of 1919, to a controlled extermination of the working class by controlling births and by deciding not to prevent deaths" (CDR, 783).

But this cannot be separated from another oppressive praxis, the refusal to expand the market (the "French solution"), for the living standard of everyone in the nation is raised by greater industrialization. So "the deliberately oppressive practice of the French bourgeoisie perpetuated an *abnormally low* standard of living" (CDR, 783).

Finally, in this context of provoked scarcity, the contradictions among the workers as individual merchants of their labor power, already somewhat overcome by labor-union practices, are transformed into oppositions between different working-class milieux, e.g., professional worker against skilled laborer, government employee versus worker in private industry, the monthly salaried against the hourly or piecemeal worker, etc. Thus the unions themselves become agents of division within the working class. Sartre maintains that "the oppression here consisted in perpetuating temporary dissensions by perpetuating the French *situation*." For the third generation, "it was a case of divide and rule. Aborting, starving, and dividing, the bourgeois class continued the massacre" (CDR, 784).

And so the Sartrean pattern for ascription of collective responsibility is realized in the third generation as it had been in the other two; an exploitative socioeconomic function (Marxist-determinist responsibility) is resolved into or at least closely linked with a deliberately oppressive praxis (existentialist-moral responsibility) under the mediating influence of class interest involving the radical negation of the other class. Class hexis is thereby grounded in individual and group praxis, and the principle of the primacy of praxis is respected.

The common, interiorized limit which defines class-being serves likewise to convict the class of oppressive praxis in whatever social or economic act its members should undertake. This is indeed hexis responsibility—the bourgeois is responsible *because of* what he is; but it is similarly voluntary responsibility—the bourgeois is responsible *for* what he is—and this because the comprehension of the significance of every Other's act (as radical refusal of the other class) mediates the praxis of each.[18]

In lines that bring Sartre's theoretical instruments to bear on the grandsons as they had probed their grandfathers, he remarks:

> [Malthusianism] is simply a matter of translating a determination that is already inscribed in the practico-inert into *practice*. But if this practice by certain groups became a class practice, involving all other groups, this is because it presented itself as immediately interpretable in the serial milieu of the objective class-spirit, and because everyone comprehended it and transcended it toward radical negation. . . . But this comprehension must be the production *over there* of other action in so far as everyone, as Other, is the Other who produces it, and it must also be the reproduction *here* (that is to say, in the elsewhere which contains my Other-Being for the Others), in so far as everyone is responsible to the class (for the radical rejection, as the limit which must never be crossed for fear of betraying the class) by and for all the Others. There was no conspiracy, no deliberation, no communication, and no com-

mon regroupment. . . . Everything took place serially. . . . But whenever possible, the activity of each local group or of each individual freely reproduced the movement of comprehension and was frequently indistinguishable from it.

He draws his own conclusion: "Thus we come back to the case of collective responsibility" (CDR, 786). At once victims and executioners, these neo-Malthusians are serially responsible for the evils the policy entails, many of which they may not have "known," but all of which they "comprehend."

Though Sartre's main purpose in citing Malthusianism is "to illustrate the *minimum* meaning which must be given to *class struggle,* if it is to be described as the motive-force of History" (CDR, 787), it is now evident that this cannot be done without appeal to his theory of collective responsibility. Indeed, the very desire to show this "minimum meaning" as well as the meaning which Sartre finally arrives at addresses a question which has pervaded all of his social and political works, namely, *Who is to blame?* And its answer in terms of collective and individual responsibility embodies all the ambiguities of the existentialist convert to Marxism who hesitates to burn his idols. Yet when allowance has been made for these difficulties inherent in Sartre's theory as a whole, a fairly consistent portrait of *the* industrial capitalist emerges from this triptych. In portraying this figure "warts and all," not only has Sartre expressed his keen sense of social justice and given vent to his antibourgeois bias, but he has afforded us a glimpse into a world where his theory of collective responsibility obtains. How closely this resembles the real world will be discussed in the concluding chapters.

> I had crossed the whole length of the salon Bordurin-Renauds. I turned back. Farewell, beautiful lilies, elegant in your painted little sanctuaries, good-bye, lovely lilies, our pride and reason for existing, good-bye you bastards!
> —Roquentin leaving the gallery.[19]

The path of argument in Part Two, leading from practice to premise and back to practice again, has clearly established the presence of a comprehensive theory of collective responsibility in Sartre. Yet it has simultaneously revealed that theory's internal tensions and suggested its external inadequacies as well. The chief internal dilemma, which we have encountered at many turns, is that of the existentialist champion of individual responsibility who must somehow account for the social facts of class action and institutionalized exploitation; who insists that each man is ultimately responsible for what is made of him, while, nevertheless, admitting that the capitalist system can reduce him to little more than an animal; and who identifies individual praxis with freedom itself before going on to affirm that only in continuing *group* praxis can the worker escape his alienating vassalage to the practico-inert. In the broader context of social philosophy in general, this is the time-honored problem of reconciling individual freedom-responsibility with collective existence and action. In view of Sartre's persistent "totalitarian" fears, this internal dilemma revolves around the question which must be answered in the final section of this study, Can there be collective responsibility without a collective subject?

Germane to the issue of the collective subject is the question of Sartre's theoretical relation to Marxist socioeconomic thought. We have noted his remarkably uncritical acceptance of basic Marxist socioeconomic theory, much of it disputed among Marxists themselves. He awards Marx's "synthetic reconstruction" of capitalism in *Capital* the highest honor in his catalogue, that of possessing a "certainty [*evidence*] . . . [which] defies commentary" (CDR, 216; F, 276). The nature of Sartre's position within the Marxist family must be assessed. Has he "Marxified" existentialism or rather existentialized Marxism?

In addition to its easy acceptance of disputed features of Marxist economics, Sartre's theory is also inadequate to account for many of the facts of social responsibility as we experience them. This stems primarily from the extremely abstract and metaphysical nature of his analysis, as witnessed by his failure to allow for degrees of responsibility in any of his discourses on the subject. In one of the few places where he does acknowledge the existence of this problem, he merely brushes it aside as the concern of casuists.[20] But even the metaphysician must submit to the criterion of adequacy or run the risk of constructing what Stuart Hampshire has termed "a piece of intellectual architecture."[21] And while the ontological and noetic senses of "responsible" as used in *Being and Nothingness* are adequate for the tasks of a "phenomenological ontology," once one turns to the social realm in order to preface a Marxist philosophy of history with a "theory of practical ensembles," a broad spectrum of evidence from history and the social sciences is called for. Indeed, want of such information and lack of time to obtain it is the reason Sartre gave for not completing the *Critique*.[22] In particular, one must be sensitive to the nuances that mark our everyday ascriptions of responsibility. Although Sartre goes to great lengths to justify some of these distinctions (witness what in chapter 7 I called the modes, the axes, the conditions, and the forms of collective responsibility), his very desire to "humanize" Marxist economism has involved him in exaggerated claims that undermine the theoretical soundness of his social ontology. For there is something antihuman, not to say untrue, about the claim that "we are all assassins" or "torturers" or whatever, when no distinction is drawn between the shocked radio audience, the frightened guardsman, and the evil genius behind the affair, if such a one exists.

There is a venerable rhetorical adage that *qui nimis probat nihil probat*. Sartre is liable to this criticism, for in maintaining that everybody is responsible he leads us to conclude that no one is more responsible than anybody else. But in practice this is tantamount to saying that no one is responsible at all—the very contrary of what Sartre wishes to maintain. Obviously, further distinctions have to be made. But Sartre is too embroiled in polemic to bother making them, even in the *Critique*. Yet such distinctions can be made without doing violence to Sartre's social theory. It is simply a matter of "carving at the joints," as William James would say. I shall attempt such surgery in the following chapter.

The problem of collective responsibility which society urges upon us, therefore, involves at least two questions, "Who is responsible?" and "To what degree?" By deliberately ignoring the latter, Sartre has rendered the response to the former difficult, if not impossible in practice. While this may be acceptable as a form of rhetorical overkill, it is clearly inadequate as a serious philosophical response. Yet the flaw need not be fatal, as the discussion in Part III will indicate.

PART THREE

Existential Marxism
or Marxist Existentialism?

We were convinced at one and the same time that historical materialism furnished the only valid interpretation of history and that existentialism remained the only concrete approach to reality.

Search for a Method

The Sartrean Dilemma
Collective Responsibility without a
Collective Subject

As soon as the collective subject reveals itself, one recognizes it in
the pressure which it exerts on its members.

Situations, 6:372

We are ready to address the fundamental question that has motivated this
investigation from the outset: Has Sartre succeeded in synthesizing ethical
existentialism and Marxist collectivism? In other words, does the theory
of collective responsibility reconstructed here warrant his being called a
Marxist, albeit an existential one? And, if so, which term deserves the
adjectival position? The answer presumes a rather clear notion of what
a Marxist is.

Sartre's Revisionist Marxism

It is perilous to attempt a distillation of the "essence" of Marxism. So
broad-ranging and variegated had the phenomenon become, even in Marx's
lifetime, that he could deny he was a Marxist.[1] Still, some limits must be
established, the boundaries to family resemblance marked off, if we are
meaningfully to locate Sartre among the Marxists.

If we take so-called orthodox Marxism-Leninism as our first set of
criteria, Sartre obviously fails to pass the test. Committed to a dialectic
of nature, epitomized by Engels' famous three laws[2] and voicing unqual-
ified faith in the dictatorship of the proletariat and in the Party's necessary
role in bringing it about—such orthodoxy has always been foreign to
Sartre. Indeed, he once remarked that the *Critique* is an anti-Communist
book.[3] It is among the "revisionists," if at all, that we must find the criteria
for Sartre's Marxism.[4]

Although standards for inclusion among the heterodox are obviously
more flexible, subscription to some form of economic "determinism" is
implicit in historical materialism (the Marxist theory of history) as Marx
conceived it, at least in the sense that economic factors are decisive "in
the long run" for the evolution of society.[5] Sartre's awareness of objective

possibility and especially his frequent appeals to material scarcity as a decisive factor in human history constitute more than a nod in the direction of economic determinism, though usually at a rather abstract level. Indeed, he claims to be "in full agreement" with Engels' dictum that economic conditions are the determining ones "in the final analysis," but adds the qualifier that "it is the contradictions within them which form the driving force of history" (SM, 31).[6] He translates these contradictions into "obscure constraints" and "exigencies" in order to maintain the primacy of praxis which saves him from the "economism" he criticizes so sharply. Whether this preserves enough "necessity" to justify his subscribing to Engels' dictum is debatable, but the question scarcely excludes him from the Marxist camp. All agree that the relation between agent and objective conditions is "dialectical." Sartre simply focuses the dialectic on individual praxis while locating counterfinality in the practico-inert. If not an adequate resolution of the freedom-necessity impasse, Sartre's response seems as satisfactory as any that Marxist humanism can offer.

Another essential Marxist thesis is that class conflict is inevitable. Here too Sartre has accepted the theory in terms of the insuperable opposition of interest and destiny between the proletariat and the bourgeoisie. No resolution of class warfare is conceivable short of a "socialism of abundance" (IF, 3:189) which will render practico-inert mediation innocuous and the interest/destiny distinction superfluous. He joins the revisionists in rejecting the dictatorship of the proletariat—"the very idea is absurd" (CDR, 662)—while sharing the Marxist vision of a classless society at the end of prehistory.

Other features that Sartre shares with Marxism include the famous unity of theory and practice,[7] the historicity of values (though, as we noted, the "notion" of freedom relieves Sartre of the problems of relativism that afflict most Marxists),[8] a concept of positive freedom, and, of course, dialectical reason itself.

But my underlying concern is the challenge leveled at Sartre by Goldmann, that he cannot consistently maintain a theory of collective responsibility because he lacks a concept of collective subject. "What seems to me to constitute the chief specific feature of Marxist thought," Goldmann declares, "is the concept of collective subject, the affirmation that, in the historical dimension, it is never individuals but social groups that act, and that it is only in relation to them that we can understand events, behavior, and institutions."[9] He goes on to insist: "It seems to me that the concept of collective or, more precisely, of trans-individual subject clearly separates Marxist thought from all other philosophies."[10] He extends this to class conflict by pointing out that social class is a privileged type of collective subject.

So the pivot point of Goldmann's Marxism is his concept of socioeconomic class. What does he mean by calling it a "transindividual" subject? Does such a concept figure prominently in Marx? Finally, can we find the equivalent in the later Sartre? If we can, the questions of his Marxism and of his theory of collective responsibility, according to Goldmann's criterion, can be settled simultaneously.

"Collective subject," for Goldmann, denotes "a certain number of individuals [who] find themselves engaged in an ensemble of mutual relations and of relations with the surrounding world, such that their behavior and their psychic lives constitute a structure that renders intelligible certain transformations of this world."[11] Although careful to deny that it is a hypostasis, he claims it is "a subject constituted by several individuals."[12] If this collective structure is the epistemic key to his theory, its ontological key is what Goldmann calls "*intra*subjective relations," that is, "relations between individuals who are each partial elements of the true subject of the action."[13] This looks suspiciously circular until we learn more about the "true subject" of the action.

Goldmann cites the example of several people lifting a table together. Their communcation within this limited undertaking can be termed *intra*subjective and their domain of operation that of the "transindividual subject." More complex but also more powerful are the examples drawn from Goldmann's ground-breaking study of Racine, Pascal, and seventeenth-century culture.[14] Their works express the tragic conflict of desire and objective condition on the part of the new nobility (*la noblesse de robe*) no longer favored by the monarchy, upon which it nonetheless continues to depend economically. Its Jansenism voices the contradiction of a class that dare not join the bourgeoisie in loyal opposition to the king. "Certain individual consciousnesses," Goldmann argues, "find themselves in relations with each other that are not intersubjective but *intrasubjective,* and so constitute the subject of all thought and all action of a social and cultural character."[15]

Thus Goldmann's collective subject, socioeconomic class, is a complex of practical and psychological relations sui generis, dubbed *intra*subjective to distinguish them from those interpersonal relations that do not constitute a social subject. In a move we recognize from Sartre, he cautions that the collective subject "has no autonomous reality outside of organic individuals and individual consciousnesses,"[16] and thus it should not be confused with Durkheim's collective consciousness.[17] Goldmann appeals to collective structures to yield both comprehension and explanation in the social realm. The former involves "descriptions of a meaningful structure and its internal bonds" whereas the latter is genetic and entails describing the development of a more comprehensive structure which incorporates the explicandum.[18]

Can we find anything like this collective subject in Marx? Since he gave no explicit consideration to social ontology, we must construct his position from occasional remarks and implicit claims.

There are numerous passages in Marx that support a collectivist reading.[19] Indeed, his basic concept of class struggle presumes that "socioeconomic class" is more than a shorthand designation of individual activities. The distinction and opposition that he marks between particular interest, class interest, and general interest within a society, for example, are clear indicators of a holistic approach to social issues.[20]

But there is also evidence to keep us from placing Marx among the collectivists *sans phrase*. In *The German Ideology* he contests the idealist social theories of the so-called Young Hegelians when he writes:

> The premises from which we begin are not arbitrary ones, not dogmas, but real premises from which abstraction can be made only in the imagination. They are real individuals, their activity and the material conditions under which they live, both those which they find already existing and those produced by their activity. These premises can thus be verified in a purely empirical way.[21]

There is a growing literature on this "humanist" dimension of even the later Marx that has appeared since the advent of his *Paris Manuscripts* and *Grundrisse* in the Western scholarly world.[22]

Marx, too, is seeking a middle ground between the atomism of the eighteenth-century social theorists and the organicism of nineteenth-century German idealists.[23] As Shlomo Avineri observes: "For Marx, socialism is about to overcome the traditional gap between individualism and collectivism. For him, the capitalist 'individualists' were as wrong as the socialist 'collectivists.' "[24] So it appears that Marx's collective subject, socioeconomic class, is no more a hypostasis than is Goldmann's. Indeed, its ontological touchstone seems to be the social individual, the agent-in-relation.[25] This is what Sartre noted when he agreed with Marx that "there are only men and *real relations* between men" (SM, 76).

Before elaborating Sartre's answer to Goldmann, let us hear two other prominent critics who believe that Sartre fails the test for membership in the Marxist family, namely, Merleau-Ponty and Raymond Aron. Their objections will help us focus Sartre's response.

Writing after the appearance of *The Communists and Peace* but before *Search for a Method,* Merleau-Ponty, with his usual perspicacity, takes Sartre to task for ignoring the specifically social: "The question is to know whether, as Sartre says, there are only *men* and *things* or whether there is also the interworld [*l'intermonde*] which we call history, symbolism, and truth-to-be-made [*vérité à faire*]."[26] The fault, he believes, lies with what I have called Sartre's existentialist model of social relations: "There is a tête-à-tête rather than common action, because the social, for Sartre, remains the relationship of 'two individual consciousnesses' who look at each other."[27] Adding his voice to the chorus of those who separate Sartre from the Marxists, he concludes: "What continues to distinguish Sartre from Marxism, even in recent times, is therefore his philosophy of the *cogito*. Men are mentally attached to history."[28] As if to invite the writing of the *Critique,* Merleau adds that Sartre lacks a social philosophy of mediations.[29]

Our third critic represents a more centrist position in the political spectrum, Sartre's erstwhile friend, Raymond Aron. Although acknowledging that Sartre now believes historical wholes to be real, he agrees with Goldmann that Sartre does so with an ontology that knows only the action of individuals: "I doubt whether Sartre succeeded [in the *Critique*] in integrating the Marxist notion of the collective salvation of humanity by the proletarian revolution into a philosophy of solitary consciousness."[30] He goes on to draw a broader moral: "A follower of Kierkegaard cannot at the same time be a follower of Marx."[31]

So a trio of Sartre's leading critics agree that he cannot achieve his projected synthesis of existentialism and Marxism because an unreconstructed Cartesian or Kierkegaardian individualism precludes the "transindividual" subject, or at least the "interworld," that Marxism requires. We now know that Sartre's social ontology is far more nuanced than his critics will allow. As we settle accounts with his adversaries in the matter of Marxist existentialism let us return a final time to the test case of collective responsibility.

Sartre before His Critics

> For a long time we believed in the social atomism bequeathed to us by the eighteenth century, and it seemed to us that man was by nature a solitary entity who entered into relations with his fellow men *afterward.* . . . We now know that this is nonsense. The truth is that "human reality" "is-in-society" as it "is-in-the-world"; it is neither a nature nor a state; it is made. (SG, 590)

Sartre's critics seem to believe either that he could not change his mind or that, if he did, the change could not favor Marxism without entailing a radical rejection of his existentialist anthropology. Avowals such as the one just cited from *Saint Genet* show that he did indeed grow in sensitivity to the social dimension of human existence. Part II of this study measures that growth in detail. In response to his critics we must weigh the success or failure of Sartre's marriage of his existentialist philosophy to a revisionist but recognizable Marxism. Within the parameters of collective responsibility, the issue turns on the nature of the collective subject.

The Collective Subject

I have noted on several occasions that much of Sartre's later social philosophy is adumbrated in the bridge essays published as *The Communists and Peace*. So it should come as no surprise that we find his first definition of the collective subject there.

> I mean by "collective subject" the *subject of the praxis* and not some kind of "collective consciousness." The subject is the group *brought together* by the situation, *structured* by its very action, *differentiated* by the objective requirements of the praxis and by the division of labor, at first random then systematic, which the praxis introduces, *organized* by the leaders which it chooses for itself or which it discovers for itself finding *in their person* its own unity. (CP, 222–23; emphasis his)

We find compressed here features of the fused, the pledged, and the organized group as he subsequently distinguishes them in the *Critique*. But the point is that he designates them a "collective subject." Sartre already perceives it as a practical, nonsubstantial, relational entity. Without mentioning the source, he even appeals to one of Durkheim's criteria for determining the collective consciousness: "[The collective subject] is recognizable by the pressure it exerts on its members" (CP, 223).

The context for these essays, like that of so many of his writings, is polemical. At the high point of his fellow-traveling, he contrasts the proletariat, galvanized by the Party, with the inert and passive masses precisely as he will later distinguish the group from the series: the proletariat, for example, "know that the efficacy of their action will be proportional to the integrating power of the group" (CP, 223).[32] He stresses the importance of thinking *en groupe* and generally argues that serial dispersion ("massification" is his term at this point) is the tool of those who would oppress the worker. Not without reason, therefore, could Merleau-Ponty cite these essays as evidence of Sartre's "ultrabolshevism."[33]

But without sacrificing his newfound sense of the power of the group, Sartre achieves a profound grasp of the internal movements of the collective subject, elaborated in terms of the dialectic of *same* and *other* in the *Critique*. We have traced those movements up to the "free alterity" within the group-in-fusion. "Ubiquity," "sameness," and "interiorized multiplicity-responsibility" were the key terms in that analysis.[34] Of course, a tension remains within the group similar to that which characterizes the conscious life of the individual. Just as the Sartrean individual is not a self but a presence-to-self, so the group subject is not a substance but a revolving set of practical relations. Total integration of the organic individual into the group is impossible. An immanence-transcendence duality characterizes both the individual and the collective subject. As there is no individual (conscious) substance, so there can be no collective substance. The group is a "practical determination of everyone by everyone, by all and by oneself from the point of view of a common praxis" (CDR, 506).

Sartre eventually puts to himself the question I have been asking: "The real critical question: what type of existence or being characterizes the common action of the organized group *in so far as it is common* (rather than in so far as it can be resolved into a multiplicity of functions)?" (CDR, 506). As we saw in chapter 7, the constituted dialectic is that specific set of rules and relations that marks the inner life of the group and its dealings with other groups and series. Sartre concludes that "group status is indeed a metamorphosis of the individual" and he sees the individual's sociality as a set of reciprocal relations mediated by the Third, such as "adopted inertia, function, power, rights and duties, structure, violence and fraternity" (CDR, 510), and, I have argued, group responsibility—all those "specific modalities of the group" discussed in chapter 6.

What, then, is the collective (group) subject? Like the ternary relation that forms its core, it is "a form of inter-individual reality" (CDR, 367). It can likewise be classified, along with practico-inert collective objects, as a phenomenon of the "interworld" (*l'intermonde*), Merleau-Ponty's term which Sartre adopts (see SM, 76).

But the discussion of the constituted dialectic and the series reveals that these phenomena resemble Goldmann's "*intra*individual" relations as well. Both authors seek to delineate those genetic and structural relations sui generis that constitute the social subject, the "we" of collective undertakings. Doubtless, Sartre is more cautious than Goldmann in referring to a "transindividual subject." But he assigns objective spirit a mediating function and a positive influence on individual praxes that Goldmann reserves to the transindividual (collective) subject. If it did not take us too far afield, we could compare Sartre's analysis of the "neurotic art" of the French bourgeoisie under the July Monarchy with Goldmann's account of the "tragic literature" of the *noblesse de robe* under Louis XIII.[35] In both cases "the subject of cultural creation," to borrow Goldmann's term, is social and collective. Neither author wishes to deny the originality of Flaubert in one case or of Racine and Pascal in the other. But each is bent on revealing the reality of objective possibility. In sum, one can say that Sartre would have little trouble accepting Goldmann's collective subject as long as it was understood in a way that respected the primacy of individual praxis: "Valéry is a petit bourgeois intellectual. . . . But not every petit bourgeois intellectual is Valéry" (SM, 56).

But, of course, there's the rub. Goldmann has tellingly underscored the fact that "for a structural and historical anthropology [such as the *Critique* claims to be] Sartre accords an excessive importance to mediation constituted by the psychological structure of individuals—from the concrete viewpoint of the investigation and explanation of social facts."[36] He finds a discrepancy between Sartre's lip service to social ensembles and his de facto emphasis on individual psychology and biographical analyses. Had Goldmann lived to see the publication of *The Family Idiot*, especially its third volume, he might have tempered his criticism. I have mentioned the role assigned to objective spirit in that opus. Indeed, if we recall that the practico-inert is a genuine force in society, albeit a derivative one, we can give a Goldmannian reading to Sartre's remark on the "contingency" of a state official's dying in a plane crash: "One can say from this point of view that contemporary society has simultaneously produced both the minister and the jet plane" (IF, 3:435n). Yet even that work, as we know, is predicated on the assumption that "a man . . . totalizes his age to the very extent that he is totalized by it" (IF, 3:426). In effect, the individual-collective relationship is dialectical and it must remain a matter of dispute whether Sartre or Goldmann better respects the terms of the dialectic.[37]

In any case, our discussion of Sartre's social ontology has revealed a breadth and a richness that allows both for those peak moments of social integration, e.g., the group-in-fusion, when multiplicity, identity, and responsibility have been almost fully interiorized, and for those more common instances of serial responsibility when, to paraphrase Rimbaud, "we are another." The latter characterizes the mass and even the class as practico-inert phenomena. To the extent that action groups[38] whip the masses into self-awareness, they make serial individuals practically conscious of their alienated condition. Still, the accoutrements of class-consciousness, e.g., day-wages, "blue collar," and lunch bucket, like class-being itself, lie in the realm of the practico-inert. The class member as such is passively active and serially responsible—both victim and accomplice. Despite his unquestionably brilliant work in the area of cultural creativity, Goldmann's "transindividual subject" conflates features of Sartre's "common" and "serial" individuals that really ought to be separated, especially when it is a question of collective responsibility.

Collective Responsibility without a Collective Subject?

We can now see that the question is ill posed. Like many such queries, however, its proper formulation constitutes the major step toward its resolution. We have established that ascriptions of collective responsibility abound in Sartre's popular writings and that he offers the elements of a theory to support them in the *Critique*. Because he is primarily a moralist, it comes as no surprise that his "collective responsibility" carries more than a Marxist-causal signification. Both his philosophical anthropology, including comprehension, "choice," and the possibility of collective bad faith, and his social ontology, with its primacy of praxis and its practico-inert mediation, render intelligible a theory of collective responsibility in the moral sense.

In a seminal essay on this topic, Joel Feinberg distinguishes between responsibility which is collective and distributed across individuals and that which is collective and not so distributed.[39] We might call the latter the "hard" case of collective moral responsibility. It claims that a social whole such as a town or an army can be morally responsible for some event, quality, or state of affairs, without the individual members being so responsible. Although worthy of consideration in its own right, this view is not ascribable to Sartre, whose principle of the primacy of praxis commits him to what may be termed the "soft" concept of collective moral responsibility, which is *distributed* across the members of the social whole. As he understands it, to say that *we* are responsible is not to claim that *I* am not responsible, but is merely to specify the mode and the scope of my responsibility. The typology in chapter 7 was introduced precisely to justify that thesis.

If the question of collective moral responsibility is posed in terms of dialectical reason, as both Goldmann and Sartre intend, the requisite dynamic interchanges, totalizatons, mediated reciprocities, and the like pertain to the standard vocabulary. It is only for analytic reason, as Sartre understands it, with its premium on binary functions and its social atomism, that such responsibility becomes problematic. For dialectical reason, the concrete reality is not the isolated individual (Aron's Kierkegaardian surd), but agents-in-relation (Marx's social individual). They are constantly constituting the social dialectic of same/other whose nature and extent I have examined.

The upshot of the previous reconstruction of Sartre's theory of collective responsibility and of the present excursion into social ontology is to indicate that one can discover a collective subject in Sartre's group and a kind of collective subject-object in his series (namely, *collectif* and institution). Neither prejudices the primacy of individual praxis and both allow for the specificity of the social. Each generates a distinct form of collective responsibility which I have labeled "group" and "serial" responsibility respectively. As social reality is a mixture of groups and series, so it is a tissue of such responsibilities distributed across social individuals according to the contingencies of multiple cross-membership.

Nor does this dissolve individual responsibility *tout court*—the hallmark of existentialism. The motto of existential humanism continues to be: "A man can always make something out of what is made of him" (BEM, 35). Ontological freedom (nonself-coincidence) guarantees it and the primacy of praxis carries it into the social realm. The claim that "we" are responsible does not exclude the possibility that I may have a quite personal, concomitant responsibility for some aspect of the same affair.

As a rather homely example of such multiple responsibility, consider a "grudge match" between two players who are personal rivals on opposing teams. Their regard for each other as individuals overlaps their roles as team members. One and the same act, a particularly vicious block, for example, could sustain two equally valid descriptions, namely, "carrying out the play" and "getting even." Responsibility in the former case would be collective since it is essentially mediated by the social whole, the team. But the latter would be an instance of individual responsibility.

Should we go so far as to claim that individual responsibility is a distillation of collective responsibility? In the social history of "responsibility" this is probably the case, and it was certainly Durkheim's view.[40] But Sartre's primacy of praxis will not allow such a reading. Not that he would deny the evidence of cultural anthropology. Again, he would simply insist that we have not looked far enough if we have settled for relations (structures) only, without regarding the praxes that dialectically sustain them. Doubtless praxis and structure are simultaneous, like the smile on the face of the Cheshire cat or the snubness of Socrates' nose. But like the faces of the feline and the philosopher, praxis is ontologically prior. Nor is this a verbal scruple. As we have seen, Sartre's existentialist humanism turns on it.

Granted that such collective subjects and subject-objects are consonant with Sartre's dialectical nominalism, are they necessary for a theory of collective moral responsibility? Since collective moral responsibility is a social fact, by definition it depends on the mediation of social ensembles such as the group, the *collectif,* and the institution. Just as the cashing of a check implies the reality of a banking system, so the ascription or the interiorization of collective responsibility presumes the reality of a social ensemble. To subsume the organic individual in some quasi-natural process would preserve collective causal responsibility at the cost of its ethical dimension, as happens in Marxist "economism." But when "collectivism'' is attacked in the name of the moral individual, collective responsibility is lost in a welter of activities of another kind. Like the aborigine describing the cashing of a check, it entirely misses the meaning of the expression, "*We* did it." It is not a matter of mere convenience or of needlessly multiplying entities. Once the ghost of twentieth-century totalitarianism has been exorcised from the discussion, it is merely a case of admitting the existence of real, practical relations that mediate our social being, binding us to each other and to our predecessors and successors. To deny the reality of such relational entities is not only to settle for a needlessly impoverished ontology, it is to leave the entire sociohistorical domain unaccounted for.

To argue that social ensembles are necessary for collective responsibility is one thing; to claim that Sartre's dialectical nominalism is necessary for such responsibility is quite another, and a stronger thesis than I care to defend. If Sartre has not given the uniquely adequate answer to this question, he has tendered a comprehensive and viable hypothesis. Moreover, he has challenged subsequent theorists to respect moral responsibility as they undertake an account of social causation. It is to his credit to have joined his ever watchful critical eye with such powerful tools of social analysis—a classic instance of the unity of theory and practice.

The Means-End Problem: Collective Responsibility and Dirty Hands

Commenting on what separated him most basically from the then recently deceased Albert Camus, Sartre wrote that for Camus: "Ethics [*la morale*] taken by itself both demands revolt and condemns it" (*Situations*, 4:127). The implication is that Sartre was a less tenderhearted realist, especially in the matter of the Algerian War. I have argued that Sartre's assessment of his "amoralist realism" is too severe, that he never abandoned his ethical concerns.

And yet the problem of ethics and politics, the means-end problem as he calls it,[41] is intensified once we take collective responsibility into account. For one thing, it makes it impossible to avoid "dirtying one's hands," as the phenomenon of serial responsibility makes clear. If the existentialist Sartre had described human reality as having a past, as coming to reflective awareness as already responsible, the existential Marxist Sartre merely expands the nature and scope of that responsibility to include the series and the group. Gone is the exculpating appeal to good intentions. Exploitative systems and collective bad faith have robbed us of our innocence. If an ethic in our present society is both inevitable and impossible (see SG, 186n), it is because the condition of material scarcity, which might well be called Sartrean original sin,[42] has made wolves of us all. It is the "bases and structures" of choice that must be altered in order to fulfill Sartre's universal freedom conditional (that I cannot be concretely free until all are free). But such disalienating praxis entails tactical counterviolence—the scandalous message of *The Wretched of the Earth*. This will continue to be the case until material scarcity is overcome.

Sartre is not sanguine about reconciling the necessary violence in an alienated society with his ideal of freedoms recognizing each other. Perhaps his retrospective "realism" was more the expression of personal frustration at the apparent incompatibility of his ethical ideal and the politics required to effect it. In one of the final interviews he gave before he died, this matter was still a major concern: "So there are two attitudes, both human but incompatible, which one must try to live at the same time. There is the effort above all else to realize man, to engender man; that is the ethical relationship. And then there is the struggle against scarcity."[43] If the reconciliation of the individual and the social remained a puzzle for Sartre, that of the ethical and the political did so as well. For a while, roughly the period of his fellow-traveling with the French Communist party, it seemed as if one had to "force people to be free"—in that popular misinterpretation of Rousseau's phrase. But he was never comfortable with the moral pragmatism implied there and his relief in finding a group (e.g., *les maos*) that conjoined social revolution to a libertarian ethic was obvious. Still, to the very end he must have felt the anguish of Camus's Tarrou before the "necessary" contradiction of using violence in the name of brotherhood.[44] One of his last public statements includes the frank avowal: "To tell the truth, I still don't see clearly the true relationship between violence and fraternity."[45]

So it seems that professional politics, which Sartre associates with the manipulation of power (see ORR, 188), necessitates dirtying one's hands. But the call to politics for him as for Camus is an ethical one: realizing an end to alienation and a life of freedom for all in the socialism of abundance—the twin values of socialism and freedom that have inspired political existentialism since its inception in the early forties.[46]

Collective moral responsibility becomes both a fact and a value for political existentialism as Sartre conceives it. As a fact, it provides the point of departure for our social relations. To be in-society is to be serially responsible and oftentimes to share group responsibility as well. His popular polemics, as we have seen, assume that as a matter of fact we are responsible for *our* world, for what "happens" to *us* and to others, and for the value-image of man that our every basic choice projects.

But collective moral responsibility is likewise a value for the political existentialist. Under the guise of "fraternity," it is the ethical aspect of that equality and reciprocity that characterizes "the reign of freedom" to which Sartre so often appeals. It constitutes that existentialist "call," to borrow from Heidegger, to become ontically what we are ontologically: free, to be sure, but free-in-society.

Can History Have a Subject?

At this point social ontology and theory of history converge. It is a commonplace among Marxists to speak of the proletariat as the "universal class" becoming the "subject of History."[47] Sartre gradually adopts this mode of discourse. "By becoming conscious of itself," he writes, "the Proletariat becomes the subject of History" (SM, 89). What is entailed by this transformation and what does he mean by "History"? His theory of collective responsibility is relevant to both questions.

It should be obvious how Sartre understands the transformation from object to subject of history. He sees it as the overcoming of passive activity and practico-inert mediation in favor of group praxis. As long as this transformation is incomplete, men remain objectified and alienated in a historical process that eludes them—at once victims and accomplices: "In this sense History, which is the proper work of *all* activity and of *all* men, appears to men as a foreign force exactly insofar as they do not recognize the meaning of their enterprise (even when locally successful) in the total, objective result" (SM, 89). This requires an ability to totalize, to grasp the *sens* of one's praxis in terms of one's class interest and ultimately in light of the moral ideal of freedoms recognizing one another. But this totalizing is no mere speculative overview; it is a praxis, a doing in terms of the whole: "all activity" and "all men."

Is this totalizing activity a mere expression of noetic freedom, of each agent's conferring the meaning-direction on the world that he wishes? Sartre's sense of objective possibility will not allow this. Alienation is real; the bases and structures of choice are truly limiting; the practico-inert actually distorting. Scarcity must be overcome for permanent brotherhood (*fraternité*) to be achieved. In this sense, Sartre does seem committed to an end-*goal* if not to an end-*terminus* of history.[48] A taste of this control over "our" future is given in the group-in-fusion and was experienced by Sartre in the streets of Paris during the events of May 1968: the exchange of serial impotence for the power of interiorized multiplicity, the "all for one and one for all" of group responsibility. But the experience must be brief, the reality ephemeral as long as scarcity reigns.

185

If we take Sartre's concept of the "subject" of history as that grouping of groups striving toward this emancipatory goal, the question of "History" becomes less problematic. Although he uses the Marxist terms, he is far from "scientific socialism" with its necessary laws, its dictatorship of the proletariat, and its inevitable advent of the classless society. The primacy of praxis that has preserved the existentialist values in Sartre's Marxism has left the historical field considerably more elastic than Marxist "economism" would allow. Accordingly, Sartre's theory of history assumes the modality of a hypothesis: *if* men would be free, they must employ every means to combat the exploitative structures and oppressive praxes of contemporary society—they must strive to replace the fractured meanings (interest-destiny) that constitute the present *sens* of history with the ethical and social ideal of true mutuality. "Thus the plurality of the *meanings* of History can be discovered and posited for itself only upon the ground of a future totalization." Sartre's hypothesis is also an imperative: "Our historical task, at the heart of this polyvalent world, is to bring closer the moment when History will have *only one meaning* [*sens*], when it will tend to be dissolved in the concrete men who will make it in common" (SM, 90).

Sartre's existentialist challenge to the Marxists lies in the "if." It is the sober affirmation that we can indeed become concretely free but that men may well choose to rest in bondage.

ten

Collective Responsibility and the Ethical Imagination

> The most radical and strenuous work of liberation may be able to be
> carried out only in the imagination, because it cannot suppress the
> original condition of total alienation.
>
> André Gorz, *Le Socialisme difficile*

Among the graffiti covering the walls of the Latin Quarter in Paris during
the events of May 1968, one seemed particularly apt. It proclaimed "All
Power to the Imagination" (*L'Imagination au Pouvoir*). This slogan captured that distrust of the actual and rage for the possible which permeated
the students' uprising. It also suggests my final perspective on Sartre's
understanding of collective responsibility, that of a social and ethical ideal.

Since his first thesis on the imagination for his diploma in advanced
studies (1926)[1] to his last major work, on Flaubert, the relation between
the real and the imaginary remained one of Sartre's prime concerns. His
intervening essays on the imagination, numerous works of imaginative
literature, and his "creative" biographies of artistic figures, including his
"true novel" on Flaubert,[2] exhibit Sartre's abiding interest in the "de-
realizing" power of consciousness. As I pointed out early in my investigation, imaging consciousness as the locus of possibility, negativity, and
lack is paradigmatic of Sartrean consciousness in general.[3] If Sartre has
been commonly acclaimed *the* philosopher of freedom in our time, he
could with equal justification be acknowledged *the* philosopher of the
imagination.

I should like to bring this study to a close by reflecting on collective
responsibility in light of Sartre's commitment to the integral role of imaginative consciousness in human affairs. I shall proceed in three stages:
by an initial, detailed analysis of Sartre's sociopolitical ideal, pausing to
make those critical observations that I have deferred to the end, in order
finally to mollify these criticisms somewhat by considering collective responsibility itself as an ingredient in Sartre's moral vision of the world
and as the ethical ideal that focuses and guides his life project.

Sartre's Sociopolitical Ideal

I argued in chapter 9 that Sartre believes that if "History" is to have a "subject" but no terminus, then it must at least have a goal, that is, a focal point and criterion from which to distinguish real and apparent successes. In other words, if "History" is a totalization of totalizations, then as such it must be unified in terms of a goal. This is all that he shares with evolutionary or providential theories of history.

We know, further, that human reality is that by which value enters the world. The goal of "History," like any value (nonbeing that "demands" to be) must be a human endeavor, indeed a human creation. I have argued throughout that freedom remains the underlying value in Sartre's philosophy and that the development of the latter can be charted by the career of the former: its "thickening" to require socioeconomic liberation and its broadening to include all people in its scope. We have witnessed a corresponding evolution in the notion of responsibility. In effect, freedom and responsibility are aspects of our facticity (we are "condemned" to be free-responsible) as well as ultimate values for Sartre—the ground of any other value that human reality may choose. In this minimal sense, Sartre approaches a philosophic tradition he professes to reject, that which subscribes to the moral maxim, "Become what you are." If he eschews essentialism and its understanding of human nature as moral norm, he is nonetheless committed to a "human condition" that makes anything less than "choice of freedom" inconsistent and alienating.

To adequately understand human reality and human "History," therefore, we must grasp what would be the full flowering of human freedom.[4] The comprehension of what humans *can* be, in turn, will cast light on what they are. These are the positive and negative functions of the Sartrean ideal to which we now turn.

Disalienation

The negative side of Sartre's sociopolitical ideal is removal of the sources of alterity (otherness) from human relations. Not that all otherness is alienating. We have seen that a kind of nonobjectifying otherness—what Sartre calls "free alterity"—obtains within the group-in-fusion. But the historical and structural factors that have intervened to separate the agent from his colleagues and from his own self must be rooted out. This aspect of Sartre's project most resembles the young Marx's diagnosis of the fourfold alienation of man.[5] In Sartre's analysis, the roots of alienation are three or, rather, there are three depths to one and the same root.

The first and most obvious level of alienation is that of the collective object, which Sartre terms "the sign of our alienation" (CDR, 307n). The other-conditioning of the mass media, the reification of the market, the reigning ideology—all are indicators of our serial impotence.

At a deeper level, alienation is rooted in the division of labor and the system of private property that contradict the basic socialist character of the forces of production—a thesis easily recognized as standard Marxist historical materialism.

At both levels alienation is a function of the practico-inert. As Sartre points out early in the *Critique:* "It is in the concrete and synthetic relation of the agent to the other through the mediation of the thing, and to the thing through the mediation of the other, that we shall be able to discover the foundations of all possible alienation" (CDR, 66n). Alienation is not a Hegelian relation of consciousness to itself, nor is it a matter of simple Marxist-causal relations. It is to Sartre's credit to have included the various forms of alienation—social, psychological, economic, and the rest— under the conceptual umbrella of the practico-inert.[6] His thesis is that all forms of alienation involve a relation between freedoms (praxes) mediated by material reality.

It is not the practico-inert as such that alienates, but as qualified by the fact of scarcity (*la rareté*). This, then, is the deepest level of alienation, the one that has turned human history into a tale of Hobbesian conflict. Sartre's point in rooting alienation in scarcity is twofold. He thereby accounts for the abiding alienation in socialist states and urges that this need not be so, that in a "socialism of abundance" true, positive reciprocity will finally replace serial otherness.

But it looks as if Sartre is liable to an objection leveled by Raymond Aron against Marx: the father of Communism commits the radical error of "attributing all alienations to a single origin and of assuming that the end of economic alienation would result in the end of all alienation."[7] Considering the paramount place accorded scarcity in Sartre's social philosophy, does he link the end of material scarcity with the overcoming of all forms of alienation?

Fortunately, Sartre has left us a clear, if open, answer to this question. It bears quoting at length.

> The real problem . . . relates not so much to the past, where recurrence and alienation have always existed, as to the future: to what extent will a socialist society do away with atomism *in all its forms?* To what extent will collective objects, the signs of our alienation, be dissolved into a true inter-subjective community in which the only real relations will be those between men, and to what extent will the necessity of every human society remaining a detotalized totality maintain recurrence, flights and therefore unity-objects as limits to true unification?

EXISTENTIAL MARXISM OR MARXIST EXISTENTIALISM?

> Must the disappearance of capitalist forms of alienation mean
> the elimination of *all* forms of alienation? (CDR, 307n)

Although he leaves us to answer the question ourselves, it is obvious that he is not about to equate socioeconomic causes with the source of alienation *simpliciter*. Scarcities of time and space, for example, seem inherent in the human condition. It is unlikely that the champion of contingency and facticity ignored these aspects of human finitude. But his remarks evidence a deeper misgiving. Will the immanence-transcendence tension that marks both personal and social integration ever be overcome? That seems impossible for ontological reasons. Must this leave us forever in a tragic state similar to that of Hegel's unhappy consciousness? Such seems to have been the "futile passion" doctrine of *Being and Nothingness,* but it is subsumed, as we have seen, in the "free alterity" of the *Critique*.[8] Still, Sartre does not exclude the possibility that people will abuse their freedom, even in abundance. To project an ideal is not to play the prophet.

The Positive Vision

The "true inter-subjective community in which the only real relations will be those between men" describes concisely Sartre's sociopolitical ideal. When "unpacked" it yields three interrelated conceptual components— reciprocity, transparency, and community. They constitute the value thread that has run throughout the previous discussion of Sartre's social ontology and his moral ascriptions. Let us examine each more closely.

Reciprocity. From the axiological viewpoint, the decisive shift in Sartre's philosophical stance after the war was the emergence of positive reciprocity as the supreme expression of concrete freedom and hence as the leading value to be fostered in all quarters. This went hand-in-hand with his gradual politicization. A developmental study such as this one must follow Sartre's growing commitment from its *terminus a quo,* the famous phenomenology of sadomasochism in *Being and Nothingness* and its infamous articulation as "Hell is other people" from *No Exit.* The transitional stage includes hints from imaginative literature that love might be more than mutual enslavement (e.g., the relation between Hilda and Goetz in *The Devil and the Good Lord*)[9] as well as reference to Genet's deliberate refusal of reciprocity, love, and hence "salvation" (SG, 114). The *terminus ad quem* of this movement is Sartre's open espousal of positive reciprocity "which excludes commands properly speaking" as "the true relationship between men" (IF, 3:48). Each of these phases merits closer scrutiny, not only because together they embody Sartre's expanding vision

190

of man-in-society, but also since they undergird and motivate his political and ethical pronouncements in the postwar era.

Recall Sartre's unequivocal denial of positive reciprocity as a possibility for human reality: "It is . . . useless for human reality to seek to get out of this dilemma: one must either transcend the Other or allow oneself to be transcended by him. The essence of the relations between consciousnesses is not *Mitsein;* it is conflict" (BN, 429). I called this "the dilemma of equality." His failure to contextualize these remarks sociohistorically left the distinct impression that this conflictive condition bore the necessity and atemporal validity of a Husserlian essence. He seemed to be describing the way human relations *had* to be, not just how they in fact were.[10]

Sartre admitted that it was his experience of the French Resistance during the Nazi occupation and of the social conflicts immediately thereafter that opened his eyes to the need for and the possibility of communal effort.[11] He came to take as his model of concrete freedom in a hostile world the small combat group where the life of each depends on the faithfulness of others. Lacking at that point a concept of the mediating Third, he was reduced to making allusions to the desirability of such positively reciprocal interpersonal relations as friendship and love.[12]

Thus in *What Is Literature?* he argues for a community of true mutuality from the nature of literary communication. He has always held that writing is an act of generosity, an invitation extended from one freedom to another. He now concludes in a manner reminiscent of *Existentialism Is a Humanism* that the act of reading presumes an ideal readership in which all men are treated as ends in themselves and not as means only. In other words, both creative writing and the reading of imaginative literature assumes as an ideal a society of full, positive reciprocity.[13]

I cite this "argument," which Sartre employs on several occasions, not to assess its validity (that would require at least as much reconstruction as did *Existentialism Is a Humanism*), but merely to illustrate his vision of a society of total reciprocity, which is beginning to take form. Years later, when imaginative literature has been set aside as seemingly irrelevant to sociopolitical concerns, Sartre remains in thrall to this vision.

Earlier I discussed the possibility of "absolute reciprocity" tantalizingly held out by Sartre toward the conclusion of *Saint Genet.* At this transitional stage, the dilemma between individual identity and collective integration is promised at least an imaginary resolution:

> If we maintain the hope and firm intention of escaping this alternative [either Bukharin, model of our will to be together, or Genet, model of our will to solitude], if there is still time to

191

reconcile, with a final effort, the object and the subject, we must, be it only once in the realm of the imaginary, achieve this latent solitude which corrodes our acts and thoughts. (SG, 599)

By experiencing the "whirligigs" of Genet's dialectic of subject and object, self and other, Sartre implies, we shall be able to live our own contradictory nature to the full. "This game of hide-and-seek will end only when we have the courage to go to the limits of ourselves in both directions at once" (SG, 599). But the method at this point is literary and the "cure" psychological, whereas the problem, Sartre has come to see, is social. True social reciprocity demands changes in those socioeconomic conditions that mediate this reciprocity. Sartre explicitly makes this proposal in the final stage of full advocacy for the ideal of reciprocity.

There are three works in which the later Sartre describes and forcefully advocates this ideal: the *Critique,* where its ontology is constructed; *The Family Idiot,* in which a counterimage is projected by Flaubert, who is incapable of reciprocity; and a series of discussions with two young Maoists entitled *On a raison de se révolter.* It is in this last that we discover Sartre's most detailed references to the positive aspect of his ideal society.

He repeats a claim made earlier in his career, that "behind socialism there is perhaps a still more important value which is precisely freedom" (ORR, 252). One of the lessons learned from the events of May 1968, is that, besides the economic reasons that Marx offered, "there are now other, personal reasons for making a revolution," such as hatred of hierarchies or love of freedom (ORR, 188). If the twin values of socialism and freedom form the arms of the anchor of political existentialism, Sartre has always insisted that socialism is for the sake of freedom, not the reverse as the Communists seem to believe.[14]

As formulated in these discussions, Sartre's vision of complete reciprocity entails an end to authority of every kind,[15] the replacing of political leaders and politicians in general by direct democracy and the power of persuasion,[16] and a total commonality of action. He believes that the true socialist society will be one in which "powers will be exercised by all equally, where there will be no more representatives of powers but where there will be free men who will decide matters of which each could be considered the author" (ORR, 350)—almost a paraphrase of Rousseau. The germ of his vision, originally stated in the Kantian terms of "freedoms recognizing themselves" (MR, 251), has flowered into libertarian socialism.

Transparency. Although full reciprocity of freedoms in eye-level relations is the focal point of Sartre's sociopolitical vision, there are other facets

192

integral to the ideal that do not figure as prominently in his remarks. One such is the value of complete openness in self-communication. This sustains positive reciprocity as Sartre understands it, while adding a psychological and an epistemic dimension left unstated under the first rubric.

Sartre allows in the *Critique* that "translucid human relations do exist . . . ; I mean immediate reciprocities" (CDR, 540). But in our current alienated state such immediacy is rare and ephemeral. With his Maoist discussants he links this transparency to the abolition of power politics: "If the politician can't say everything, it is while he functions as mediator. But when the time comes that one can say everything, the politician will disappear; he will no longer exist" (ORR, 289). Sartre's point, shared by Foucault and others,[17] is that secrecy and even privacy are forms of power retention and hence are alienating; they undermine true reciprocity. Total honesty and openness seem to be components of Sartre's ideal social relation. Yet he remains enough of a rationalist to demand direct evidence and objective criteria in these relationships rather than settling for trust and faithfulness, at least if "trust" implies faith in another's word.

It is one of the blind spots in his anthropology and in the ethics he builds upon it that Sartre considers fiducial faith a form of passive activity, an essentially alienating phenomenon—"the Other in me" (IF, 1:166).[18] For even the relation fraternity-terror, proper to the pledged group, presumes that the other parties will respect their oaths, though the appeal is more to fear than to faithfulness. Admittedly, "terror" is chiefly an extrapolation from one's own fear of violent death and to that extent is also a matter of evidence. But it at least presumes a confidence that people will act according to enlightened self-interest and keep their word, and that is a kind of faith.

No doubt, by calling for complete transparency, Sartre is being true to his existentialist anthropology of absolute freedom and self-luminosity. But as freedom was concretized in society via praxis (which entails the "opacity" of the practico-inert), could not luminosity gain concreteness in more than "comprehension"? Or rather, does not the "comprehension," which in the group implies "You can count on me and I on you," optimally rest not on some extrinsic factor (e.g., fear of consequences, the way perfect strangers form self-interest groups) but on the *trust* that the other party would be faithful even to the point of self-sacrifice (i.e., beyond the Hobbesian limit)? The absurdity of nonelective self-sacrifice aside, this element of supererogation is strangely lacking in Sartre's philosophy, though scarcely absent from his personal life.[19]

Sartre's most extensive remarks on the ideal of transparency occur in the course of an interview when he is asked whether highly personal questions disturb him:

> As far as I'm concerned, what vitiates relations among people is that each keeps something hidden, secret from each other—not necessarily from all, but from the one to whom he is presently speaking. I think that transparency ought to replace secrecy at all times, and I well imagine the day when two men will have no more secrets from each other because subjective life as well as objective life will be totally offered, totally given.

Sartre's reason for expecting such transparency will surprise those raised on popular readings of his "dualism": "It is impossible to admit that we should deliver our bodies as we do and that we should hide our thoughts—given that, for me, there is no difference in nature between body and consciousness" (*Situations,* 10:141–42). Sartre's reason is obscure because even a "psychic" body, as he calls our physical being in *Being and Nothingness,* can dissemble. But such concealment would be an exercise of power, he seems to be saying, in opposition to the disalienated spirit of the ideal. Transparency, too, belongs to "that far-off time" when man will be free "from the yoke of scarcity" (SM, 34).

Community-Fraternity. Raymond Aron observes that, in his opinion, Marx "secretly [*sourdement*] dreamt of a community beyond Saint-Simonian industrialization for which Rousseau entertained a certain nostalgia and whose advent would be made possible by an abundance of goods."[20] Sartre's Rousseauistic nostalgia is quite pronounced, as we have seen. Recall the contrariety he posits between collective objects and "a true inter-subjective community" (CDR, 307n). A necessary condition for the latter in any permanent state is the end of material scarcity.

Again, it was in his contacts with the *groupuscules* of the ultra Left that Sartre found in the sixties and seventies the comradeship he had valued in the Resistance. Their cooperative spirit, their friendship (*l'amitié*), "the relation of reciprocity" that marked their dealings with each other, were particularly attractive to him. He could say to his Maoist friends: "For these different reasons I believe that I can find among you, and not only among you but in the anti-hierarchical and libertarian movement, the heralding of a new politics and the roots of the new man who will undertake it" (ORR, 77).

The importance he attaches to the related concept of fraternity emerges in those interviews published shortly before his death. Due allowance made for the interviewer's own interest in the topic and for his control of the discussion, it is clear that Sartre recommends "fraternity" as the ideal around which the leftists (*gauchistes*) can rally. But he means a radical fraternity, one based on affective identity, mutual support, and sharing of goods (as in Marx's famous slogan: "From each according to his ability, to each according to his need"). It is distinctive of Sartre's ideal that this fraternity, first experienced *en famille,* is more basic than the productive relation emphasized by Marx; it stands as the model for all interpersonal relations.[21] He assumes a prophetic tone in summarizing this aspect of his ideal. The full experience of fraternity will be possible only at the end of a long historical development toward our common goal, which he terms simply "Man." That teleology is prefigured now in our moral judgments which, in effect, demand that we treat each other as true brothers: "What is required for an ethic [*une morale*] is to extend the idea of fraternity to the point that it becomes a unique and evident relationship among all men, that relationship being first of all a properly group relation, one of small groups bound in one way or another to the family idea."[22] This is what gives the problem of violence its particular poignancy for Sartre: on the one hand, terror (violence) is necessary to guarantee fraternity in this place of scarcity and possible betrayal; on the other, violence of itself will never further the advent of "Man." We noted in chapter 9 his uncertainty as to the "true" relationship between fraternity and violence.

But the primacy of individual praxis is respected even in the ideal community. Sartre reminds us of the "untranscendability of the ontological and practical status of the regulatory third party." We now know that this is not some de facto limit assigned to communities. "We have seen how [the third] arises . . . in the course of development of the constituent dialectic, as a free, organic praxis and as a human relation of reciprocity" (CDR, 662). These reciprocal praxes reach maturity in the positive mutuality and fraternity of the true intersubjective community.

Sartre's sociopolitical ideal is thus one of a community of fully disalienated individuals, voluntarily engaged in perfectly mutual, practical, nonhierarchical relations, where rationality is the criterion for all decisions and where openness, sympathy, and a spirit of fraternity prevail.

Raymond Aron, who has followed the later Sartre more closely than most French critics, has clearly grasped this ideal and its function in Sartre's thought. He observes that, "lacking a concept of human nature, Sartre uses reciprocity as the criterion for judging the inhuman."[23] The image which I have been sketching is that of the fully human relationship as Sartre conceives it—the "Man" of his final interviews. It reminds us of the normative role that his anthropology has played from the outset, grounding first his ethics and subsequently his politics as well, a sequence canonized in ancient Greek philosophy. If his ideal of the "fully human" can serve Sartre as a moral norm and do so consistently, it is because of the abiding force of the primacy of praxis: if we continue to live inhuman lives, it is as much because of the abuse of freedom as it is due to "force of circumstance." That our alienation is a function of both, but with the accent on the former, is the message of his Marxist existentialism.

The Balance Sheet: Sartre, Philosopher of Dichotomies

With few exceptions, I have refrained from critical assessments of Sartre's work thus far in the belief that a thorough and sympathetic exposition would enhance the credibility of any subsequent evaluation. Moreover, my primary task has been to determine whether Sartre has a theory of collective responsibility based on a coherent social philosophy and, if so, how this exhibits his amalgamation of existentialism and Marxism. We have seen that he does indeed hold such a theory and that it incorporates, though not always with complete consistency, essential features both of existentialism and of Marxism. Yet the primacy of praxis and his revisionist Marxism lead us to conclude that *Sartre remains an existentialist.* No doubt, we may now call his existentialism "Marxist." He has succeeded in marrying a kind of Marxism to his brand of existentialism. His theory of collective responsibility witnesses this brokerage.

As I assume a critical stance toward the material discussed thus far, I shall stay with the root issues. To do otherwise would risk becoming engrossed in an endless series of interesting but secondary questions that have arisen along the way. Fortunately, the basic issues can be seen as five variations on a single theme, that of unresolved dichotomies.

Existentialist Responsibility: All/None

Those who call Sartre a Cartesian dualist are only half wrong. He never accepted a two-substance ontology or an inside-outside epistemology. Yet neither did he reject the cogito as a philosophic point of departure (see IF, 1:162), even if he insisted on its prereflective nature. To that extent, his valuing of intuitive evidence presumes a lingering philosophy of consciousness (Descartes, Husserl) in the midst of his conversion to praxis. Nowhere is this more evident than in the utter translucency that he claims for that inner gap, presence-to-self, which grounds Sartrean freedom.

Despite remarks indicating that "at the very level of nonthetic consciousness, intuition is conditioned by individual history" (IF, 1:148)—a claim whose compatibility with his epistemology of vision he never weighed—Sartre remained committed to a theory of complete self-transparency, both in the individual and, as we have seen, among individuals in the ideal society. Courting paradox, I should like to call this Sartre's angelism, by which I mean his demand that each of us be ontologically free, prereflectively translucent, and totally responsible. I am aware of the paradox, in that Sartre's praxis philosophy centers on interiorization and exteriorization among organic individuals in a field of material scarcity, whereas angels never get hungry. I call it angelism, not because he considers us disembodied spirits (we have just seen him embrace a kind of materialism) but because Sartre ascribes to us a responsibility that medieval thinkers reserved to angels.[24]

Like the angels, Sartrean man seems incapable of minor offenses (venial sins). The typology of individual and collective responsibilities listed in chapters 1 and 7 respectively admits of no degrees. No doubt there are exits from this dilemma. One could argue, for example, that "responsibility" is an analogous term or that it denotes a family resemblance. Room could then be found for more standard uses. But Sartre does not bother with such niceties. Consequently, he is frequently forced to overstate his case to the dismay of those who seek practical applications for his theory of responsibility.

Existentialist Ontology: Spontaneity/Inertia

The dichotomy that most thoroughly pervades Sartre's thought is doubtless that of spontaneity versus inertia. This characterizes the *pour-soi/en-soi* relation of his earlier works and continues as praxis/practico-inert later on. Although the relationship is more clearly dialectical in his later writings, none but a practical "synthesis" is ever achieved. On the contrary, the negative relationship is merely intensified as culture/nature. This bars Sartre from continuing on the trail blazed by the Marxists and John Dewey toward a full praxis philosophy. Sartre's commitment to a praxis philosophy seems halfhearted. In this ontological sense, he remains insuperably dualistic, as the list of oppositions drawn at the close of chapter 6 attests.

Sartre's particular form of dualism leaves in doubt the adequacy of his dialectical reason at several junctures. Chief among these for our purposes is the ambiguity of "situation" that we noted at the outset. This leaves the relation between the "given" and the "taken" indeterminable, which in turn clouds the issue of objective possibility so vital to his theory of collective responsibility and to his Marxism generally. For until a real dialectical exchange is established between practical organism and environment, both natural and "cultural," Sartre's appeal to objective conditioning can be regarded with a certain skepticism. In other words, the freedom-in-situation of the forties having become the freedom-in-conditions of the fifties and sixties, one is entitled to ask, "Are we conditioned or are we free?" "An analytic question," he will answer; "we are both together: totally conditioned yet totally free." At this point, dialectical reason is employed to engender reciprocity out of seeming nonsense. This carries a certain plausibility in the Hegelian tradition, including Marx and Dewey, that is denied Sartre. For, given his uncompromising spontaneity/

inertia dichotomy, Sartre owes us an explanation of the meaning of "conditioned." Otherwise, his appeal to dialectic looks simply verbal.

Existentialist Social Theory: Same/Other

I have argued that Sartre's dialectical nominalism marks a real advance in the controversy between holists and individualists in social theory. It is here he achieves a genuine dialectic of same and other that clarifies the possibilities and the limits to social integration in series and group. The difficulty here is not that Sartre failed to offer any but a practical synthesis of the same and the other—no other social synthesis seems possible. Rather, it is that he fails to examine the nature of the relations that constitute the reality of the group. Since agents-in-relation are for him as for Marx the ultimate constituents of social reality,[25] each owes us an ontology of relations but neither provides it. In Sartre's case the lack is more pronounced because it leads him to the erroneous contrast of the ontological and the practical. Had he given the theory of relations the slightest attention, he would have hesitated to attach the nominalist epithet to his dialectic. Moreover, he would have had no difficulty with the interworld or even with the intrasubjective.

Existentialist Politics: Socialism/Freedom

It has gradually become clear that Sartre is a libertarian socialist. We are now in a position to see why this is the natural politics for such an existentialist. To the degree that he grounds freedom on presence-to-self and defines "sovereignty" in the abstract as coterminous with individual praxis, he cannot help but be libertarian. And to the extent that scarcity which leads to serial dispersion is viewed as the source of unfreedom (alienation), the existentialist's concrete freedom, this side of abundance, must be achieved within the group. But, given that concrete freedom requires the recognition of other freedoms, socialism must obtain even in conditions of abundance. Finally, insofar as politics deals primarily with power relationships and power, at least outside the group, is alienating, existential "politics" is really an antipolitics (as is the politics of Marx)[26]—it aims for the day when it can self-destruct.

Now this "anarchist" model of society as a town meeting writ large seems inapplicable to a community that significantly exceeds Plato's limit of 5,040 citizens.[27] This standard objection of the anarchist's foes assumes particular force in a complex and highly technological society such as ours.

But my criticism is leveled at Sartre's assumption that *all* power is alienating, unless exercised within the group, and particularly that all

198

authority is a form of subjection to an alien will. I have called this his command theory of authority. We can prescind from the difficulties this entails by virtue of its affinity to the command theory of law, and see that it is a corollary to his all-or-none concept of responsibility and its "angelic" anthropology criticized above. As no room is left in his theory of responsibility for the ambiguous, the uncertain, and the attenuated, so his politics assumes that mutuality (reciprocal autonomy) and authority necessarily exclude each other. Yet it is clear that some submission to rules (to authority in a minimal sense) is a necessary condition for the epistemic and social community Sartre advocates. How else can one make sense of that "power of persuasion" which is to supplant coercion in the free society?

Furthermore, as the *mot d'ordre,* though practico-inert, still functions as a "vehicle of sovereignty" (CDR, 380) because each "gives it to himself" in Rousseau's phrase, so a limited fidelity-trust relationship seems quite compatible with mutuality in a less than angelic world. Sartre dismisses both belief and authority because of the otherness (heteronomy) they entail. I would contend rather that their common feature is a reliance on extrinsic evidence which, when adequate, renders both belief and "obedience" reasonable. Since the reason for proffering belief or obedience is not the intrinsic evidence of the proposition or imperative itself but the warrant of the one who utters the statement or issues the command, the corresponding act on the part of the agent is one of trust, a communication of freedoms that extends beyond, but not counter to, the limits of intrinsic evidence.

This is a far cry from that "sacrifice of intellect and will" which Sartre and rationalists in general so sharply denounce, for the agent maintains his criteria of intrinsic evidence. If the one to be trusted violates these norms, it is possible and advisable to withdraw allegiance. Reciprocity no longer obtains. Indeed, it is difficult to understand how the society Sartre advocates can exist solely on intrinsically evidential situations. The friendship and communion he prizes are themselves the fruit of fidelity-trust relations. This may spell the end of a kind of power politics, but not the end of authority.

Rather than speak of command-obedience, therefore, we should refer to fidelity-trust. My claim is that it is not counter to mutuality; indeed it is one of its highest expressions, to place one's trust in another (not as other, but as "the same," as alter ego), provided only that this be a reasonable act and not a blind or impulsive "leap." Here as elsewhere, Sartre's "angelism" demands the rational, when the reasonable is what we require.

199

Existentialist Marxism: Freedom/Necessity

Sartre seems never to have felt comfortable with his Marxism. His support of the Communist party in the early fifties was based, as he put it, "on *my* principles and not *theirs*" (CP, 68; emphasis his). By 1974 he could avow to Michel Contat, "I am *no longer* a Marxist."[28] Doubtless the command-obedience relationship that obtained between the party and the individual repelled him, though it did not prevent his recommending the party to the workers, presumably as the least of the evils that they could choose. But the growing demand for concrete freedom that led him to Marxism kept him from casting his lot there unconditionally. If the Marxists gave him the necessary concepts of objective possibility and collective causal-responsibility, he found them insensitive to the crucial existentialist category of contingency and without moral respect for the individual as a sovereign praxis. To the extent that political expediency motivated a certain "amoralist realism" during the late forties and early fifties, this can be read as an example of Sartre's "thinking against himself," a characteristic tendency, confirmed by his subsequent moves.

At a more abstract level, the chief barrier to Sartre's wholehearted conversion to Marxism is the freedom/necessity dichotomy. Despite reference to the decisive influence of economic conditions "in the final analysis," Sartre and the Marxists remain on opposite sides of the distinction. I suggested in chapter 9 that this may be merely a matter of emphasis since both sides appeal to a "dialectical" resolution. But it has become clear that the term "dialectical" doesn't have the same meaning for Sartre as for Marx. Even the most liberal reading of the latter ascribes to him a "soft" determinism that Sartre must reject.[29] Much turns on the precise meaning that can be given those synonyms he offers for "condition" such as "exigency" and "obscure constraint." But as I noted, Sartre never gave himself to such specificities. No matter how deforming the circumstance, Sartre continues to insist that we can always make something out of what others have made of us. Objective possibility has limited that "something" but it can never destroy it. Yet if Sartre is to be left with more than noetic freedom-responsibility, the nature of that limit must be explained. As long as his basic spontaneity/inertia dichotomy prevails, we seem to be dealing with occasions and not with dialectical (reciprocal) conditions at all.

As we reflect on these various unresolved dichotomies, we might well ask what happened to Althusser's "philosopher of mediations." The mediating factors, of course, are present in full force. As we have seen, his entire social ontology turns on them. But at almost every juncture Sartre exhibits a certain "failure of nerve" as the naturalists would say. Or is it

200

robust common sense? In either case, these dichotomies, all/none, same/other, socialism/freedom, freedom/necessity and, most radically, spontaneity/inertia exist not in simple opposition, much less in dialectical resolution (*Aufhebung*), but in creative tension. Sartre seems to be telling us that if the positivists explain too little, the Hegelians account for too much; that whether it be in the individual-social, the ethical-political, or the more basic freedom-necessity relationships, we must not settle for brute fact or for easy reductions but must "have the courage to go to the limits . . . in both directions at once" (SG, 599). He has led the way in this respect by his treatment of collective responsibility. His theory has incorporated the foregoing dichotomies, pushing them to the limits and thereby revealing important facets both of responsibility and of the collective.

But there remains a final dichotomy that permeates Sartre's work and especially his thinking on collective responsibility. It affords a last perspective on this issue and suggests a reading that tames the hyperboles and softens many of the paradoxes we have encountered along our way. I mean the essential opposition of the real and the unreal.

Collective Responsibility as Socioethical Ideal

Mounting his incisive critique of surrealism in *What Is Literature?* Sartre admitted that "the only poetic movement of the first half of the 20th century" contributed to human liberation. "But what it frees," he continued, "is neither desire nor human totality; it is the pure imagination. Now pure imagination and praxis are difficult to make compatible" (*Situations,* 2:324).

I have criticised Sartre's theory of collective responsibility from the viewpoint of unresolved dichotomies and have assessed its success in combining Marxist and existentialist insights. I shall bring this investigation to a close with some reflections on collective responsibility as an ideal in the Kantian sense, as a point of reference for totalizing society. Like the value-image discussed in chapter 3, such an ideal, though not descriptively accurate, can lead to model citizens and fully moral social relations, provided each person acts *as if* it were true. As Sartre achieved a practical "synthesis" of self and other in the group, so it is precisely as a practical ideal that collective responsibility can bridge the gap which he observes between praxis and the purely imaginative.

Sartre has consistently championed the power of the negative and, with it, that of the imaginary. The revolutionary philosopher, for example, must appeal to the future society as a value, that is, as "the appeal of what does not yet exist" (MR, 235). What Sartre dislikes about "political positivism," that realism which is "the favorite thesis of the collaborator," is that it rejects this power of the negative, which is likewise that of human freedom. A typically Sartrean lesson drawn from the Resistance (and, we might add, from the events of May 1968) is that "the role of man is to know how to say *no* to the facts, even when it seems one ought to submit to them" (*Situations,* 3:61). This is the function of his "city of ends," three of whose features I analyzed earlier. But if we regard Sartre's sociopolitical ideal as an ethical vision, the aspect of collective responsibility comes to the fore. Let us review several examples in this light, under the aspect of collective responsibility as an ethical ideal. Some otherwise exaggerated claims should then appear less offensive.

"We are all assassins" is the title of an essay written at the height of the Algerian war of independence. Earlier I dealt with Sartre's argument there and in related works. Given the practico-inert bonds linking all parties to the colonialist system and the fact that everyone in the mother country benefits from the exploitation of the native which that system entails (claims that presumably can be empirically established), Sartre's cry of collective guilt is not mere rhetoric. But if read in the sense I am now suggesting, it can serve to spur the metropolitan populace to active support of the Algerians' cause. Sartre's failure to speak of degree of responsibility in such remarks tends to weaken their descriptive force. But if we read them in the hortative mode of an ethical ideal, they assume a legitimate meaning and a special force. They translate into something like the following: "Act as if you were each responsible for the assassinations carried out in the colony by your soldiers in your name. Only then will your consciousnesses be raised to move you to serious action against such atrocities." This is more than a form of Plato's "noble lie." It is a call to heightened moral sensitivity and, as such, constitutes a clear moral imperative.

My second example is the implicit command to "interiorize multiplicity" given in the midst of the fusing group. As we know, this enables each to say, "We are a hundred strong!" and by that very claim to make it so. I should like to reiterate that the crucial phenomenon of "interiorizing multiplicity," which bears more than merely psychological import for Sartre, should be read as the imperative: "Accept responsibility for the whole." This exhortation to collective responsibility is, I believe, Sartre's social imperative par excellence. It challenges particularist, self-centered consciousnesses to judge and act in terms of meanings larger than themselves. In Rousseau's sense, it turns men into citizens.[30]

A final example to be read in the light of collective responsibility as an ethical ideal is taken from Sartre's last major interview mentioned earlier. He had been collaborating with his young Maoist friend Benny Lévy (alias Pierre Victor) on a book to be called *Pouvoir et liberté* which, as he claimed elsewhere, would "leave nothing standing from *Being and Nothingness* and the *Critique*." Its chief innovation, he insisted, would be to construct "an ethic of the *We*."[31] In the final interview he enunciates some aspects of that ethics. It will be based, not on the futile desire to be God made famous in *Being and Nothingness,* but on a kind of "desire for society," for a new relation among men (fraternity). These are not "the socioeconomic relations that Marx envisaged." Rather, they are "the true social goals of ethics" and at the same time "the true principle of the Left." In this respect, he still insists on the ideal of the *Critique:* "Our goal is to arrive at a veritable constituted body where each person would be a man and where the collectivities would *be equally human.*"[32] To be man "truly and totally" means developing certain seeds that are already growing in that direction, despite our present "subhuman" condition. With persistent optimism he insists that a kind of humanism which appeals to that authentic tendency is already possible. Counter to a narcissistic egoism, it advocates "essentially the ethic of relationships with the Other. And that is a moral theme which will last once man truly comes to be." Sartre recommends that even we, living in a less than human era, should embrace this humanism "as . . . our effort to be beyond ourselves, in the circle of men."[33]

Again, if we read this recommended effort at self-transcendence in terms of the ideal of collective responsibility, we can understand how the goal aimed at and its present anticipation do not voice simply an individualistic respect for the rights and duties of all—fruit of the bourgeois humanism he detests—but ground a genuine *ethics of the We* as he had promised. By judging and acting in terms of the collective, one is truly going beyond oneself and entering "the circle of men." Sartre implies this when he continues: "This self considering itself as self for the other, having a relationship with the other, is what I call moral consciousness." The image of brotherhood to which Sartre appeals in these final interviews is best articulated as the appropriation of collective responsibility: each is his brother's keeper.

This vision of what man can be—of what men can be together—gave Sartre hope in his blindness and old age. His final temptation to despair came from the thought that we shall never be done with invasions, cold wars, exploitation, and the rest; that the most we can hope for are minor rebellions, limited goals, and momentary respites. Yet he courageously rejected this notion: "That's the tranquil despair of an old man who will die in it. But that's precisely what I'm resisting, and I know that I shall die in hope—but we must ground this hope."[34]

These are among his last recorded words in a lifetime of struggling by means of art and argument to keep hope afloat in a sea of injustice, failure

203

(*l'échec*), and despair. Significantly, his words hold forth the prospect of a time when men will be as brothers, and they are words that sound the call to bring it about—Sartre's moral legacy to us.

What at the start of this inquiry seemed like an attempt to square the circle (finding in Sartre's thought an ideal of collective responsibility as well as the ontology to ground it) can now be perceived as a sort of half-fulfilled promise uttered by a moral leader as he dies with intimations of his goal. Such is Sartre, the lonely thinker, apostle of individual responsibility, for whom the Other's existence was man's original fall, gradually discovering in the contingencies of history the need and the joy of communal action. It is as if the small boy who so wanted an invitation to play with the others in the Luxembourg Gardens[35] had finally, at mid-life, been allowed to join in and, in his old age, had come to champion this hard-won sense of brotherhood as the model and goal of what it is to be human: "A whole man, composed of all men and as good as all of them and no better than any,"[36] but in the company of men.

Jean-Paul Sartre *Vivant:* The Existentialist as Social Theorist

"To be dead is to be a prey for the living" (BN, 543). It is we who take (noetic) responsibility for the dead. This conviction doubtless motivated Sartre's life-long concern with the judgment of future generations. Not that he was hungry for the immortality of fame—he declined to be enrolled among the "immortals" of the Académie française—but because he was keenly sensitive to the fact that meaning (and hence "History") is an ongoing, human construct. Sartre's work, upon his death, remains alive only in our projects. And yet in fashioning that project, we cannot ignore the objective features of his work—some rocks do not lend themselves to scaling. One final time we are faced with the ambiguity of the given and the taken in Sartre's philosophy, now reflected in that legacy itself.

At the outset I spoke of the challenge of producing an existentialist social philosophy. Has Sartre carried it off? Does he leave us a coherent and plausible answer to the ground question of social theory, the individual-social relation? And since the meaning is that of *our* project, not his, is there promise of future development in his concepts and categories or must we regard his social theory as merely a sterile hybrid, a philosophic cul de sac?

We have witnessed the conceptual moves in Sartre's shift from the interpersonal (the dual) to the social properly speaking, especially his adoption of the praxis model for social relations and his introduction of the mediating Third. This marks the true "birth of humanity" (CDR, 436) and of man as a social being. The praxis model along with objective possibility opens him to Marxism; the mediating Third is pivotal to a social ontology based on dialectical reason. Sartre thereby joins the dialectical sociologists and eo ipso shares their tradition of methodological holism. Yet his "dialectical nominalism," as we know, keeps the holists at bay by asserting the threefold primacy of individual praxis, thus preserving the "existentialist" values of individual freedom and moral responsibility in the midst of social causation. It is failure to take seriously the dialectical nature of Sartre's "nominalism" that misled Raymond Aron into reading the *Critique* as a defense of methodological individualism.[1] Sartre's ultimate agents are individuals-in-relation like Marx's social individuals. It is the reality of these relations that separates Sartre from nominalists *simpliciter.*

If the "mediating Third" carries existentialist values into social life, the "practico-inert" brings the corresponding disvalues, alienation and flight from responsibility, to the Marxist realm of economic and technological determinism.[2] This concept embraces not only those "material conditions of life" which Marx located at the base of social existence, but the institutions, practices, and "milieux" of the superstructure itself. If the ideal of "science" since Aristotle has been to gather the many into one, Sartre's concept of the practico-inert raises the "material conditions of life" to a new level of generality, while underscoring their grounding in individual praxis. No doubt "practico-inert" is even more abstract than "forces and relations of production." But it enjoys a correspondingly broader scope; as modified by scarcity, for example, it accounts for continued alienation in socialist societies.

The promise of Sartre's social theory lies first in the space it creates for phenomenologies of social being such as his own arresting descriptions of the revolutionary group-in-fusion and the Flaubert family. Many such analyses are called for, but they need not remain isolated in the realm of eidetic description. By dialectical linkage with praxis and the practico-inert, they can share the explanatory power of these concepts. Likewise, the progressive-regressive method incorporates existential psychoanalyses such as those of Genet, Flaubert, and Sartre himself. Because individual praxis is primary, we can and should understand the agent's project in joining the group or "choosing" to remain a passively active, serial individual. Rom Harré notes "the striking absence of a plausible social psychology" in Marx's social thought.[3] Members of the so-called Frankfurt school of social theory have sought to correct this fault. Sartre, who excelled in psychological descriptions, has further remedied this defect and, characteristically, has done so in a manner that highlights the moral responsibility of the agents involved.

So it should be clear that Sartre has established himself as a social theorist without abandoning his existentialist commitments. Indeed, the genius of his pivotal concepts is precisely to bring these values to bear on the "impersonal" domain of social causation. Still, the slope of his thinking continues to incline toward the individual. That is why we should characterize him as a "Marxist" *existentialist*. But the understanding of human sociality, far from "eluding Sartre's grasp," as Aronson insists,[4] is furthered by appeal to (practico-inert) structure and counterfinality and by reference to "synthetically enriched" praxis with its specific modalities. What Sartre's theory lacks most basically, I have said, is an ontology of relations. But that is absent from most contemporary social theories. It is missing in Marx as well.

Still, the tensions remain, and appropriately so for a philosopher of dichotomies. Does this mean the ultimate failure of a philosophy of mediations, of a dialectical philosophy? Yes and no. Yes, to the extent that his dichotomies preclude "ultimate" synthesis. His oppositions leave us with ongoing "surpassings" (*dépassements*) of distinctions in creative tension. We can expect totalization, not totality, as long as praxis is included as an integral part. Yes, too, insofar as the relation between the objective and the subjective (the given and the taken) remains inherently obscure.

But if Sartre has failed to bring his dialectical philosophy to any but an imaginative term (collective responsibility as socioethical ideal), this could well be because none but a practical "synthesis" of his dichotomies is possible. This will appear scandalous only to those whose dialectic is omnivorous; who hope for more than a practical synthesis; who expect to "subsume" the inert in the spontaneous, immanence in transcendence, the other in the same, and the individual in the social. Sartre, as we have seen, always displayed a healthy respect for the individual's radical "No!", that is, for ontological freedom as the power to betray. Appropriately, he crowns his social theory with reference to an end-goal, not an end-terminus, of history. But how better to limn the moral configuration of his entire project? And what more fitting "synthesis" to the social thought of an existentialist, moralist, and philosopher of the imagination?

Notes

Introduction

1. Lucien Goldmann, *Marxisme et Sciences Humaines* (Paris: Gallimard, 1970), p. 327. All translations, unless otherwise noted, are my own.

2. Karl Jaspers, *The Question of German Guilt,* trans. E. B. Ashton (New York: Dial Press, 1947), and Roman Ingarden, *Über die Verantwortung* (Stuttgart: Reclam, 1970).

3. Mary Warnock, *The Philosophy of Jean-Paul Sartre* (London: Hutchinson University Library, 1965), pp. 135 and 157, and George Kline, "The Existentialist Rediscovery of Hegel and Marx," in Edward N. Lee and Maurice Mandelbaum, eds., *Phenomenology and Existentialism* (Baltimore: Johns Hopkins University Press, 1967), p. 137.

4. That is the point of Sheridan's *Sartre: The Radical Conversion* (Athens, Ohio: Ohio University Press, 1973).

5. Marjorie Grene, *Sartre* (New York: New Viewpoints, 1973), p. 270.

6. Ronald Aronson, *Jean-Paul Sartre* (London: New Left Books, Verso Editions, 1980), pp. 11 and 285ff.

7. See, for example, Theodor Schwarz, *Jean-Paul Sartres 'Kritik der Dialektischen Vernunft'* (Berlin: Veb Deutscher Verlag der Wissenschaften, 1967), pp. 133–34.

8. Hazel E. Barnes, *Sartre* (Philadelphia: Lippincott, 1973), p. 105. Yet she contends that "the basic ontology which serves as [the *Critique*'s] philosophical foundation is still that of *Being and Nothingness*" (p. 135).

9. István Mészáros, *The Work of Sartre,* vol. 1, *Search for Freedom* (Atlantic Highlands, N.J.: Humanities Press, 1979), pp. 14 and 77.

10. Fredric Jameson, *Marxism and Form* (Princeton, N.J.: Princeton University Press, 1971), p. 209.

11. Jameson, *Marxism,* p. xv.

12. Mark Poster, *Sartre's Marxism* (London: Pluto Press, 1979), p. 80.

13. Raymond Aron, *History and the Dialectic of Violence,* trans. Barry Cooper (Oxford: Blackwell, 1975), p. 200; for Warnock and Kline, see n. 3 above.

14. Mészáros, *Work,* p. 144.

15. See Jameson, *Marxism,* pp. 287 ff., Aronson, *Philosophy,* pp. 207 ff., and Wilfrid Desan, *The Marxism of Jean-Paul Sartre* (Garden City, N.Y.: Doubleday Anchor Books, 1965), p. v.

16. See, e.g., Joel Feinberg's seminal *Doing and Deserving* (Princeton, N.J.: Princeton University Press, 1970) and Peter A. French, ed., *Individual and Collective Responsibility* (Cambridge, Mass.: Schenkman, 1972).

17. In an interview in *Der Spiegel* on the German premier of *The Condemned*

of Altona, Sartre admits to having been influenced by Jaspers's *The Question of German Guilt* in the matter of collective responsibility. See below, chap. 5, n. 16.

Chapter One

1. See Søren Kierkegaard, *Philosophical Fragments,* trans. David Swenson, rev. Howard V. Hong (Princeton, N.J.: Princeton University Press, 1967), pp. 93ff.

2. See Martin Heidegger, *Being and Time,* trans. John Macquarrie and Edward Robinson (New York: Harper and Row, 1962), par. 64; and Jean-Paul Sartre, *Being and Nothingness,* trans. Hazel E. Barnes (New York: Philosophical Library, 1956), pp. 308 and 322; hereafter cited as BN. Where I employ my own translations from Sartre's works available in English versions, I shall follow the English citation by a reference to the original, designated by "F" and the page number. Publication information for the originals will be found after that of their translations in the bibliography.

Already in his *The Emotions: Outline of a Theory,* trans. Bernard Frechtman (New York: Philosophical Library, 1948), hereafter cited as EMO, Sartre speaks of the possibility of drawing up "a 'hodological' map of our *umwelt,* a map which varies as a function of our acts and needs" (p. 57).

3. Translated by Forrest Williams and Robert Kirkpatrick (New York: The Noonday Press, 1957); hereafter cited as TE.

4. See his essay, "Intentionality: A Fundamental Idea of Husserl's Phenomenology," trans. Joseph P. Fell, *Journal of the British Society for Phenomenology* 1, no. 2 (May 1970), pp. 4–5.

5. Translated by Bernard Frechtman (New York: Washington Square Press, 1966); hereafter cited as PI.

6. This is a thesis which I develop at length in my "The Role of the Image in Sartre's Aesthetic," *Journal of Aesthetics and Art Criticism* 33 (1975), pp. 431–42.

7. For a discussion of constitution and meaning-giving (*Sinngebung*) in Husserl, see Robert Sokolowski, *The Formation of Husserl's Concept of Constitution* (The Hague: Martinus Nijhoff, 1970).

8. See Edmund Husserl, *Ideas,* First Book, *General Introduction to a Pure Phenomenology,* trans. F. Kersten (The Hague: Martinus Nijhoff, 1982), pars. 27–32.

9. "Materialism and Revolution," in *Literary and Philosophical Essays,* trans. and ed. Annette Michelson (New York: Collier Books, 1962), p. 225; see also pp. 235–36 (hereafter cited as MR).

10. Many commentators erroneously conflate what Sartre distinguishes, at least when he is being careful, namely, the *pre*reflective and the *ir*reflective. It is the former which I have been discussing. The latter, technically speaking, is no longer prereflective but neither is it "positional" of a reflective object. Rather, it resembles Husserl's "neutrality" thesis where the world's reality status is held at bay in order to describe its various modes of givenness; see Husserl, *Ideas,* pars. 109–17. For Sartre's use of the distinction, see PI (F) pp. 204 and 223, and *L'Idiot de*

la Famille, 3 vols. (Paris: Gallimard, 1971–72), 2: 1544 (hereafter cited as IF).

11. In *The Transcendence of the Ego* Sartre concedes that I will be more familiar with my own ego than with that of others (!), despite its objective status, and in *Being and Nothingness* allows it the status of "quasi object," thus distinguishing it from other objects of consciousness.

12. Sartre distinguishes knowledge from simple awareness or prereflective consciousness. The former is a phenomenon of reflective consciousness where the subject-object distinction obtains. The latter is prior to such a distinction. Hence, it can occur that someone will later come to know what he has been aware of all along—Sartre's way of dealing with psychoanalytic data without appealing to an unconscious.

13. Thus Hazel Barnes translates *est été* as "is made-to-be" (BN, 78); Maurice Natanson renders it "is-was" (see *A Critique of Jean-Paul Sartre's Ontology* [The Hague: Martinus Nijhoff, 1973] p. 59); and Peter Caws offers us "is been," explaining that this turning of "to be" into a reflexive verb captures Sartre's nuance that the for-itself is "a self-sustaining reflection of Being upon itself" (*Sartre* [London: Routledge and Kegan Paul, 1979], p. 82).

14. One should not be misled by Sartre's claim, equally true, that "it is because human reality *is not* enough [i.e., exists as lack] that it is free" (BN, 440; F, 516). As world-surpassing, human reality is dynamically "more" than what it actually is, precisely because it is not all that it could and desires to be. Aristotle grasped this well in another context when he attempted to understand motion in terms of matter, form, and a third principle called "privation" (see *Physics* I, 5–7).

15. See R. M. Hare, *The Language of Morals* (New York: Oxford University Press, 1964), chap. 4, "Decisions of Principle."

16. The difficulty in translating *motif/mobile* into English lies in the fact that they do not fit exactly any of the terms in our already rather well-established vocabulary of reasons, causes, motives, and motivations. I have chosen "reason" and "motive" to render "motif" and "mobile" because they correspond to Sartre's similar distinction between these terms as objective and subjective respectively. Here is how he explains that distinction:

> By *motif* one ordinarily understands the reason [*la raison*] for an act; that is to say, the ensemble of rational considerations that justify it. . . . The *motif* is characterized . . . by an objective appreciation of the situation. . . . So we shall call *motif* the objective grasp of a determined situation in so far as that situation reveals itself in the light of a certain end as able to serve as means toward that end.
>
> *Mobile,* on the contrary, is ordinarily considered as a subjective fact. (BN, 445–46; F, 522)

Of course, even the reason (*le motif*) depends on the original "choice" of an end. As Sartre's explanation makes clear, "reason" (*motif*) denotes the factual situation as means to that chosen end, as in the adage: "Who wills the end wills the means." In this sense, Sartre's "reason" (*motif*) is similar to the "rational" in Max Weber's purposive-rational (*Zweckrational*) and value-rational (*Wertrational*) action.

NOTES TO PAGES 9–12

The novelty of Sartre's position in this matter consists in his linking the motif/ mobile distinction with that between nonreflective and reflective consciousness. He writes: "The voluntary act is distinguished from the nonvoluntary spontaneity in that the latter is purely unreflective [one of his less precise uses of "irréfléchie"] consciousness of reasons [*motifs*] via the project of the act pure and simple. As for the motive [*mobile*], it is not at all an object for itself in the unreflective act, but is simply nonpositional consciousness (of) self" (BN, 451; F, 529–30).

17. Jean-Paul Sartre, *Search for a Method,* trans. Hazel E. Barnes (New York: Random House, Vintage Books, 1968), p. 151; hereafter cited as SM.

Although he likens original choice to what psychologists term "selective attention" (see BN, 462), Sartre's most extended analogy to original choice is that of the Gestalt-shift operative in the figure-ground relationship of visual perception. My attention can focus on either of two alternatives but not on both at once. Thus I can see the book on the table or the table supporting the book. Whichever I see is my free choice; but the distribution of "givens" is a function of the "facticity," to borrow a common existentialist term, of my upsurge. We are faced with the ambiguity of the given and the taken in Sartre's epistemology, a direct reflection of the ambiguity in the relation between the for-itself and the in-itself in his ontology (see BN, 316–17).

18. Concluding his brief essay on intentionality in Husserl, Sartre exclaims: "We are delivered from Proust. We are likewise delivered from the 'internal life' " ("Intentionality: A Fundamental Idea," p. 5).

19. Sartre notes that the infinity of this reflection-reflecting relationship occurs with the *reflective* attempt to grasp the reflection-reflecting as totality (see BN, 78).

20. See below, chap. 5.

21. From the viewpoint of ekstatic temporality, "presence to—indicates existence outside oneself near to—" (BN, 121).

22. A position that Sartre maintained throughout his career: "You know how I conceive of the self [*le moi*]. I haven't changed: it is an object before us. That is to say, the self appears to our reflection when it unifies the reflected consciousness. Thus there is a pole of reflection that I call the self, the transcendent self, which is a quasi-object" (*Situations,* 10 vols. [Paris: Gallimard, 1947–76], 10:100).

23. "Our intention is . . . to reconquer man within Marxism" (SM, 83). For his criticism of "economism," see SM, 43ff.

24. Years later, in his brilliant study of Jean Genet, he explains that what he is calling "presence-to-self" is "this vague sense of a want of exact correspondence between the subjective and the objective" (*Saint Genet. Actor and Martyr,* trans. Bernard Frechtman [New York: George Braziller, 1963], p. 592; hereafter cited as SG).

25. Simone de Beauvoir renders this into less technical language when she writes: "To attain his truth, man must not attempt to dispel the ambiguity of his being but, on the contrary, accept the task of realizing it. He rejoins himself only to the extent that he agrees to remain at a distance from himself" (*The Ethics of Ambiguity,* trans. Bernard Frechtman [Secaucus, N.J.: The Citadel Press, 1948],

p. 13).

26. Correcting a mistaken impression which he had left in *The Transcendence of the Ego,* Sartre now admits that the prereflective consciousness is prepersonal, not impersonal, as he had claimed in that earlier work. See *La Transcendence de l'Ego,* intro., nn., and apps. Sylvie Le Bon (Paris: J. Vrin, 1965), p. 55n.

27. "Selfness" (*l'ipséité*) is the translation of Heidegger's *Selbstheit,* a neologism Sartre attributes to Heidegger's French translator, M. Cobin. In *Situations,* Sartre describes it succinctly as "the existential return from project to self . . . which gives birth to the self" (1:148).

28. Almost thirty years later he will repeat substantially this claim, using the categories of *L'Idiot* when he observes that "selfness [is] the lived [*le vécu*] as perpetual reference-to-self through time and space" (IF, 2:1295–96). For his discussion of selfness in terms of praxis and the practico-inert; that is, in the language of the *Critique of Dialectical Reason,* see IF, 2:1294.

29. For an interesting discussion of pervasive responsibility, see Stephen David Ross, *The Nature of Moral Responsibility* (Detroit: Wayne State University Press, 1973), pp. 226–35.

30. Nothing illustrates the range of responsibility as Sartre conceives it so clearly as does the following brief catalogue from the pages of BN. Throughout that work Sartre insists that consciousness is responsible: (a) for the fact that "there is" an Other, "In so far as I am conscious (of) myself as one of my free possibilities and in so far as I project myself toward myself in order to realize this selfness, to that extent I am responsible for the existence of the Other. It is I who by the very affirmation of my free spontaneity make there to be an Other and not simply an infinite reference of consciousness to itself" (BN, 287); (b) for the fact that "there are" things, "It is our freedom which is responsible for the fact that *there are* things with all their indifference, their unpredictability, and their adversity, and for the fact that we are inevitably separated from them; for it is on the ground of nihilation that they appear and that they are revealed as bound one to another" (BN, 509); (c) for being an object, "And when I naively assume that it is possible for me to be an objective being without being responsible for it" (BN, 309); (d) for my being, "It is facticity that causes me to apprehend myself simultaneously as totally responsible for my being and as totally unjustifiable" (BN, 309); "for the for-itself can *be* only if it has chosen itself" (BN, 445); (e) for my past, "It is the future which decides whether the past is living or dead. . . . But it depends on my actual freedom to confirm the meaning of these anticipations by again accepting responsibility for them—i.e., by anticipating the future which they anticipated—or to invalidate them by simply anticipating another future" (BN, 499); (f) for my situation, "Thus I am absolutely free and absolutely responsible for my situation. But I am never free except *in situation*" (BN, 509); (g) for the existence of the human race, "and the necessary connections which accompany the essential elements of man appear only on the foundation of a free choice; in this sense each for-itself is responsible in its being for the existence of a human race" (BN, 520); (h) for techniques, "Thus the for-itself is responsible for the fact that the Other's conduct is revealed in the world as techniques" (BN,

213

521); (i) for my death, "By being interiorized, it [my death] is individualized. . . . Hence, I become responsible for *my* death as for my life" (BN, 532); (j) for the dead, "Of course the dead choose us, but it is necessary first that we have chosen them. . . . Thus by its very facticity the for-itself is thrown into full 'responsibility' with respect to the dead; it is obliged to decide freely the fate of the dead" (BN, 542); (k) and finally for the existence of my possessions, "Thus I am responsible for the existence of my possessions in the human order. Through ownership I raise them up to a certain type of functional being. . . . I draw the collection of my surroundings into being along with myself. If they are taken from me, they die as my arm would die if it were severed from me" (BN, 509).

31. For a brief history of both aspects of the term, see Richard McKeon, "The Development and the Significance of the Concept of Responsibility," *Revue Internationale de Philosophie* 11 (1957), pp. 3–32.

32. "Existentialism Is a Humanism," in *Existentialism from Dostoevsky to Sartre,* ed. Walter Kaufmann (Cleveland: Meridian Books, 1956), p. 291 (hereafter cited as EH).

33. Elaborating on this claim that I am "as profoundly responsible for the war as if I had myself declared it," Sartre concedes that "this responsibility is of a very particular type" (BN, 555). That type, as we shall now see, is specifically noetic responsibility.

34. See H. L. A. Hart, "The Ascription of Responsibility and Rights," in Antony Flew, ed., *Logic and Language,* 1st and 2d series (Garden City, N.Y.: Anchor Books, 1965), pp. 151–74. The "defeasibility" thesis was later repudiated by Hart; see Joel Feinberg, *Doing and Deserving* (Princeton, N.J.: Princeton University Press, 1970), p. viii.

35. Elsewhere in BN he identifies this power to be, i.e., to make a situation exist, with freedom itself: "*Freedom* is an objective quality of the Other as the unconditioned power of modifying situations. This power is not to be distinguished from that which originally constitutes the Other and which is the power to make a situation exist in general. In fact, to be able to modify a situation is precisely to make a situation exist" (BN, 350).

36. The problematic Sartrean self intervenes here to render an apparently straightforward issue ambiguous. In the matter of self-determination, which "self" is determining the choice to abjure, the empirical ego or the presence-to-self? If it is the empirical ego (the ideal subject pole of reflective awareness), then "I could have done otherwise" is true only if "I" had been another empirical ego, with another character, other dispositions, habits, and the like—just as the determinists claim. But, of course, Sartre's contention is that, because of original choice, I can in effect be someone else, at least in the sense of being able to change my individuating project by conversion. Sartre, as usual, achieves dramatic effect by conflating these two levels of selfness. Yet he succeeds in placing the contrast in relief when, in another context, he asks: "Could I have done otherwise without perceptibly modifying the organic totality of the projects which I am? . . . I could have done otherwise. Agreed. But at what price?" (BN, 454). The determinists admit that I could have done otherwise (indeed, that I would have done so) if "I"

had been someone else, paradoxical as this expression remains. But they simply deny that "I" could have been someone else. Sartre, on the contrary, asserts that the "I" (empirical ego) is a product of original choice (presence-to-self) and that the latter, as shot through with otherness, the inner distance whereby the for-itself is self-nihilating, can always "choose" another basic project. Conversion is always a possibility, which is not to say that it is a common phenomenon.

37. We must be careful to distinguish this use from Sartre's technical term, "appropriation," which signifies the inauthentic project of the for-itself's becoming at the same time in-itself by assimilating the latter through knowledge, eating, sex, material possessions, and the like.

Chapter Two

1. See his *The Rules of Sociological Method*, trans. Sarah A. Solovay and John H. Mueller, 8th ed. (New York: The Free Press, 1966), p. 13.

2. It is not clear how seriously we should take his claim that being-for-others is as fundamental as being-for-itself (see BN, 218), since being-for-others is obviously dependent on being-for-itself, which seems to be independent of it. Given the Hegelian inspiration not only of these terms but also of much of the analysis in BN, and the paradigmatic role of Hegel's Master/Slave dialectic for Sartre's theory of self-consciousness, it is clear that the for-itself is basically dependent on the for-others in order to arrive at self-consciousness.

3. The best-known incident is that of the person spying on a couple through a keyhole, who is suddenly frozen by the sound of footsteps behind him. His visual "objectification" of the others has itself been objectified, the *sens* which he had imposed on them has been incorporated in another's *sens;* their possibilities, which he had "stolen" by his look, have themselves been "robbed" along with his own by the other's gaze. In sum, his shame-consciousness articulates an (ontologically) prior awareness of another as subject. He could not have experienced himself as a transcendence transcended if there had not been such a prior awareness of another freedom. Even if the "footsteps" turn out to be nothing but the rustle of the curtains before an open window, the experience of another subjectivity is the precondition for the possibility of the shame-consciousness that surfaced at that moment.

4. In the example of someone's being mistakenly "seen" by another, it is the awareness of the other's original, prenumerical presence that serves as the condition for shame-consciousness, even erroneous shame-consciousness (see above, n. 3).

5. See below, chapter 8, and CM, 487.

6. In a spoken preface to a recording of *No Exit*, for example, the post-*Critique* Sartre explains the line from that play, "Hell is other people," which hounded him for years: "I mean that *if* relations with the Other are contorted, corrupt, then the Other can only be hell" (as quoted in Francis Jeanson, *Sartre dans sa Vie* [Paris: Editions du Seuil, 1974], p. 114; emphasis added). Everything hangs on the hypothesis and on the conditions for its realization. Scarcely a hint is given in BN that these conditions are socioeconomic. He admits this in CM, 430.

7. This point constitutes a major portion of his analysis of Jewish consciousness in the essay *Anti-Semite and Jew,* written shortly after the publication of *Being and Nothingness.* See *Anti-Semite and Jew,* trans. George J. Becker (New York: Schocken Books, 1965), p. 137; hereafter cited as AJ.

8. In fact Sartre will introduce the "oath" in the *Critique* in order to harness these relations via "fraternity-terror." But by then the looking/looked-at model will have been subsumed in a praxis model of society.

9. See *The Sociology of Georg Simmel,* trans. and ed. Kurt H. Wolff (New York: The Free Press, 1964), p. 129.

10. *Sociology of Simmel,* p. 145.

11. On the relation between objectification and alienation in the early and in the later Sartre, see below, p. 242 n.8. The Third constitutes the "Us,"as Sartre calls it, and we experience our "Us" status as a "community [*communautaire*] alienation," as "being-objects in common" (BN, 415; F, 486), and as "a still more radical alienation" than that felt in the face of the Other, because I am now constrained "to assume also a totality which [I] am not although [I] form an integral part of it" (BN, 419). See CM, 137–40.

12. For a discussion of objective possibility and class consciousness, see below, chap. 5.

13. "Thus whereas in the experience of being-for-others the upsurge of a dimension of real and concrete being is the condition for the very experience, the experience of the We-subject is a pure psychological, subjective event in a single consciousness; it corresponds to an inner modification of the structure of this consciousness but does not appear on the foundation of a concrete ontological relation with others and does not realize any *Mitsein*" (EN, 425).

14. Years later Sartre will rely heavily upon such "comprehension" of both individual and collective undertakings. See below, chap. 7.

15. But it would be a mistake simply to equate methodological individualism with one of its (more vulnerable) subspecies, "psychologism," as J. W. N. Watkins points out in a series of essays reprinted in *Modes of Individualism and Collectivism,* ed. John O'Neill (London: Heinemann, 1973), especially pp. 173ff. On the holist/individualist distinction, see below, chap. 7.

16. See Jean-Paul Sartre, David Rousset, and Gerard Rosenthal, *Entretiens sur la Politique* (Paris: Gallimard, 1949), p. 38.

17. Years later, commenting on his existentialist doctrine of unlimited choice, Sartre explained its genesis in terms of the limited experience of the Resistance where every Frenchman, he believed, had a simple option, either for or against the Germans: "The real political problems, of being 'for,' but' or 'against, but' were not posed by this experience. The result was that I concluded that in any circumstances, there is always a possible choice. Which is false." "Questioning Jean-Paul Sartre," *New Left Review,* no. 58 (November/December, 1969), p. 44.

18. "It is finally impossible for me to distinguish the unchangeable brute existence from the variable meaning [*sens*] which it includes" (BN, 498).

19. Pietro Chiodi, *Sartre and Marxism,* trans. Kate Soper (Atlantic Highlands, N.J.: Humanities Press, 1976), p. 15.

20. See below, chapter 5.

21. At this stage Sartre seems innocent of Saussure's *Cours de Linguistique Generale* and his famous langue/parole distinction, a lacuna which he will subsequently fill; see below, chap. 6, n.8.

22. In the *Critique* where choice becomes praxis, I shall refer to this as an instance of Sartre's principle of the primacy of (individual) praxis. Then as now it will serve as the bastion for the existentialist values of individual freedom and responsibility.

23. See AJ, 67, 89–101 and 136–38.

Chapter Three

1. "The Itinerary of a Thought," in Jean-Paul Sartre, *Between Existentialism and Marxism,* trans. John Mathews (New York: William Morrow, 1974), p. 34; hereafter cited as BEM.

2. See *Sartre, un Film,* produced by Alexandre Astruc and Michel Contat (Paris: Gallimard, 1977), pp. 99–103; Jeanson, *Sartre,* p. 230n.

3. His "amoral realism" during this time was more apparent than real. For Sartre's claim, see ORR, 78, and *Sartre, un film,* 99–101; for alternative views of the matter, see Jeanson, *Sartre,* 230, and my "L'Imagination au pouvoir," 171.

4. See Sartre, Rousset, and Rosenthal, *Entretiens,* especially p. 39. For a step-by-step analysis of Sartre's relations with the Communist movement since the Second World War, see Franco Fe, *Sartre e il communismo* (Florence: La Nouva Italia, 1970).

5. Simone de Beauvoir shares this vision in her *Ethics of Ambiguity:* "Perhaps it is permissible to dream of a future when men will know no other use of their freedom than this free unfurling of itself; constructive activity would be possible for all; each would be able to aim positively through his projects at his own future" (EA, 81). Sartre's socioethical ideal, treated briefly later in this chapter, will be discussed at length in chapter 10. See CM, 421–42 and 487.

6. See SM, 34. The two moments, disalienation and reciprocity, are described as essential to the "revolutionary movement," the latter as its *terminus ad quem* (see MR, 218). An insight into the relation between ethics and politics as Sartre conceives them as well as an explanation for his "amoral realism" of several years is gained from his early *What is Literature?* (1947). Consider, for example, the following: "At present, a good will is not possible or rather it can only be the intent to render the good will possible" (*Situations,* 2:297).

7. Among the bridge essays between Sartre's existentialist and his Marxist periods, I am considering the following, with date of original publication: "Présentation des *Temps modernes*" (1945), *Anti-Semite and Jew* (1946), *Existentialism Is a Humanism* (1946), "Materialism and Revolution" (1946), "The Responsibility of the Writer" (1947), *What Is Literature?* (1947), and *Entretiens sur la Politique* (1949). For relevant passages in CM, see 54, 95, and 484–544.

8. See *Sartre, un film,* pp. 94–95, and Francis Jeanson, *Sartre and the Problem of Morality,* trans. Robert V. Stone (Bloomington: Indiana University Press, 1980), p. 22, and translator's note.

9. This is similar to what John Findlay describes in axiological ethics as a certain "loose logic of analogy or affinity similar to the logic of inductive arguments" (*Axiological Ethics* [London: Macmillan, 1970], p. 88).

10. In addition to the citations in chapter 2, consider, for example: "The deep meaning of choice is universal and . . . thereby the for-itself brings a human-reality into existence as a species" (BN, 550–51; F, 636); and "The Other whom I hate actually represents all Others" (BN, 411).

11. "All existence as soon as it is posited is surpassed by itself. But it must retreat *towards something*. The imaginary is in every case the 'something' concrete toward which the existent is surpassed" (PI, 244). "All apprehension of the real as world implies a hidden surpassing towards the imaginary. . . . The imaginary thus represents the implicit meaning of the real" (PI, 245).

12. Writing against American "war crimes" in Vietnam, Sartre takes his accustomed turn toward valuational humanism when he adds: "And the commitment . . . must be total. Each one sees the whole of the struggle and places himself on one side or the other according to motivations which develop from his objective situation into a certain idea which he forms for himself of human life" (Sartre's interview with Vladimir Dedijer, *War Crimes in Vietnam*, Spokesman Pamphlet no. 12 [Nottingham: The Bertrand Russell Peace Foundation, 1971], p. 1).

Offering what could be a gloss on the foregoing, he writes in *The Family Idiot*, "In every collectivity the individuals have a certain representation of the human person in common . . . which defines what they are by what they ought to be and what they ought to be by what they are" (IF, 1:811).

13. Max Scheler is included among the authors whom Sartre read during his year's residence at the Maison Française in Berlin, 1933–34 (see SM, 38). Although we do not know the works he read, he was certainly familiar with Scheler's famous theory of the material a priori in ethics, for he remarks in BN: "As Scheler has shown, I can achieve an intuition of values in terms of concrete exemplifications" (BN, 93). Sartre is doing something like this in EH.

14. In this sense, it is perhaps closer to the "iconic sign" of a value property such as Charles W. Morris finds in the work of C. S. Peirce (see the former's *Signs, Language, and Behavior* [New York: Prentice-Hall, 1946], pp. 190–92). Indeed, Sartre's talk of free commitment's "realizing a type of humanity" (EH, 304), reminds us immediately of C. S. Peirce's famous type/token distinction (see *Collected Papers of Charles Sanders Peirce*, ed. Charles Hartshorne and Paul Weiss, 6 vols. [Cambridge: Harvard University Press, 1931–35], 4: pars. 537ff.).

15. I have developed this point at length in my "Vision, Responsibility, and Factual Belief in Existentialist Ethics," *Journal of Chinese Philosophy* 7 (1980), pp. 27–36. What I term Sartre's "value-image" approximates the concept of ideal theme formulated by Antonio Cua. He distinguishes ideal norms from ideal themes, the latter offering "a life unity without a life plan" (see Antonio Cua, *Dimensions of Moral Creativity* [University Park, Pa.: Pennsylvania State University Press, 1978], pp. 123–25 and 133–49).

16. Thus Peter Caws sees it as "clearly a form of . . . the 'generalization argument,' " but one that lacks "a class over which the generalization can operate."

He concludes that Sartre's use of moral generalization "is more a matter of evangelistic rhetoric than of philosophical reasoning" (*Sartre* [London: Routledge and Kegan Paul, 1979], pp. 119–20). A trio of German critics considers the entire choosing-for-all-men principle to be respectively: "a postulate" (von Krosigk), "unbegründetes Sollen" (Hartmann), and "a mere postulate" (Kampits). See F. von Krosigk, *Philosophie und Politische Aktion bei Jean-Paul Sartre* (Munich: Beck, 1969), p. 86; Klaus Hartmann, *Sartres Sozialphilosophie* (Berlin: de Gruyter, 1966), p. 35; and Peter Kampits, *Sartre und die Frage nach dem Anderen* (Vienna: R. Oldenbourg, 1975), pp. 239 and 294. In the most extensive study of the problem to date, Thomas Anderson concedes that "neither in his essay *Existentialism and Humanism* nor elsewhere does Sartre advance much to support his claim that a man is obliged to will the freedom of others" (*The Foundation and Structure of Sartrean Ethics* [Lawrence: The Regents Press of Kansas, 1979], p. 78).

17. This is merely a gloss on a text from *Being and Nothingness:* "The other accomplishes for us a function of which we are incapable and which nevertheless is incumbent on us: *to see ourselves as we are*" (BN, 354).

For a similar claim in the context of Brice Piran's theory of language, see *Situations,* 1:219.

18. Ph. Gavi, Jean-Paul Sartre, and P. Victor, *On a raison de se révolter* (Paris: Gallimard, 1974), p. 342; hereafter cited as ORR.

19. Employing the wisdom of hindsight, one of Sartre's leading French commentators, Michel Contat, characterizes *Being and Nothingness* as "above all, a phenomenology of bad faith" (*Explication des Séquestrés d'Altona de Jean-Paul Sartre* [Paris: Minard, 1968], p. 15).

20. See AJ, 17, 21, and 54. Among the critics who air this objection are Henry Veatch, *For an Ontology of Morals* (Evanston, Ill.: Northwestern University Press, 1971), pp. 76–77; Mary Warnock, *Existentialist Ethics* (London: Macmillan, 1967), pp. 47–48; and Richard Bernstein, *Praxis and Action* (Philadelphia: University of Pennsylvania Press, 1971), pp. 151–54.

21. Anderson argues that consistency emerges from this lecture as a more basic value for Sartre than freedom (see *Sartrean Ethics,* pp. 63–64 and 145).

22. See his "Cogito, ergo Sum: Inference or Performance?" in Alexander Sesonske and Noel Fleming, eds., *Meta-Meditations: Studies in Descartes* (Belmont, Calif.: Wadsworth, 1965), pp. 50–76.

23. In an interview given to *Comoedia* as early as 1943, Sartre had distinguished freedom in-consciousness (our "ontological" and "noetic" freedoms) from freedom in-situation. The latter, he admitted, required others' freedom. See the definitive "bibliographical life" compiled by Michel Contat and Michel Rybalka, *The Writings of Jean-Paul Sartre,* 2 vols., trans. Richard C. McCleary (Evanston, Ill.: Northwestern University Press, 1974), 1:87.

24. In the discussion following the lecture, Sartre concedes that "the real problem . . . is to define the *conditions for universality* [since there is no human nature] (EH, 135; emphasis mine). He makes an initial move in that direction with premise 6. As we know, "situation" figures centrally in any discussion of universality for

him. Responding to questions from the audience, he develops the social aspect of this term: "What we call 'situation' is precisely the set of material and even psychoanalytic conditions which exactly defines an ensemble in a given epoch" (EH; F 137). His Communist interlocutor, Pierre Naville, is skeptical about the conformity of this definition to Sartre's existentialist texts. Naville has put his finger on the major turning point that this lecture represents, namely, the definition of "situation" in terms of "ensembles" and "psychoanalytic" and "material" conditions. Though we now recognize these as developments of ideas whose germ is found in BN, they are more accurately seen as anticipations of Sartre's subsequent social theory and of his biographical studies.

25. "For us, man is defined first of all as a being 'in a situation.' That means that he forms a synthetic whole with his situation—biological, economic, political, etc. He cannot be distinguished from his situation, for it forms him and decides his possibilities but, inversely, it is he who gives it meaning by making his choices within it and by it" (AJ, 59–60).

26. Referring to anti-Semitism as a product of bourgeois culture, Sartre opines: "In a society whose members feel mutual bonds of solidarity, *because they are engaged in the same enterprise*, there would be no place for it" (AJ, 150; emphasis mine).

For Sartre's response to François Mauriac's subsequent challenge to comment on anti-Semitism in socialist states, see Michel-Antoine Burnier, *Choice of Action*, trans. Bernard Murchland (New York: Random House, 1968), p. 88.

27. He appeals to the socioeconomic dimension of the analytic/synthetic distinction shortly before the *Existentialism* lecture when he claims that "one makes oneself bourgeois . . . by choosing a certain analytic vision of the world . . . that excludes the perception of collective realities" (*Situations*, 2:19).

28. As early as *Anti-Semite and Jew* Sartre had realized that "the choice of authenticity is not a solution of the social aspect of the Jewish problem" (AJ, 138). We have created the Jew's situation in which he must choose between Jerusalem and France. It is the "bases and structures" of such choice, Sartre is beginning to see, that must be changed; see below, chap. 4.

29. See CDR, 662. Expressing what seems to be Sartre's view as well during his "realist" period of fellow-traveling with the French Communist party, de Beauvoir avows: "Without crime and tyranny there could be no liberation of man; one can not escape that dialectic which goes from freedom to freedom through dictatorship and oppression" (EA, 155). For his similar view on this means-end issue, see the interview, "A Long, Bitter, Sweet Madness," *Encounter* 22 (June 1964), pp. 61–63. Indeed, as early as 1946 he had argued that "there must be . . . complete liberation on the economic and social plane before the principles of *habeas corpus*, political freedom, and freedom of thought regain a meaning" ("Responsibility of the Writer," reprinted in *Reflections on Our Age* [New York: Columbia University Press, 1949], p. 79).

30. For the immense influence of Alexander Kojève's Marxist humanist reading of the *Phenomenology* on Sartre's generation of French intellectuals, see Vincent Descombes, *Le Même et l'autre. Quarante-cinq ans de Philosophie Française*

(1933–78) (Paris: Minuit, 1979), pp. 21–70.

31. Although he has reservations about "history as totality," Jürgen Habermas acknowledges that "on the basis of industrial society and its technically mediated commerce, the interdependence of political events and the integration of social relations have progressed so far beyond what was even conceivable two centuries ago that within this overall complex of communication particular histories have coalesced into the history of *one* world" (*Theory and Practice,* trans. John Viertel [Boston: Beacon Press, 1973], pp. 250–51; emphasis his).

32. "Socialisme et Liberté" was the name which he and Merleau-Ponty had given their short-lived Resistance group of intellectuals in 1941. Their enterprise did not last nine months, and Sartre returned to his own form of resistance, the unmasking of bad faith, by completing *The Flies;* see Jeanson, *Sartre,* pp. 133–34.

Chapter Four

1. A gallery of such portraits could be collected from Sartre's writings. Besides those about to be examined, namely, the anti-Semite, the neocolonialist, and the torturer, consider the following: the writer—the locus classicus is *What Is Literature?* but a briefer sketch with all the essentials represented can be found in his brief address to the opening session of UNESCO in Paris, November 1, 1946, "The Responsibility of the Writer," reprinted in *Reflections on Our Age* (New York: Columbia University Press, 1949); the intellectual, both new (socialist) and classical (bourgeois)—see "A Plea for Intellectuals" and "A Friend of the People" in BEM.

2. For a discussion of anti-Semitism under the Vichy regime, see Paul A. Gagnon, *France Since 1789* (New York: Harper and Row, 1964), pp. 439ff. The Vichy government has been called "the revenge of the anti-Dreyfusards."

3. See his analysis of "being Jewish" as an elective assumption (interiorization) of being-for-others (BN, 526ff.).

4. He later admitted the superficiality of such a claim if taken in an exclusive sense (see his interview with Benny Lévy, "L'Espoir, Maintenant . . . ," Le Nouvel Observateur, no. 802 (24 March 1980), pp. 57–59. But the claim remains true if the only social ontology available is that of the looking/looked-at. It is the inadequacy of the model itself that underlies Sartre's change of mind. But seeds of that change are already present in the essay AJ.

5. See below, chap. 5.

6. All the articles I am considering date from 1956 to 1958, except for the Fanon preface, published in 1961.

7. Karl Marx, *Capital: A Critique of Political Economy,* trans. S. Moore, E. Aveling, and E. Untermann (Chicago: Charles H. Kerr, 1906–9), p. 15.

8. The means-end problem, as he calls it, has been the focus of his attention from the outset of his political and social concerns. His "solution" is summarized in the general thesis that one cannot do politics without dirtying one's hands; see my *"L'Imagination au Pouvoir. The Evolution of Sartre's Political and Social Thought,"* *Political Theory* 7, no. 2 (May 1979), p. 177 n. 34.

9. Jean-Paul Sartre, *The Communists and Peace,* with *A Reply to Claude Lefort,* trans. Martha H. Fletcher and Philip R. Berk (New York: George Braziller, 1968), p. 138; hereafter cited as CP.

10. That Marx does in fact advocate the moral superiority of socialism over preceding systems is demonstrated quite clearly by Eugene Kamenka, *Marxism and Ethics* (New York: St. Martin's Press, 1969), pp. 5ff. Sartre is well aware of the inconsistencies of Communist "moralizing" from such a determinist position; see MR, p. 235n.

11. This is the moral of two of the most powerful tracts to come out of the Algerian civil-war experience, Henri Alleg's *The Question* and Sartre's *A Victory* published together in English translation by John Calder (New York: George Braziller, 1958).

12. Sartre's true view of representative bourgeois democracy is captured in the title of his essay, "Elections: A Trap for Fools," reprinted in *Life/Situations. Essays Written and Spoken,* trans. Paul Auster and Lydia Davis (New York: Pantheon, 1977), pp. 198–210; hereafter cited as L/S.

13. Judicious distinctions, which Sartre fails to make, in this matter can be found in Karl Jaspers, *The Question of German Guilt,* pp. 31ff. Sartre admits to having been influenced by Jaspers's study, especially regarding "points which concern collective guilt as such" (interview in *Der Spiegel,* in *Sartre on Theatre,* ed. Michel Contat and Michel Rybalka, trans. Frank Jellinek (New York: Pantheon, 1976), p. 298 (hereafter cited as ST).

14. Frantz Fanon, *The Wretched of the Earth,* trans. Constance Farrington (New York: Grove Press, 1968); hereafter cited as WE.

15. As executive president of the "Russell Tribunal" which met in Stockholm in the summer of 1967 to determine the question of American guilt for war crimes in Vietnam, Sartre had occasion to express his position on collective responsibility in a formally judicial context. Except for a heavier emphasis on what he termed the admonitory and genocidal aspects of the conflict, his conclusions, including his summary essay "On Genocide" written at the end of the second session, are strikingly similar to those of his treatment of the Algerian war. See Jean-Paul Sartre, *On Genocide,* introduction by Arlette El Kaïm-Sartre (Boston: Beacon Press, 1968).

16. I have developed this point at length in several essays, namely, "The Role of the Image in Sartre's Aesthetic," *The Journal of Aesthetics and Art Criticism* 33 (Summer 1975), pp. 431–42; "L'Imagination au Pouvoir" and "Sartre-Flaubert and the Real/Unreal," in *Jean-Paul Sartre: Contemporary Approaches to his Philosophy,* ed. Hugh Silverman and Frederick Elliston (Pittsburgh: Duquesne University Press, 1980), pp. 105–23.

17. Sartre is less ambiguous in distinguishing these two realms than he is in respecting his distinction. He denies that theater is a "philosophical vehicle" precisely because it stresses what escapes philosophy, "the particular as such." And yet he does aim for what he terms "the philosophical myth" in his plays: "it is a way of presenting in a drama a moment of social and personal reality as a single whole. But it must be so thoroughly integrated with the story, the dramatic

aspect and the development of the story, that the play cannot be said to be valid by virtue of certain principles and that one piece of it cannot be accepted and another rejected" (ST, 280; trans. emended). This resembles the singular universal, the goal of his synthetic, later "dialectical," reasoning. And the two domains are simply superimposed in his "true novel" on Flaubert, *L'Idiot de la Famille*.

18. Michel Contat, *Explications*, p. 13.

19. Jean-Paul Sartre, *The Condemned of Altona*, trans. Sylvia and George Leeson (New York: Vintage Books, 1961), p. 65; hereafter cited as CA.

20. Hannah Arendt, *Eichmann in Jerusalem* (New York: Viking Press, 1965), p. 282.

21. As he comments to a French interviewer on the occasion of the play's original production: "Naturally, the spectator has not been a torturer, but that's not the point; like all of us, he has been an accomplice in one thing or another, you know all the objective complications we have; and consequently, if the spectator is affected, he is affected through this kind of *compelled, objective*—or however you like to describe it—*complicity*" (ST, 284; emphasis mine).

22. Jean-Paul Sartre, *"The Wall" and Other Stories* (New York: New Directions, 1969). This early story (written in 1938) anticipates not only Sartre's castigation of bourgeois humanism but also his later sense of the decisive influence of early, familial experiences on a person's life project.

23. This exemplifies the practico-inert necessity analyzed in the *Critique* (see below, chapter 6, "The Practico-Inert"). After the war, the father, though still owner, is no longer manager of the firm. He feels himself helplessly subject to an inertia carried by the firm itself. In fact, such inertia ("exigencies") had required that he denounce his son at the start of the play.

24. "Itinerary of a Thought" (BEM, 35).

25. Sartre had once avowed that he would commit suicide if the only alternative was to torture someone; see Michel Contat, *Explications*, p. 75 n. 35.

26. In an interview given a year earlier (17 September 1959) regarding *The Condemned*, he expressed this view succinctly: "It is my belief that the world makes man and man makes the world. I have not wished merely to put characters on the stage, but also to suggest that *objective circumstances condition* the make-up and behavior of a particular person at a particular moment" (ST, 270; emphasis mine).

27. This pattern for ascribing responsibility to collectives continues in the sixties and seventies. It occurs in a quasi-judicial context in the Russell Tribunal of which, as we noted, Sartre was a leader. His statements in that setting reflect the ongoing tension between Marxist-determinist and existentialist-moral uses of "responsibility." Thus, he argues that the struggle between the U.S. and the people of the Third World "is determined by the *structure* of the groups confronting one another. The imperialist policy is a *necessary historical reality* and it escapes for this reason every juridical or moral condemnation."

Yet this thought could lead one to judge events as people did in Stalin's day, "only from the angle of efficiency, and to accept a *passive complicity* while judging the acts of a government only in a practical perspective." But "doesn't a political fact likewise have an ethico-juridical structure?'' he asks, voicing his abiding concern for the means-end problem. He adds that it is good ''to remind the working class, who have been led too often into considering only efficiency, that there is an ethico-juridical structure for every historical action'' (Sartre and Dedijer, *War Crimes in Vietnam*, pp. 1–2; emphasis mine).

Chapter Five

1. I discuss the nature and development of that hermeneutic in my ''Existential Hermeneutics: The Progressive-Regressive Method,'' *Eros* 8, no. 1 (1981), pp. 3–24.

2. L/S, 112; see *Situations*, 10:94; emphasis his.

3. Consider the relatively minor role accorded these conditioning factors in his early Baudelaire study, their increasing importance in *Saint Genet* and his autobiography, *The Words*, and their dominance in *The Family Idiot*.

4. Roger Garaudy, *Humanisme Marxiste* (Paris: Editions Sociales, 1957), p. 193.

5. See Merleau-Ponty, *Adventures of the Dialectic*, trans. Joseph Bien (Evanston, Ill.: Northwestern University Press, 1973), pp. 153–54.

6. Ibid., pp. 158–59.

7. It was awareness of Sartre's current work and her conviction that Merleau-Ponty was aware of it as well that brought Simone de Beauvoir so caustically to Sartre's defense with her ''Merleau-Ponty et le pseudo-sartrisme,'' *Les Temps modernes* 114–15 (June–July 1955), pp. 2072–2122.

8. *Karl Marx: Selected Writings*, ed. David McLellan (Oxford: Oxford University Press, 1977), p. 300. *The Eighteenth Brumaire of Louis Bonaparte* is a work that Sartre cites several times.

9. The locus classicus for this elaboration is Marx's brief *Preface to a Critique of Political Economy*, in McLellan, ed., *Selected Writings*, pp. 388–91. Another important text in this regard is his letter to Annenkov, 28 December 1846 (ibid., pp. 191–94).

10. The premises for the materialist conception of history are: ''real individuals, their activities and the material conditions under which they live, both those which they find already existing and those produced by their activity'' (Marx and Engels, *The German Ideology*, partially reprinted in McLellan, ed., *Selected Writings*, p. 160).

11. See McLellan, ed., *Selected Writings*, pp. 317–22.

12. Sartre cites the famous remark by Plekhanov that ''influential personages can . . . modify the particular physiognomy of events and certain of their partial consequences, but they cannot change the orientation of the events'' (SM, 130).

13. One vehicle for this schooling in German thought was Aron's *German Sociology*, published in France in 1938 (English translation by Mary and Thomas Bottomore [London: Heinemann, 1957]); another was his *Introduction to the Philosophy of History*, trans. G. J. Irwin (London: Weidenfeld and Nicolson, 1961), which was also published in France in 1938.

14. Although he credits the term originally to the physiologist von Kries and the jurists and criminologists with whom he worked in the late 1800s; see Max Weber, *Selections*, ed. W. G. Runciman (Cambridge: Cambridge University Press, 1978), p. 113 n. 2.

15. See Maurice Weyembergh, "M. Weber et G. Lukács," *Revue Internationale de Philosophie* 27, no. 106 (1973), p. 483.

16. See Runciman, ed., *Selections*, p. 128.

17. Ibid., p. 3.

18. Ibid., p. 4.

19. Merleau-Ponty underscores the concept of totality in Lukács but, since he wrote prior to the *Critique*, misses the parallel in Sartre. See *Adventures*, pp. 31ff.

20. Georg Lukács, *History and Class Consciousness*, trans. Rodney Livingstone (Cambridge, Mass.: M.I.T. Press, 1971), p. 10; see p. 27.

21. In an interesting essay on this topic, Iring Fetscher observes that "the ideal of adequate class consciousness . . . is 'constructed' by Lukács in a manner similar to Max Weber's [construction] of the rational, objectively possible behavior of a historical personality." But he notes that Lukács uses objective class interest and class situation in relation to the objective structure of society as a whole, whereas Weber deals with the individual person in light of hypothetical knowledge of circumstances, consequences, and *Nebenwirkungen*. Of relevance to our general topic is his additional observation that in this regard Lukács's sociology differs from Weber's, which "doesn't know such a 'collective subject' [i.e., class] as being also a 'subject of responsibility' " ("Zum Begriff Der 'Objektiven Möglichkeit' bei Max Weber und Georg Lukács," *Revue Internationale de Philosophie* 27, no. 106 (1973), p. 509.

22. Lukács, *Consciousness*, p. 51; emphasis his.

23. Ibid., p. 79.

24. Ibid., p. 153.

25. Ibid., p. 186.

26. Ibid., pp. 315–16.

27. See above, chapter 2.

28. Merleau-Ponty, *Adventures*, p. 132.

29. Thus he maintains his Husserlian conviction that "essence" is an objective rule for appearances. Such appearances are not just psychological phenomena: "They are strictly objective and derive from the nature of things" (BN, 317).

30. The nature and career of this movement is traced in dependable studies by Michel-Antoine Burnier, *Choice of Action*, trans. Bernard Murchland (New York: Random House, 1968), and by Mark Poster, *Existential Marxism in Postwar France* (Princeton, N.J.: Princeton University Press, 1975).

31. Sartre, *Entretiens*, pp. 38–39; emphasis mine.

32. Sartre continues: "At the moment, good will is not possible, or rather, it is and can only be the project [*dessein*] of rendering good will possible" (ibid.). It is this project of "rendering good will possible" that I referred to previously as Sartre's "ethic of disalienation." See CM, 54–55.

33. Sartre, *Entretiens,* p. 158.

34. Ibid., p. 38. For objective possibility in CM, see 342–62, 412, and 447–53.

35. See McLellan, ed., *Selected Writings,* p. 389. The precise meaning of "forces" and "relations" in this context is disputed among Marxist scholars. Typically, Sartre does not bother with such details. Raymond Aron is on target when he points to "Sartre's facile acceptance of all those aspects of Marxist thought in which he is not particularly interested, but which were the essential things for Marx himself—for instance, the synthetic reconstruction of capitalism" (Raymond Aron, *Marxism and the Existentialists,* trans. Helen Weaver, Robert Addis, and John Weightman [New York: Harper and Row, 1969], p. 167).

36. Klaus Hartmann sees in scarcity "a dialectical principle" and indeed "a universal a priori" (*Sartres Sozialphilosophie,* p. 87). While this emphasizes the general applicability of the fact of scarcity to human history thus far, it seems to leave Sartre's hope for a "socialism of abundance" as one more futile passion.

37. For Sartre's discussion of objective contradiction in terms of collective praxis and counterfinality, see CDR, 193ff.

38. On the "triple objective exigency" for "neurotic art" on the part of French society in the second quarter of the nineteenth century, see IF, 3:662–63.

39. Because of the stratification of nineteenth-century bourgeois society, a system of "equivalences and hierarchies" which "vary according to the place a particular family occupies in the bourgeois class," Sartre explains, it happens that "a child, even before birth, is designated by a certain field of rather stringent and clearly organized possibles that reflects to him the social needs defined by his class and finally . . . by the will of his father" (IF, 2:1477). Applied to the young Flaubert, this means that "Gustave is *made* but not by a conscious experience; [rather] by an ensemble of processes which precede experience and condition it" (IF, 2:1509).

Sartre reaffirms this point emphatically in a film interview several years later where he insists: "Flaubert was free to become Flaubert, but he didn't have so many possibilities outside of that. He had a few. . . . Thus historical conditioning exists at every instant. One can question this but it remains true nonetheless. Even those who contest their formation nowadays are no less victims of that formation. And it's evident in the very way they deny it" (*Sartre, un film,* p. 76). Recall Sartre's humanist motto: ". . . out of what is made of him," indeed!

40. Sartre's discussion of class "comprehension" suffices to disprove Goldmann's contention that he lacks the central Marxian category of "possible consciousness" (*Marxisme et sciences humaines* [Paris: Gallimard, 1970], p. 258).

41. See "Jean-Paul Sartre Répond," *L'Arc* 30 (October 1966), pp. 88–89. I develop the concept of the practico-inert in chapter 6.

42. L. W. Nauta, for example, charts the beginning of Sartre's dialectical thinking in his studies of the imagination in the 30s; see his "Dialektik bei Sartre," *Studium Generale* (17 July 1968), pp. 591–607. Georges Gurvitch criticizes what he calls Sartre's "domestication" of the dialectic in BN, i.e., its impressment into the service of a "pessimistic individualism"; see his *Dialectique et Sociologie* (Paris: Flammarion, 1962), p. 21. If Merleau-Ponty presumes that Sartre has re-

jected the dialectic in this period, it is the dialectic of nature and a date-progressive, historical dialectic that he has in mind; see his *Adventures,* p. 98 and passim.

43. Parallels between Fichte and Sartre have been the topic of several dissertations over the years. See, for example, Aldo Masullo, *La Communità come fondamento: Fichte, Husserl, Sartre* (Naples: Libreria Scientifica Editrice, 1965).

44. See Nauta, "Dialektic," pp. 549ff.

45. Hartmann, *Sartres Sozialphilosophie,* p. 31.

46. "The dialectic is both a method *and* a movement in the object. For the dialectician, it is grounded on a fundamental claim both about the structure of the real and about that of our praxis. We assert simultaneously that the process of knowledge is dialectical, that the movement of the object (whatever it may be) is *itself* dialectical, and that those two dialectics are one and the same" (CDR, 20).

47. Sartre explicitly distinguishes dialectic from a mere play of reciprocities by reason of the absence of totalities in the latter (see CDR, 99–100). A fine discussion of totalization can be found in William L. McBride's *Fundamental Change in Law and Society* (The Hague: Mouton, 1970), pp. 176–86.

48. For an excellent survey of issues in the holist-individualist controversy in the social sciences, see John O'Neill, ed., *Modes of Individualism and Collectivism* (London: Heinemann, 1973). I deal with the matter from the viewpoint of collective responsibility in chapter 6.

49. See Raymond Aron, *History and the Dialectic of Violence,* trans. Barry Cooper (Oxford: Basil Blackwell, 1975), p. 200.

50. As early as *The Psychology of Imagination* (1940) Sartre writes of the power of consciousness "to posit the world in its synthetic totality" in order to posit the imaginary as beyond that totality (PI, 239).

51. Double negation is the dialectical principle that, since negative relations are internal, i.e., constitutive, the negation of a negation constitutes a *new* affirmation and not a mere return to the original thesis. So Sartre is lax in stating *sans phrase* that "the negation of a negation is necessarily an affirmation" (CDR, 47).

52. See my "Praxis and Vision: Elements of a Sartrean Epistemology," *Philosophical Forum* 8 (1976), especially pp. 33–34.

53. See below, chap. 7, as well as "Praxis and Vision," p. 30, and IF, 1:148.

54. See, for example, his analysis of what it means to comprehend class action (CDR, 701ff.). On comprehension in CM, see 91 and 287–306.

55. "Cartesian Freedom," *Literary and Philosophical Essays,* p. 191.

56. "I am using the term 'abstract' here in the sense of *incomplete*. The individual is not abstract from the point of view of his individual reality (one could say that he is the concrete itself); but only *on condition* that the ever deeper determinations which constitute him in his very existence as a historical agent and, at the same time, as a product of History, have been revealed" (CDR, 52 n.).

57. Sartre wrote an essay entitled "Kierkegaard: The Singular Universal" (BEM, 141–69), and he claims at least to approximate this notion in his study of Flaubert as the author of *Madame Bovary* (see IF, 1:7–8).

58. Jean-Paul Sartre, "Consciousness of Self and Knowledge of Self," trans. Mary Ellen and Nathaniel Lawrence, *Readings in Existential Phenomenology,* ed. Nathaniel Lawrence and Daniel O'Connor (Englewood Cliffs, N.J.: Prentice-Hall, 1967), p. 131; hereafter cited as CSKS.

59. On diachronic totalization and class solidarity through history, see IF, 3:342.

60. The expression is Iris Murdoch's; see her *Sartre, Romantic Rationalist* (New Haven: Yale Universtiy Press, 1953), p. 114.

61. "Jean-Paul Sartre Répond," *L'Arc,* p. 94. In an interview given several years later, Sartre avows: "Personally, I have been compelled, in order to criticize Althusser, to look again at the idea of 'notion' and to draw a series of conclusions in the process" (BEM, 134). Already in "Materialism and Revolution" he had contrasted the *concept* of science with the *notion* of dialectic (see MR, 209).

62. See my "Praxis and Vision," p. 34.

63. Claude Lévi-Strauss, *The Savage Mind* (Chicago: University of Chicago Press, 1966), pp. 245–46.

64. See Nauta, "Dialektik bei Sartre," p. 603.

Chapter Six

1. Vincent Descombes makes this the guiding thread for his survey of forty years of recent French philosophy. He joins the chorus of those who emphasize the influence of Alexander Kojève's Hegel lectures from 1933 to 1939 in setting this tone. See *Le Même et l'autre. Quarante-cinq ans de philosophie française (1933–78),* (Paris: Minuit, 1979), especially pp. 21–63. See CM, 53–54.

2. In a most perceptive essay, Dina Dreyfus points out that the practico-inert is the ground of all alienation in the later Sartre, but only in the form of scarcity can it be considered "radical evil." In other words, Sartre has not lapsed into Manichaeism, as some of his critics have suggested. See "Jean-Paul Sartre et le mal radical," *Mercure de France* 341 (January 1961), pp. 154–67.

After criticizing Hegelians and pseudo-Marxist "mechanistic determinism," Sartre insists that "it is in the concrete and synthetic relation of the agent to the other through the mediation of the thing, and to the thing through the mediation of the other, that we shall be able to discover the foundations of all possible alienation" (CDR, 66 n.).

3. I have noted his opposition to a dialectic of nature such as Engels constructed on Hegel's natural philosophy. But Sartre does allow a kind of dialectic even here, due to the negations introduced by individual and collective praxis: "If one can nevertheless apply the term 'dialectical' to this material field of the anti-dialectic, it is precisely because of this double negation" (CDR, 319). Still, he later adds that "the practico-inert field is in itself a caricature of the dialectic and its alienating objectification" (CDR, 556).

4. "Alterity creates its own laws; they are the *rules of belief*" (CDR, 342).

5. Sartre offers his usual weighty definition of process: "A development which, though oriented, is caused by a force of exteriority which has the result of actualizing the series as the temporalization of a multiplicity in the fleeting unity of a violence of impotence" (CDR, 304).

6. Another milieu of recurrence is public opinion. Sartre analyzes it in terms of the Other thinking it "elsewhere." "At this level," he concludes "the Idea is a process; it derives its invincible strength from the fact that nobody thinks it" (CDR, 300). It is another instance of action without an agent.

7. Commenting favorably on the language theory of his friend Brice Parain, Sartre notes: "Language has become the most penetrating [*insinuant*] of the instruments of oppression" (*Situations,* 1:187).

8. See Ferdinand de Saussure, *Course in General Linguistics,* trans. Wade Baskin (New York: The Philosophical Library, 1959), especially pp. 17–20. "Langue" refers to the natural language with its rules for phonology, morphology, and syntax. "Parole" denotes the datable use of this language by acts of speaking. By focusing on the former rather than on the latter, de Saussure sets the stage for subsequent "structuralist" analyses of synchronic structures, free of the unscientific contingencies of actual expressive acts. This is a direct violation of Sartre's principle of the primacy of praxis and, as such, constitutes his chief quarrel with structuralism in general; see "Jean-Paul Sartre Répond," *L'Arc,* pp. 87–96.

Recall that in *Being and Nothingness* his scheme is Hegelian; the act of speaking is the "reality" of language whereas language is the "truth" of speech (see above, chap. 2).

9. "These verbal structures, in so far as they have been invented by nobody and in so far as they are language organizing itself as passive activity in the milieu of alterity, are, in a collective, the collective itself" (CDR, 304–5).

10. At its most concrete, class incorporates all the elements of Sartre's social ontology: "Class manifests itself not only as an institutionalized apparatus, but also as an ensemble (serial or organized) of direct-action groups, and as a collective which receives its status from the practico-inert field (through and by productive relations with other classes) and which received its universal schema of practical unification from the groups which constantly form on its surface" (CDR, 685).

11. "Other-comprehension" should be distinguished from comprehension of the Other, which has as its aim, when direct, to comprehend the Other as the same. Other-comprehension is indirect and aims at comprehending the Other as other, i.e., as liberating me from myself and my responsibilities. Consider the person who is always aware of what "they" are wearing this season.

12. See Albert O. Hirschman, *The Passions and the Interests* (Princeton, N.J.: Princeton University Press, 1979) on the gradual evolution of "interest" to mean economic well-being. Thus Helvetius claims: "As the physical world is ruled by the laws of movement so is the moral universe ruled by the laws of interest" (in Hirschman, p. 43).

13. Sheldon S. Wolin, *Politics and Vision* (Boston: Little, Brown, 1960), p. 274.

14. Disclaiming any desire to add to "the certainty of the reconstruction which Marx carried out in *Capital,*" Sartre merely wishes "to define the type of intelligibility which is involved in the Marxist reconstruction" at a higher level of generality (CDR, 216).

15. Sartre speaks of "ideological interests," a term he borrows from Isaac Deutscher, such as the author's attachment to his published works and concern

about their subsequent career (see CDR, 203ff.). He has even described his own relation to *L'Idiot de la Famille* in these terms (see ORR, 68 and 71).

16. See Marx's famous thesis on the fourfold alienation of the worker in the *Paris Manuscripts* of 1844 (*Selected Writings*, pp. 77ff.). Viewed in terms of the practico-inert collective object, this alienation affects the owner of the machine as well. "The seriality of class," Sartre notes, "makes the individual (whoever he is and whatever his class) into a being who defines himself as a humanized thing and who, in the practico-inert universe, is strictly interchangeable, in given conditions, with some material product" (CDR, 316).

17. Sartre suggests, "It may be that [interest] reveals itself fully, in human history, only with what is called real property" (CDR, 197).

18. Marx is in effect defining "praxis" in *The German Ideology* when he refers to "the material activity and the material intercourse of men, the language of real life" (*Selected Writings*), p. 164).

As Shlomo Avineri points out: "*Praxis* means man's conscious shaping of the changing historical conditions." In this sense, it is for Marx "both a tool for changing the course of history and a criterion for historical evaluation" (*The Social and Political Thought of Karl Marx* [Cambridge: At The University Press, 1968], p. 138).

19. Sartre defines "praxis" rather ponderously as "an organizing project which transcends material conditions towards an end and inscribes itself, through labor, in inorganic matter as a rearrangement of the practical field and a reunification of means in the light of the end" (CDR, 734).

20. See my "Praxis and Vision."

21. In contradistinction to what I have called "practico-inert" structures, such as kinship relations studied by structural anthropologists, Sartre introduces the concept of existential structure, a kind of halfway house between constituent praxis and static, abstract (practico-inert) structures. Examples of existential structures are transcendence, negativity (negation of negation), surpassing-toward (rudimentary project), and especially need, which summarizes the others (see SM, 171n.). Introduced in *Search for a Method*, these structures are revealed by what he calls "indirect knowing," a form of his now familiar "comprehension," described as a "regressive denoting of existence" (see SM, 171 and 180). Thus existential structures are dependent both semantically and ontologically upon praxes, which they illumine.

22. Speaking of Flaubert, who had little self-knowledge (*connaissance de soi*) but exceptional comprehension of his inmost movements, Sartre describes the latter as "an obscure grasp of the *sens* of a process beyond its signification; in other words, it is itself lived and we shall call it *prereflective* (and not irreflective) because it appears as a doubling of interiorization without distance. Intermediate between nonthetic consciousness and reflective thematization, it is the dawning of a reflection. But when the latter arises, with its verbal tools, it frequently falsifies the comprehended [*compris*]: other forces intervene . . . that divert it or force it to substitute a set of significations, i.e., superficial, verbal generalities, for the deep meaning [*sens*] just glimpsed" (IF, 2:1544).

23. See my "Sartre-Flaubert and the Real/Unreal," pp. 107–9.

24. The following points are developed more fully in my "Existential Hermeneutics: Sartre's Progressive-Regressive Method."

25. Sartre anticipates the ontological primacy of praxis, as he does so many other theses of the *Critique,* in *The Communists and Peace,* where he writes: "Of course, the system of production is for a class the necessary condition of its ability to exist. . . . But this condition is not *sufficient:* praxis is necessary" (CP, 99). And again, "The class, a *real* unity of crowds and historical masses, manifests itself by an operation that can be located in time and referred to an intention. The class is never separable from the concrete will which animates it nor from the ends it pursues. The proletariat forms itself by its day-to-day action. It exists only by acting. . . . If it ceases to act, it decomposes" (CP, 97). No doubt, for Sartre at this early stage of his social thought, these remarks constitute a kind of plaidoyer for the Communist party. The *Critique,* on the contrary, is a Marxist criticism of the party, especially as it has developed in the Soviet Union.

26. See Merleau-Ponty, *Adventures,* p. 155.

27. There is a certain fluidity in Sartre's use of *le collectif* and its derivatives. Sometimes he will use "collectivity" in a generic sense synonymous with "social ensemble" as when he speaks of groups as "active collectivities" (CDR, 250). But he reserves "collective" (*le collectif*), as we have seen, to denote "the two-way relation between a material, inorganic, worked object and a multiplicity which finds its unity of exteriority in it" (CDR, 269). The multiplicity so united is what Sartre calls the "series" and the relations between individuals in this multiplicity are "serial." Taking part for whole, Sartre tends to use "collective" and "series" synonymously and even extends the term *le collectif* to designate the "collective object." Context usually makes clear which aspect of this complex of relations he has in mind. For "collective realities" in CM, see 34–36 and 117–23.

28. Sartre's most complete anticipation of the series/group distinction occurs in his discussion of mass and class in *The Communists and Peace.* Seriality is foreshadowed by what he describes as "the strange formal reality which is called 'anyone at all' [but which] is only commutative isolation" (CP, 216). Even "the same" (*le même*) of group action is anticipated. After distinguishing cooperation from mere imitation, he writes: "What I imitate in my neighbor is not the Other, it is myself become my own object; I do not repeat this act because *he* did it, but because *I,* in him, have just done it" (CP, 207–8).

29. Sartre's ultimate concern in making history, as we know it, intelligible is "to explain the transition of oppressed classes from the state of being collectives to revolutionary group praxis" (CDR, 349).

30. Sartre calls the *mot d'ordre* the "inert vehicle of sovereignty" (CDR, 308). Sometimes translated as "order" or, worse, as "password" or "watchword," *mot d'ordre* is clearly intended by Sartre in an extended sense such as "word" in the expression "the word got around that . . ."—not as denoting a rumor (which would be a form of *pensée-autre*) but as signifying the practical self-understanding of a closely knit group. As he observes: "The *mot d'ordre* is not *obeyed.* Who would obey? And whom? It is simply the common praxis becoming, in some third

party, regulatory of itself in me and in all the other third parties, in the movement of a totalization which totalizes me and everyone else" (CDR, 380).

31. It is sometimes called the "regulating Third" when its directive function is being discussed.

32. Occasionally, even in the *Critique,* Sartre will refer to individual praxis as "presence to self" (see CDR, 220; F, 279).

33. For Sartre's second (and final) thoughts on the relation between fraternity and terror, see his interview with Benny Lévy, "L'Espoir Maintenant," *Le Nouvel Observateur* nos. 800–802 (March 1980), especially no. 801, pp. 53–58.

34. "From the structural point of view," Sartre writes, "the third party is the human mediation through which the multiplicity of epicenters and ends (identical and separate) organizes itself directly as determined by a synthetic objective" (CDR, 367). This "synthetic objective" differs from the collective object as the group differs from the collective. Sartre speaks of it either as common danger, e.g., the advancing royal troops, or as common need (see CDR, 350). It is the task of historians to show and evaluate "the urgency, the imperious clarity, and the totalizing force of *the objective* (that is to say, of the danger which has to be avoided, of the common means which has to be found)." The method Sartre suggests, of course, is a "progressive-regressive decoding" (CDR, 387).

35. Georges Gurvitch, *Dialectique et sociologie* (Paris: Flammarion, 1962), p. 170.

36. Sartre sees community as the transformation of total sovereignty into quasi-sovereignty, "and this determination in interiority of the regulating Third, as a transition from the Other to the Same, is a fundamental structure of praxis as community" (CDR, 612).

37. Active passivity is "the regulated production of pledged inertia and . . . a condition for common activity" (CDR, 603). Sartre is not in secure possession of this crucial term, however, for in *L'Idiot,* he uses "active passivity" to denote the actualization in his body of Flaubert's mental attitudes under autosuggestion. In this case, the passive activity/active passivity distinction assumes a purely personal, not a social significance (see IF, 2:1736–49).

38. "What Is Literature?" (*Situations,* 2:298). He expected the Revolutionary People's Assembly to reconcile the conflict between individual and society (see EP, 40).

Chapter Seven

1. *Oxford English Dictionary,* s.v. "Responsibility."

2. For discussions of status and role responsibility as forms of collective responsibility see, respectively, John Silber, "Being and Doing," in *Phenomenology in America,* ed. James Edie (Chicago, Ill.: Quadrangle Books, 1967), pp. 197–254, and R. S. Downie, "Responsibility and Social Roles," in *Individual and Collective Responsibility,* ed. Peter A. French (Cambridge, Mass.: Schenkman, 1972), pp. 68–80.

3. See Maurice Mandelbaum's much anthologized essay, "Societal Facts," in *Theories of History,* ed. Patrick Gardiner (Glencoe, Ill.: The Free Press, 1959),

pp. 476–88. His thesis is discussed below, in chapter 9.

4. See respectively F. A. Hayek, *The Counter-Revolution in Science* (Glencoe, Ill.: The Free Press, 1952), p. 56, and Karl R. Popper, *The Poverty of Historicism* (New York: Harper Torchbooks, 1964), p. 140. Still, there are a number of parallels between Hayek's position and Sartre's. For instance, he writes: "It has, indeed, rightly become one of the first maxims which the student of social phenomena learns (or ought to learn) never to speak of 'society' or a 'country' acting or behaving in a certain manner, but always and exclusively to think of individuals as acting." From *Scientism and the Study of Society,* excerpted in John O'Neill, ed., *Modes of Individualism and Collectivism* (London: Heinemann, 1973), p. 45. This resembles Sartre's principle of the primacy of individual praxis.

5. Hayek and Popper are known primarily as methodological rather than as ontological individualists, though the former species seems to imply the latter for individualists in a way that is not required of holists. In other words, although methodological holism is growing in popularity, ontological holism continues to be in disrepute among English-speaking philosophers.

6. Emile Durkheim, *The Rules of Sociological Method,* p. 14.

7. Ibid., p. 13; emphasis mine.

8. Sartre could be pressed to reconcile the internality of relations within the group with *any* significant independence of the latter at all. For if we take the internal negations of his philosophical anthropology as continuing to hold in his philosophy of praxis (and we have several reasons to do so and none not to), then it can scarcely be *this* group that perdures when a single member joins or leaves. This is one of many instances where the lack of any Sartrean ontology of relations is felt. To claim that the relations within the group are dialectical, as Sartre does, merely indicates where a solution might be found; it is not to give one.

9. He criticizes "organicist idealism" which sees the group functioning "as a hyper-organism in relation to individual organism" (CDR, 346). He urges us to "reject organicism in every form" (CDR, 348).

10. He sees class as "a fundamental [social] structure [which] represents at a certain level the very substance of which groups and passive socialities are determinations." He studies collectives in their ontological intelligibility the better "to understand and fix this more fundamental reality, class" (CDR, 252).

11. Sartre insists that these "social objects" are not mere symbols but true "practical realities, with their exigencies, to the extent that they realize in and through themselves the interpenetration of a multiplicity of unorganized individuals *within them* and that they produce every individual in them in the *indistinction* of a totality" (CDR, 252).

12. See above, chap. 1.

13. Such preontological comprehension is an unusually fecund source of primitive, infallible awareness for Sartre. Thus in BN he speaks of a preontological comprehension of being (17), of nonbeing (7), of the futility of "sincerity" (63), of the criteria of truth (156), of the existence of the Other (251), of human reality (561), of the human person (568), and of one's fundamental project (570).

14. Although his terminology is often fluid, the awareness just discussed being designated "practico-theoretical knowledge [*savoir*]," Sartre usually distinguishes three uses of "knowledge" in his praxis epistemology: the fundamental comprehension that is praxis-as-conscious and that plays the same foundational role in his Marxist writings that prereflective consciousness plays in his phenomenological works; reflective knowledge (*connaissance*) at one remove from comprehension and the locus of conceptual, analytical rationality; and an existentialized historical materialism (*savoir*) which "illumines and deciphers" the concrete, historical situation. See n. 17 below.

15. See ORR, 342.

16. He distinguishes two forms of knowledge (*savoir*) in terms of the substructure and superstructure respectively. The "theoretico-practical" belongs to the latter and hence is infected with ideology and allied to objective spirit; see IF, 3:45–46.

17. This is the point of the title of his *Against the Self-Images of the Age* (London: Duckworth, 1971). For Sartre's rather cumbersom definition of ideology, see IF, 3:222.

18. Sartre draws on his existentialist heritage when speaking of appetites for *savoir* and for *nonsavoir:* fear of discovering that "questioning is the practical basis of our being" (IF, 3:224). Earlier in the same work he takes "ideology" in what he claims rather curiously is its Marxist sense "as commodity," but adds that this practico-inert determination is unrelated to the practice of those post-Marxian philosophers whom he called "ideologues" in the *Critique* "in order to indicate that they were trying to refine in its details a philosophy they had not created" (IF, 3:212 n.).

For a discussion of comprehension as potentially falsified by verbal expression (and hence by ideology), see IF, 2:1544 and my remarks in chapter 6.

19. Although there are obvious parallels between Sartre's "objective spirit" and Karl Popper's "objective knowledge," the category of the practico-inert affords Sartre's term a greater range than that of Popper's. See Karl Popper, *Objective Knowledge: An Evolutionary Approach* (Oxford: Clarendon Press, 1972).

20. As we might expect, he distinguishes two imperatives: "the first, frustrated, obscure and solitary, is bound to seriality''; e.g., one must do it because "everybody's doing it." "The second, which refers us to the combat group and to its unity, is the imperative of freedom—at least in principle" (IF, 3:54).

21. Hannah Arendt, *Eichmann in Jerusalem,* p. 287.

22. Recall Leibnitz's famous division of evils into physical, metaphysical, and moral forms, the latter requiring our standard cognitive and conative conditions. He was merely canonizing a common distinction in the previous literature. See his *Essais de théodicée* (Paris: Aubier, 1962), par. 21.

23. "The passive agent," Sartre insists, "though alienated, nevertheless remains free; that is, he retains the initiative of changing direction but he cannot orient the process of interiorization and of exteriorization except by revealing himself in the dark," e.g., through dreams and vain wishes (IF, 2:1689).

24. Thus in *The Family Idiot* he describes false consciousness as "a filter of thoughts—common to all individuals of the class—which is born of their incapacity to assume a true consciousness of their class as such and whose purpose [*l'intention téléologique*] is to render such awareness impossible" (IF 3:223). Sartre sees false consciousness, not primarily as the product of simple historical class praxis, but as the result of a contradictory need to know and to not-know (see above, n.19). In a fine example of the marriage of vocabulary and concepts from BN and from the *Critique,* a distinctive feature of *L'Idiot,* he explains: though human reality is praxis, it is also "a being in question." These two features are, in fact, inseparable: "Praxis presumes questioning and questioning is . . . the practical quest to recuperate oneself as a living being, reproducing one's life" in a hostile environment (scarcity) (IF, 3:223).

25. McLellan, ed., *Selected Writings,* p. 487.

26. See David Hume, *A Treatise of Human Nature,* ed. L. A. Selby-Bigge, rev. P. H. Nidditch (Oxford: Clarendon Press, 1978), bk. II, pt. III, secs. 1 and 2.

27. By "orthodox Marxism" I mean dialectical and historical materialism as interpreted by the Communist party of the USSR and diffused throughout the world by the party apparatus.

28. McLellan, ed., *Selected Writings,* p. 417.

29. See ibid., pp. 389–90. A recent interpreter, defending Marx's "technological" or "productive-force" determinism, believes he can make the theory more palatable by including labor-power (skill, knowledge, and experience) among productive forces. In any case, he insists that for Marx it is clear that "not only [do] societies form integrated totalities but . . . these functionally related social wholes are determined by their economic base" (William H. Shaw, *Marx's Theory of History* [Stanford: Stanford University Press, 1978], pp. 81 and 67).

30. See, among numerous examples, Bertell Ollman, *Alienation* (Cambridge: Cambridge University Press, 1971).

31. As H. L. A. Hart observes, "it is difficult to conceive of a morality, as the term is presently used, which would not regard as a necessary condition for blame a subject's capacity to understand, reason about, and control his conduct" (*Punishment and Responsibility* [New York: Oxford University Press, 1968], pp. 227–30).

32. *Sartre, un film,* p. 99.

33. McLellan, *Selected Writings,* p. 487.

34. See, e.g., his inaugural editorial for *Les Temps modernes* (*Situations,* 2:27–28).

35. A recent case for the negative responsibility thesis is offered by John Harris in *Violence and Responsibility* (London: Routledge and Kegan Paul, 1980). Sartre appeals to such a thesis when, referring to serial responsibility as what people call "collective responsibility," he explains: "Its being depends on the absence of a negation: if [the passive agent] tried to regroup democratic bourgeois in order to protest against the massacres [of 1848], and to oppose the repressive measures, he would escape this passive qualification" (CDR, 761).

36. See above, chap. 4.

37. For his discussion of "group memory," see CDR, 414n.

38. The author and the reader of bourgeois literature, e.g., have the same goal: "each wishes to forget and to cause to be forgotten a history/story [*une histoire*] by destroying the historicity of human societies." Each sees himself making and undergoing his destiny in a praxis-process that pulls him toward his fall. "It is beginning with a historically lived story and *against it*—against the idea that 'men make history on the basis of prior circumstances'—that they in connivance have wished to surpass historialization as a dialectic of necessity and freedom in human praxis and, in order to free themselves of all responsibility, have in the final analysis contested this praxis itself" (IF, 3:429).

39. "The seriality of class makes the individual (whoever he is and whatever his class) into a being who defines himself as a humanized thing and who, in the practico-inert universe, is strictly interchangeable, in given conditions, with some material product" (CDR, 316).

40. See below, chapter 9.

41. Elsewhere he elaborates this claim: "What one man expects from another, if their relation is human, is defined in reciprocity, for expectation is a human act. There can only be such a thing as passive exigency between them if, within a complex group, divisions, separations, and the rigidity of the organs of transmission replace living bonds by a mechanical status of materiality. . . . No praxis as such can even formulate an imperative simply because exigency does not enter into the structure of reciprocity" (CDR, 187). This is why Sartre speaks of "invitation" rather than "demand" when describing the artwork, the *mot d'ordre*, and what I have called the "evidential situation"; see my "The Role of the Image," pp. 431–42, and "An End to Authority," pp. 450–52.

Chapter Eight

1. See above, chap. 3.

2. "The bourgeoisie has been amusing us for two hundred years with its propaganda for 'rugged individualism' which it calls 'social atomism'; but its purpose is to confuse the poor classes: for the bourgeoisie forms by itself alone a strongly integrated collectivity which exploits them" (CP, 122).

3. See McLellan, ed., *Selected Writings,* pp. 132 and 168.

4. See above, chapter 7, and IF, 3:45.

5. Working out the mechanics of bourgeois refusal, Sartre observes: "It is as if everyone's praxis had two components: one horizontal and opposed to the praxis of the adverse group; and the other vertical, an oppressive and repressive force against the proletariat. But this oppression by a group is never direct: it depends on mediation by the State, by public force, or by the series themselves" (CDR, 751). Sartre's popular writings abound with examples of such mediated oppression.

These instruments of repression are the standard Marxist ones: the state as arm of the ruling class and the "forces of order" whose prime concern is the protection of private property, augmented by the Sartrean set of serializing collectives—popular press, the labor market, and the like. All operate within the "chosen necessity" of the capitalist system and bear the "otherness" of the practico-inert on which they rely.

6. "The contradiction of early capitalism . . . is that the employer, under cover of proclaimed reciprocity, treats the worker as an enemy: the free contract, at this period, concealed what was really forced labor" (CDR, 740).

7. Sartre is supported with regard to the fact of economic Malthusianism, if not its motive, by economic historian David Landes. See his essay, "French Business and the Businessman," in *Modern France: Problems of the Third and Fourth Republic,* ed. E. M. Earle (Princeton, N.J.: Princeton University Press, 1951). Landes develops the point in a larger context in his *The Unbound Prometheus: Technological Change and Industrial Development in Western Europe from 1750 to the Present* (London: Cambridge University Press, 1969).

8. A similar thesis is defended at length by C. P. Macpherson in his *The Political Theory of Possessive Individualism: Hobbes to Locke* (Oxford: Oxford University Press, 1962).

9. Jean-Paul Sartre, *Nausea,* trans. Lloyd Alexander (New York: New Directions, 1959), p. 114.

10. The first of these occurs in *The Communists and Peace* (148ff.); it is more fully developed in the *Critique* (758ff.) and is extended to the provincial bourgeois, mutatis mutandis, in *The Family Idiot* (IF, 1:1022ff. and 2:1348).

11. With the fall of the July Monarchy of Louis-Philippe, a new Republic was declared in February of 1848. The socialist, Louis Blanc, was placed at the head of a commission to inquire into economic and social problems. National Workshops (Blanc's term) were created as a measure against unemployment. A few months later, "because of their distant socialistic implications, the National Workshops were suppressed with as much clumsiness as they had been managed. This was intended to be a showdown. On June 23, the Paris masses rose in formidable insurrection. . . . Cavaignac, a general trained in Africa to ruthless warfare, defeated the insurgents in the bloodiest street fighting Paris had even known. . . . The regime which nominally survived until December, 1852, was guided, far more than Louis-Philippe ever was, by its hatred and dread of the proletariat" (Albert Guerard, *France. A Modern History,* new ed. rev. by Paul A. Gagnon [Ann Arbor: The University of Michigan Press, 1969], p. 301).

12. A certain ambiguity results from Sartre's claim that the bourgeois democrat could have absolved himself from complicity by protesting these massacres. For he adds that this crucial concept of identity in alterity must not be reduced to a mere negation, to the failure to resist. For "this identity-alterity is really opaque plenitude"; i.e., though lacking the intellectual transparency of praxis, it is a positive feature of serial being that each acts as Other in the Other. "And since his *Other-Being* merges with his *class-being* here, the class as a collective of oppression is produced in him as *oppressive-being.* . . . In alterity he reveals what he is as inert becoming through what he has done as passive activity" (CDR, 761).

13. Throughout the *Critique* Sartre employs the phrase "pressure groups" (*groupes de pression*) in a broader sense than we are accustomed to. For him it

designates any actively organized interest group seeking to influence class or governmental policy.

14. On "subjectivity" as the limit to reflexive recoil, see above, chapter 1. In the *Critique,* Sartre applies the concept to class consciousness: "Reflection is the *means* of unifying [reflected and reflector]; but, at the same time, it is itself the unifying praxis: through it, the free, practical organism mediates between synchronic class-being and diachronic class-being from the point of view of a totalization. . . . The reflexive totalization is not characterized by class *knowledge*— since class is a quasi-object—but rather, expresses the general schemata of a situated comprehension; and the relations we have analyzed [e.g., exploitation, oppression, obduracy] become orientations of comprehension" (CDR, 768).

15. "Their fathers had denied themselves so that their sons could adopt puritan humanism in freedom. Respectability justified the heir's inheritance" (CDR, 774).

16. As recently as 1952, Sartre referred to Malthusian practices as "the constitutional vice of our economy" (CP, 142). At that time he distinguished social from economic Malthusianism, something he failed to do in the *Critique,* but added that "economic Malthusianism bases itself on social Malthusianism and accelerates it" (CP, 164). If the French are forced to act miserly, "the meanness is in the system"—a familiar claim (CP, 183). In a reprint of this essay Sartre later conceded: "This Malthusianism is outdated today (1964). But it will take a long time," he was quick to add, "before the social structures which proceed from it can give way to new structures" (CP, 231n).

17. In CP he had included statistics on infant mortality in France in 1939 according to socioeconomic class. Though he omits these here, they undoubtedly form the factual basis for the interpretation which he now delivers in the *Critique.*

18. See above, chapter 7, on hexis responsibility, as well as n.2 of the same on status and role responsibility.

19. Sartre, *Nausea,* p. 129.

20. On my responsibility for "my" war, he writes: "Of course others have declared it, and one might be tempted perhaps to consider me as a simple accomplice. But this notion of complicity has only a juridical sense, and it does not hold here" (BN, 554).

21. Stuart Hampshire, *Spinoza* (Baltimore: Penguin Books, 1951), p. 210.

22. See L/S, p. 75, and Contat and Rybalka, *Writings,* 2:373. In fact, more than seven hundred manuscript pages of volume 2 do exist and will eventually appear in print (see Ronald Aronson, "Sartre's Turning Point: The Abandoned *Critique de la raison dialectique,* Volume Two," in P. A. Schilpp, ed. *The Philosophy of Jean-Paul Sartre,* pp. 684–708). Initial portions of the manuscript appear in translation as "Socialism in One Country," *New Left Review* 100 (November 1976–January 1977), pp. 143–63.

Chapter Nine
1. Quoted by Engels in a letter to Bernstein, 2–3 November 1882; Marx/Engels, *Werke,* vol. 35 (Berlin: Dietz Verlag, 1956–68), p. 388. I thank Professor Tom Rockmore for this reference.

2. See Lewis S. Feuer, ed., *Marx and Engels. Basic Writings on Politics and Philosophy* (Garden City, N.Y.: Doubleday Anchor Books, 1959), pp. 224–42.

3. See L/S, 18.

4. I am using "revisionism" in its broad sense of heterodox Marxism generally, and not in its technical sense denoting the position of Eduard Bernstein and his followers within the socialist movement. See the editor's introduction to *Revisionism. Essays on the History of Marxist Ideas,* ed. Leopold Labedz (London: George Allen and Unwin, 1962), pp. 9ff.

5. In his letter to Joseph Bloch, September 21–22, 1890, Engels writes: "We make our history ourselves, but, in the first place, under very definite assumptions and conditions. Among these the economic ones are ultimately decisive" (Feuer, *Marx and Engels,* p. 398).

6. Thus the Communist commentator Adam Schaff is a bit hasty in his assessment of Sartre's Marxism when he announces:

Sartre, however, who declares his avowal of Historical materialism, rejects what is the foundation stone of that materialism, namely, historical determinism with its specific conception of the laws of social development, of the derivative character of social consciousness, and of the dialectic inherent in understanding the individual as both the product and at the same time the maker of society. (*A Philosophy of Man,* [New York: Delta Books, 1963], p. 40)

7. See my "Praxis and Vision" for the inconsistencies that this entails in his epistemology.

8. See above, p. 36.

9. Lucien Goldmann, *Marxisme et sciences humaines* (Paris: Gallimard, 1970), p. 327.

10. Ibid., pp. 330–31. "[Affirmation of] the collective subject," he insists, "constitutes the chief opposition between dialectic and Sartrean thought" (p. 249n).

11. Ibid., p. 249n.

12. Ibid., p. 102.

13. Ibid. The distinction between the inter- and the intra-individual was previously drawn by Tarde, but in a different and more obvious sense. See R. Toulemont, "La Spécificité du social d'après Husserl," *Cahiers internationaux de sociologie,* 25 (July–December 1958), p. 147.

14. Lucien Goldmann, *The Hidden God. A Study of Tragic Vision in The Pensées of Pascal and the Tragedies of Racine,* trans. Philip Thody (New York: Humanities Press, 1964).

15. Goldmann, *Marxisme,* p. 104; emphasis his. He argues this thesis at length both in this essay, "The Subject of Cultural Creativity" (*Marxisme,* pp. 94–129), and in "Dialectical Thought and Transindividual Subject," *Cultural Creation,* trans. Bart Grahl (Saint Louis: Telos Press, 1976), pp. 89–107.

16. Goldmann, *Marxisme,* p. 249n.

17. Of course, it is questionable whether Durkheim ever held the position which Sartre, Goldmann, and others implicitly attribute to him. See Edward A. Tiryakian, *Sociologism and Existentialism* (Englewood Cliffs, N.J.: Prentice-Hall, 1962),

p. 20 n. 27.

18. Goldmann in his later years referred to his position as "genetic structuralism" (see *Marxism*, p. 30).

19. Thus his famous preface to the first edition of *Capital* avows that "here individuals are dealt with only in so far as they are the personifications of economic categories, embodiments of particular class relations and class interests" (McLellan, ed., *Selected Writings*, p. 417).

20. See *The German Ideology* in McLellan, ed., *Selected Writings*, pp. 169–70.

21. McLellan, ed., *Selected Writings*, p. 160.

22. For a brief account of the history of these most recent additions to the Marxian corpus, see David McLellan's introduction to his translation and edition of Marx's *The Grundrisse* (New York: Harper Torchbooks, 1971), pp. 1–15.

23. Thus Lukács, explaining Marx's social ontology, insists: "It is necessary to understand and maintain this duality [of independently operating processes and their arising only through individual intentions], if the specificity of social being is to be understood: the simultaneous dependence and independence of social [for "special" in the English] patterns and processes on the individual acts that directly give rise to them and perpetuate them" (*Toward the Ontology of Social Being,* vol. 2, *Marx,* trans. David Fernbach [London: Merlin Press, 1978], p. 76).

24. Shlomo Avineri, *The Social and Political Thought of Karl Marx,* p. 92.

25. "To Marx, the 'subject' is always social man, the individual viewed in his actual relationships with groups, classes, society as a whole" (Henri Lefebvre, *The Sociology of Marx,* trans. Norbert Guterman [New York: Random House Vintage Books, 1968], p. 8). Carol C. Gould develops this thesis in her *Marx's Social Ontology* (Cambridge, Mass.: The M.I.T. Press, 1978); see especially pp. 30–39.

26. Merleau-Ponty, *Adventures,* p. 200.

27. Ibid., p. 204 (translation altered).

28. Ibid., p. 158.

29. Ibid., pp. 153–54.

30. Raymond Aron, *Marxism and the Existentialists* (New York: Harper and Row, 1969), p. 12. In words that could scarcely have been uttered after reading the *Critique,* Aron notes: "Sartre, in spite of everything, never transcended the Cartesian duality as reinterpreted by Husserl. . . . The rejection of intermediary situations underlies both the Sartrian dualism and the critique made of it by Merleau-Ponty" (p. 9).

31. Ibid., p. 30.

32. This "collectivist" position remains a constant feature of Sartre's subsequent thought. In the 70s he still claims: "I think that an individual in the group, even if he is a little bit terrorized [sic], is nonetheless better than an individual alone and thinking separately. I do not believe that an individual can accomplish anything by himself" (ORR, 171).

33. Merleau-Ponty, *Adventures,* p. 96 n. 2.

34. See above, chap. 6.

35. See IF, 3, book 1, and Goldmann, *The Hidden God.*

36. Goldmann, *Marxisme,* p. 255.

37. Even Lukács, whose thought Goldmann always championed, defends a version of the primacy of praxis: "If the determination of distribution by production is considered . . . from the standpoint of the primacy of man forming and transforming himself in production, then this relationship appears immediately evident. It is only when, as is often the case within Marxism, as is still the case today, economic relations are not conceived as relationships between men, but are fetishized and 'reified' . . . that this relationship becomes puzzling" (*History and Class Consciousness,* p. 66).

38. In CP he argued for "an organization which is the pure and simple incarnation of Praxis" (CP, 128). At that time he had in mind the French Communist party (see CP, 129ff.).

39. Joel Feinberg, *Doing and Deserving* (Princeton, N.J.: Princeton University Press, 1970), pp. 243ff.

40. Durkheim claimed that every individual 'I' was in fact a "we"; see Tiryakian, *Sociologism,* p. 22. From a more clearly structuralist perspective, though he would deny the term, Michel Foucault insists, contra Sartre, that "relations constitute the subject, not vice versa" (conversation, July 21, 1981).

41. In a lecture delivered at the opening session of UNESCO at the Sorbonne, November 1, 1946, Sartre delineated the responsibility of the writer in our time: "He must . . . give his thoughts without respite, day in, day out, to the problem of the end and the means; or, alternatively, the problem of the relation between ethics and politics." ("The Responsibility of the Writer" in *Reflections on Our Age,* p. 83).

42. In BN our being-for-others was likened to our original fall; now this original evil is historicized by appeal to scarcity.

43. "L'Espoir, maintenant . . . ," *Le Nouvel Observateur* 801 (17 March 1980), p. 58.

44. Albert Camus, *The Plague,* trans. Stuart Gilbert (New York: Random House, 1948), pp. 226ff.

45. "L'Espoir, maintenant . . . ," p. 58.

46. See my "From '*Socialisme et Liberté*' to '*Pouvoir et Liberté*': Sartre and Political Existentialism," in *Phenomenology in a Pluralistic Context,* ed. William L. McBride and Calvin O. Schrag (Albany, N.Y.: State University of New York Press, forthcoming). Also see above, chap. 3, n.30.

47. Lukács, for example, sees the proletariat as the "we" which is the subject of history (see *History and Class Consciousness,* pp. 145–49).

48. Sartre shares the aversion to closures that typifies the existential dialectic generally (see Robert Denoon Cumming, *Starting Point. An Introduction to the Dialectic of Existence* [Chicago: The University of Chicago Press, 1979], especially part IV, pp. 399ff.). So he will not accept the Hegelian-Marxian end-*terminus* of history. Replying to the Communist Claude Lefort (1953), Sartre insists that the truth of a dialectical movement can be established in only two ways: if you are caught up in the movement, it is praxis which decides: "Action and idea being

but one, the true idea is an efficacious action''; but if you are outside the action and immobile, as he accuses Lefort of being, then "you must be placed precisely at the end of history" (*Situations*, 7:21). But it is by implicit appeal to an end-goal of history, a future totalization, that he can speak of a subject of history at all. I shall discuss this goal in chapter 10.

Chapter Ten

1. Unfortunately, this essay remains among Sartre's unpublished works.

2. He describes it as "un romain vrai," literally "a novel which is true" (*Situations*, 9:123). For a discussion of Sartre's trading on the ambiguity of this phrase, see my "Sartre-Flaubert and the Real/Unreal," p. 122.

3. See above, chap. 1, as well as my "The Role of the Image," p. 440.

4. The limit to this grasp of what human freedom can become will mark the limit to our understanding of human reality and "History" as well as to Sartrean "rationalism" from the perspective of the future, just as facticity and the practico-inert set those limits from the other temporal perspectives.

5. See his *Economic and Philosophical Manuscripts of 1844* in McLellan, ed., *Karl Marx: Selected Writings*, pp. 81ff.

6. To an orthodox Marxist such as Theodor Schwarz, this is, of course, a distinct liability. See his *Jean-Paul Sartres 'Kritik der dialektischen Vernunft,'* pp. 77–84, 91–93.

7. Aron, *Marxism and the Existentialists*, pp. 87–88. An orthodox Marxist would answer by distinguishing antagonistic and nonantagonistic contradictions. The latter, not based on class distinction, remain even under socialism. Examples of these would be such personal tragedies as sickness, death, and natural disaster. See Schwarz, *Sartres 'Kritik'*, pp. 89–90.

8. The concept of "free alterity" (CDR, 366) should suffice to prove alienation distinct from otherness *sans phrase*. As for objectification, the matter is less clear. The gamut of opinions among Sartre's commentators regarding its identification with alienation runs as follows: clearly yes (Pietro Chiodi, *Sartre and Marxism*, pp. 21 and 93, and app. 2), more yes than no (Raymond Aron, *History and the Dialectic of Violence*, trans. Barry Cooper [Oxford: Basil Blackwell, 1975], pp. 42, 101, and 232), and emphatically no (André Gorz, *Socialism and Revolution*, trans. Norman Denny [Garden City, N.Y.: Doubleday Anchor Books, 1973], pp. 253–56).

9. See Joseph H. McMahon's analysis in *Humans Being. The World of Jean-Paul Sartre* (Chicago: The University of Chicago Press, 1971), pp. 227ff. McMahon characterizes Nasty, another protagonist in the play, as incarnating "a new category in the Sartrean system, a kind of harmonization of the subject-object conflict" (p. 242). For positive reciprocity in CM, see 224 and 294–301.

10. See above, chap. 2.

11. "After the war came the true experience, that of *society*" (BEM, 34). "Every man is political," Sartre told an interviewer, "but I did not discover that for myself until the war, and I did not truly understand it until 1945" (L/S, 44–45).

12. In addition to the references from *The Devil and the Good Lord* and *Saint Genet* mentioned above, consider: "Love desires reciprocity," but Genet remains incapable of reciprocity (SG, 527). On authentic love, see CM, 434, 493–98, and 523.

13. In accord with his ideal of *concrete* freedom, the politicized Sartre concludes that the denizens of this literary world must "historicize themselves," i.e., that they should "transform their formal exigencies into material, dated demands." Otherwise, he warns, the city of ends will last only the length of our reading; as we pass from the imaginary life to the real, we shall forget this abstract, implicit community, which rests on nothing," i.e., on the "nothing" of imaginative consciousness (*Situations*, 2:293).

14. "The Communists . . . say: 'If you talk Justice to the people, they'll march.' But [they] don't give a damn for Justice; [they] first of all want power" (ORR, 76).

15. "The true relation among men is reciprocity, which excludes commands properly speaking" (IF, 3:48). See my "An End to Authority," pp. 452ff.

16. "If you supposed a veritable socialism in act, a real one, the notion of the politician would disappear in the sense that everyone would be political. . . . If we suppose a classless society, I don't think this category of person is necessary. I think that each one becomes mediator of the ensemble" (ORR, 288). "The political man whom we retain . . . possesses only one technique, that's the technique of persuasion" (ORR, 301).

17. Foucault gradually came to see that his "genealogies" are really "analytics of power." See his *The History of Sexuality,* vol. 1: *An Introduction,* trans. Robert Hurley (New York: Pantheon, 1978), p. 82. But he stands in opposition to Sartre by not considering all forms of power (at least outside the group) as alienating. See my "Sartre and Foucault on Reason and History," forthcoming.

18. "[Belief] is the presence in us of a foreign will, unifying words in an assertoric synthesis that both fascinates and alienates us to the point that we make it our own will" (IF, 1:163). I develop this in my "An End to Authority," pp. 449–52.

19. Sartre once avowed that, if faced with the choice of torturing another or being killed, he would commit suicide. See above, chap. 4, n. 29.

20. Aron, *D'une sainte famille à l'autre: Essais sur les marxismes imaginaires* (Paris: Gallimard, 1969), p. 373.

21. See "L'Espoir, maintenant . . . ," no. 801, especially pp. 55–57.

22. Ibid., p. 58.

23. Aron, *Marxism and the Existentialists,* p. 169.

24. See, for example, Thomas Aquinas, *Summa Theologiae,* I, 64, 2. In another context but in a manner applicable to Sartre's "noetic freedom," Jean Granier refers to "the angelism of absolute spiritual freedom" (*Penser la praxis,* p. 261).

25. One commentator even speaks of Marx's "social nominalism" due to Feuerbach's influence (James Miller, *History and Human Existence* [Berkeley: University of California Press, 1979], p. 44).

26. See Wolin, *Politics,* pp. 416–17.

27. A question raised, analyzed, but not resolved by Peter Laslett in his "The Face-to-Face Society," *Philosophy, Politics, and Society,* 1st series, ed. Peter Laslett (Oxford: Blackwell, 1970), pp. 157–84.

28. Quoted by Jeannette Colombel, *Sartre ou le parti de vivre* (Paris: Grasset, 1981), p. 88.

29. See, e.g., Miller, *History,* pp. 72–97.

30. This social imperative was first conceived as a democratic ideal at the time of Sartre's entry into mass politics via the short-lived Revolutionary Democratic Assembly. In its quasi-manifesto he explains how, with the help of the directing committee, "the base will learn to see that each of its particular problems, which is in effect an aspect of a general problem, can be resolved only in the general positing of the problem. . . . Thus democracy will consist in formulating each-particular problem in the perspective of general problems" (EP, 31). Sartre seems always to have believed that the "particular" and the "general" problems could be clearly distinguished, a sign of his political idealism.

31. Interview with Michel Sicard in the first of two special "Sartre" issues of *Obliques,* nos. 18–19 (1979), p. 15.

32. "L'Espoir, maintenant . . ." no. 800, pp. 57–58.

33. Ibid., p. 60.

34. Ibid.

35. See Jean-Paul Sartre, *The Words,* trans. Bernard Frechtman (New York: Braziller, 1964), pp. 84–85.

36. Sartre, *Words,* p. 160.

Jean-Paul Sartre Vivant

1. Aron, *History,* p. 200.

2. For a recent attempt to defend Marx's "technological" determinism, see Shaw, *Marx's Theory of History,* especially chapter 2.

3. Rom Harré, *Social Being* (Totowa, N.J.: Littlefield, Adams and Co., 1979), p. 97.

4. Aronson, *Sartre,* p. 345.

Bibliography

The following are works cited in the present study or consulted in its preparation. Where available, English translations are listed followed by the original version when the latter is cited in the text.

Writings of Sartre

Anti-Semite and Jew. Translated by George J. Becker. New York: Schocken Books, 1948.

Between Existentialism and Marxism. Translated by John Mathews. New York: William Morrow and Company, 1974.

Being and Nothingness. Translated by Hazel E. Barnes. New York: Philosophical Library, 1956. *L'Être et le Néant.* Paris: Gallimard, 1943.

Cahiers pour une morale. Paris: Gallimard, 1983.

Les Carnets de la drôle de guerre. Paris: Gallimard, 1983.

The Communists and Peace with *A Reply to Claude Lefort.* Translated by Martha H. Fletcher and Philip R. Berk respectively. New York: George Braziller, 1968.

The Condemned of Altona. Translated by Sylvia and George Leeson. New York: Random House, Vintage Books, 1961.

"Consciousness of Self and Knowledge of Self." In *Readings in Existential Phenomenology.* Edited by Nathaniel Lawrence and Daniel O'Connor. Englewood Cliffs, N.J.: Prentice-Hall, 1967.

Critique of Dialectical Reason. Translated by Alan Sheridan-Smith. London: New Left Books, 1976. *Critique de la raison dialectique,* précédé de *Question de méthode.* Paris: Gallimard, 1960.

The Devil and the Good Lord. Translated by Kitty Black. New York: Random House, Vintage Books, 1960.

Dirty Hands. See *"No Exit."*

The Emotions. Outline of a Theory. Translated by Bernard Frechtman. New York: Philosophical Library, 1948.

Entretiens sur la politique. With D. Rousset and G. Rosenthal. Paris: Gallimard, 1949.

"Existentialism Is a Humanism." In *Existentialism from Dostoevsky to Sartre.* Selected and introduced by Walter Kaufmann. Cleveland: World Publishing, Meridian Books, 1956. *L'Existentialisme est un humanisme.* Paris: Nagel, 1970.

L'Idiot de la famille. 3 vols. Paris: Gallimard, 1971–72. *The Family Idiot.* Vol. 1. Translated by Carol Cosman. Chicago: University of Chicago Press, 1981.

"Intentionality: A Fundamental Idea of Husserl's Phenomenology." *Journal of the British Society for Phenomenology* 1, no. 2 (May 1970): 4–5.

Life/Situations: Essays Written and Spoken. Translated by Paul Auster and Lydia Davis. New York: Pantheon, 1977.

Literary and Philosophical Essays. Translated by Annette Michelson. New York: Crowell-Collier, Collier Books, 1962.

"A Long, Bitter, Sweet Madness." *Encounter* 22 (June 1964): 61–63.

"L'Espoir, maintenant. . . ." *Le Nouvel Observateur,* no. 800 (10 March 1980), p. 19; no. 801 (17 March 1980), p. 52; and no. 802 (24 March 1980), p. 55. English translation with some omissions in *Dissent* 27 (Fall 1980): 397–422.

Marxisme et existentialisme. Controverse sur la dialectique. With R. Garaudy, J. Hyppolite, J. P. Vigier, and J. Orcel. Paris: Plon, 1962.

"Materialism and Revolution." See *Literary and Philosophical Essays.*

"Merleau-Ponty vivant." *Les Temps modernes* 184–85 (September–October 1961): 304–76.

Nausea. Translated by Lloyd Alexander. New York: New Directions, 1959.

"No Exit" and Three Other Plays. Translated by Lionel Abel. New York: Random House, Vintage Books, 1955.

Oeuvres Romanesques. Edited by Michel Contat and Michel Rybalka with Geneviève Idt and George H. Bauer. Paris: Gallimard, 1981.

On a raison de se révolter. With Ph. Gavi and P. Victor. Paris: Gallimard, 1974.

On Genocide. Introduction by Arlette El Kaïm-Sartre. Boston: Beacon Press, 1968.

"Présentation des *Temps modernes.*" *Situations* (1948), 2:7–30.

The Psychology of Imagination. Translated by Bernard Frechtman. New York: Washington Square Press, 1966. *L'Imaginaire.* Paris: Gallimard, 1940.

"The Responsibility of the Writer." In *Reflections on Our Age.* Introduction by David Hardman. New York: Columbia University Press, 1949.

Saint Genet, Actor and Martyr. Translated by Bernard Frechtman. New York: George Braziller, 1963.

Sartre on Theater. Edited by Michel Contat and Michel Rybalka. Translated by Frank Jellinek. New York: Pantheon, 1976.

Sartre, un film. Produced by Alexandre Astruc and Michel Contat. Paris: Gallimard, 1977.

Search for a Method. Translated by Hazel E. Barnes. New York: Random House, Vintage Books, 1968.

Situations. Vols. 1–10. Paris: Gallimard, 1947–76.

"Socialism in One Country." *New Left Review* 100 (1976–77): 143–63.

The Transcendence of the Ego. Translated by Forest Williams and Robert Kirkpatrick. New York: The Noonday Press, 1957. *La Transcendence de l'ego.* Introduction, notes, and appendixes by Sylvie Le Bon. Paris: J. Vrin, 1965.

A Victory, preceded by Henri Alleg's *The Question.* Translated by John Calder. New York: Braziller, 1958.

"The Wall" and Other Stories. Translated by Lloyd Alexander. New York: New Directions, 1969.

War Crimes in Vietnam. With Vladimir Dedijer. Nottingham: The Bertrand Russell Peace Foundation, 1971.

What Is Literature? Translated by Bernard Frechtman. New York: Washington Square Press, 1966.

The Words. Translated by Bernard Frechtman. New York: Braziller, 1964.
Preface to *The Wretched of the Earth* by Frantz Fanon. Translated by Constance Farrington. New York: Grove Press, 1968.

Bibliographies
Belkind, Allen J. *Jean-Paul Sartre and Existentialism in English: A Bibliographical Guide.* Kent, Ohio: Kent State University Press, 1970.
Contat, Michel, and Rybalka, Michel. *The Writings of Jean-Paul Sartre.* 2 vols. Evanston, Ill.: Northwestern University Press, 1974. Updated in *Magazine Littéraire* no. 55–56 (September 1971): 36–47, and no. 103–104 (September 1975): 9–49; and in *Obliques* no. 18–19 (1979): 331–47.
Lapoint, François and Claire. *Jean-Paul Sartre and His Critics: An International Bibliography (1938–1980).* 2d ed., rev. Bowling Green, Ky.: Philosophy Documentation Center, 1981.
Wilcocks, Robert. *Jean-Paul Sartre: A Bibliography of International Criticism.* Edmonton: University of Alberta Press, 1975.

Studies on Sartre
Anderson, Thomas C. *The Foundation and Structure of Sartrean Ethics.* Lawrence: Regents Press of Kansas, 1979.
Aron, Raymond. *D'une sainte famille à l'autre: Essais sur les marxismes imaginaires.* Paris: Gallimard, 1969.
———. *German Sociology.* Translated by Mary and Thomas Bottomore. London: Heinemann, 1957.
———. *History and the Dialectic of Violence.* Translated by Barry Cooper. Oxford: Basil Blackwell, 1975.
———. *Introduction to the Philosophy of History.* Translated by G. J. Irwin. London: Weidenfeld and Nicolson, 1961.
———. *Marxism and the Existentialists.* Translated by Helen Weaver, Robert Addis, and John Weightman. New York: Harper and Row, 1969.
Aronson, Ronald. *Jean-Paul Sartre.* New York: New Left Books, 1980.
Barnes, Hazel E. *Sartre.* New York: Lippincott, 1973.
———. *Sartre and Flaubert.* Chicago: University of Chicago Press, 1981.
Bernstein, Richard. *Praxis and Action.* Philadelphia: University of Pennsylvania Press, 1971.
Biemel, Walter. "Das Wesen Der Dialektik bei Hegel und Sartre." *Tijdschrift voor Philosophie* 20 (1958): 269–300.
Briosi, Sandro. *Il Pensiero di Sartre.* Ravenna: Longo, 1978.
Burnier, Michel-Antoine. *Les Existentialistes et la politique.* Paris: Gallimard, 1966. Translated by Bernard Murchland as *Choice of Action.* New York: Random House, 1968.
Caws, Peter. *Sartre.* London: Routledge and Kegan Paul, 1979.
Cera, Giovanni. *Sartre tra ideologia e storia.* Bari: Laterza, 1972.
Chiodi, Pietro. *Sartre and Marxism.* Translated by Kate Soper. Atlantic Highlands, N.J.: Humanities Press, 1976.

Collins, Douglas. *Sartre as Biographer*. Cambridge: Harvard University Press, 1980.

Colombel, Jeannette. *Sartre ou le parti de vivre*. Paris: Grasset, 1981.

Contat, Michel. *Explication des Séquestrés d'Altona de Jean-Paul Sartre*. Paris: Minard, 1968.

Craib, Ian. *Existentialism and Sociology: A Study of Jean-Paul Sartre*. Cambridge: Cambridge University Press, 1976.

Cranston, Maurice W. *The Quintessence of Sartrism*. New York: Harper Torchbooks, 1969.

Cumming, Robert Denoon, ed. *The Philosophy of Jean-Paul Sartre*. New York: Random House, Modern Library, 1965.

Danto, Arthur C. *Jean-Paul Sartre*. New York: Viking Press, 1975.

De Beauvoir, Simone. *All Said and Done*. Translated by Patrick O'Brian. New York: G. P. Putman's Sons, 1974.

———. *La Cérémonie des adieux*, followed by *Entretiens avec Jean-Paul Sartre (août-septembre 1974)*. Paris: Gallimard, 1982.

———. *The Prime of Life*. Translated by Peter Green. New York: World, Lancer Books, 1962.

———. *Pyrrhus et Cinéas*. Paris: Gallimard, 1944.

———. "Merleau-Ponty et le pseudo-sartrisme." *Les Temps modernes* nos. 114–15 (June–July 1955): 2072–2122.

Desan, Wilfrid. *The Marxism of Jean-Paul Sartre*. Garden City, N.Y.: Doubleday Anchor Books, 1965.

———. *The Tragic Finale*. New York: Harper Torchbooks, 1954.

De Waelhens, Alphonse. "Sartre et la raison dialectique." *Revue philosophique de Louvain* 60 (1962): 79–99.

Dreyfus, Dina. "Jean-Paul Sartre et le mal radical." *Mercure de France* 341 (January 1961): 154–67.

Fe, Franco. *Sartre e il communismo*. Florence: La Nouva Italia, 1970.

Fell, Joseph P. *Heidegger and Sartre: An Essay on Being and Place*. New York: Columbia University Press, 1979.

———. *Emotion in the Thought of Sartre*. New York: Columbia University Press, 1965.

Fetscher, Iring. "Der Marxismus im Spiegel der französischen Philosophie." *Marxismusstudien* 1 (1954): 173–213.

Flynn, Thomas R. "An End to Authority: Epistemology and Politics in the Later Sartre." *Man and World* 10 (1977): 448–65.

———. "Existential Hermeneutics: The Progressive-Regressive Method." *Eros* 8, no. 1 (1981): 3–24.

———. "From '*Socialisme et Liberté*' to '*Pouvoir et Liberté*': Sartre and Political Existentialism." In *Phenomenology in a Pluralistic Context*. Edited by William L. McBride and Calvin O. Schrag. Albany, N.Y.: State University of New York Press, forthcoming.

———. "*L'Imagination au Pouvoir*: The Evolution of Sartre's Political and Social Thought." *Political Theory* 7, no. 2 (May 1979): 175–80.

248

———. "Mediated Reciprocity and the Genius of the Third." In *The Philosophy of Jean-Paul Sartre*. Edited by P. A. Schilpp. La Salle, Ill.: Open Court, 1981.

———. "Praxis and Vision: Elements of a Sartrean Epistemology." *The Philosophical Forum* 8 (Fall 1976): 21–43.

———. "The Role of the Image in Sartre's Aesthetic." *The Journal of Aesthetics and Art Criticism* 33 (Summer 1975): 431–42.

———. "Sartre-Flaubert and the Real/Unreal." In *Jean-Paul Sartre. Contemporary Approaches to His Philosophy*. Edited by H. Silverman and F. Elliston. Pittsburgh: Duquesne University Press, 1980.

Garaudy, Roger. *Humanisme marxiste*. Paris: Editions Sociales, 1957.

Goldmann, Lucien. *Marxisme et sciences humaines*. Paris: Gallimard, 1970.

Gorz, André. *Le Socialisme difficile*. Paris: Le Seuil, 1967. Translated with abridgment by Norman Denny as *Socialism and Revolution*. Garden City, N.Y.: Doubleday Anchor Books, 1973.

Greene, Norman N. *Jean Paul Sartre. The Existentialist Ethic*. Ann Arbor: The University of Michigan Press, 1960.

Grene, Marjorie. *Sartre*. New York: New Viewpoints, 1973.

Gurvitch, Georges. *Dialectique et sociologie*. Paris: Flammarion, 1962.

———. "Dialectique et sociologie selon Jean-Paul Sartre." *Cahiers internationaux de sociologie* 31 (1961): 113–28.

Hana, Ghanem-George. *Freiheit und Person: Eine Auseinandersetzung mit der Darstellung J.-P. Sartres*. Munich: Beck, 1965.

Hartmann, Klaus. *Sartre's Ontology*. Evanston, Ill.: Northwestern University Press, 1966.

———. *Sartres Sozialphilosophie. Eine Untersuchung zur "Critique de la raison dialectique, I."* Berlin: de Gruyter, 1966.

Hayim, Gila J. *The Existential Sociology of Jean-Paul Sartre*. Amherst: University of Massachusetts Press, 1980.

Jameson, Fredric. *Marxism and Form*. Princeton, N.J.: Princeton University Press, 1971.

Jeanson, Francis. *Sartre and the Problem of Morality*. Translated with Introduction by Robert V. Stone. Bloomington: University of Indiana Press, 1981.

———. *Sartre par lui-même*. Paris: Le Seuil, 1967.

———. *Sartre*. Paris: Desclée de Brouwer, 1966.

———. *Sartre dans sa vie*. Paris: Le Seuil, 1974.

Kampits, Peter. *Sartre und die Frage nach dem Anderen*. Vienna-Munich: R. Oldenbourg Verlag, 1975.

Krosigk, F. von. *Philosophie und politische Aktion bei Jean-Paul Sartre*. Munich: Beck, 1969.

Kline, George L. "The Existentialist Rediscovery of Hegel and Marx." *Phenomenology and Existentialism*. Edited by Edward N. Lee and Maurice Mandelbaum. Baltimore: Johns Hopkins Press, 1967.

LaCapra, Dominick. *A Preface to Sartre*. Ithaca, N.Y.: Cornell University Press, 1978.

Laing, R. D., and Cooper, D. G. *Reason and Violence: A Decade of Sartre's Philosophy, 1950–1960.* London: Tavistock, 1964.

Lawler, James. *The Existentialist Marxism of Jean-Paul Sartre.* Amsterdam: Grüner, 1976.

Lévi-Strauss, Claude. *The Savage Mind.* Chicago: University of Chicago Press, 1966.

Lukács, Georg. *Existentialisme ou marxisme?* 2d ed. Paris: Nagel, 1961.

McBride, William L. *Fundamental Change in Law and Society: Hart and Sartre on Revolution.* The Hague: Mouton, 1970.

———. *Social Theory at a Crossroads.* Pittsburgh: Duquesne University Press, 1980.

McMahon, Joseph J. *Humans Being: The World of Jean-Paul Sartre.* Chicago: University of Chicago Press, 1971.

Manser, Anthony R. *Sartre: A Philosophic Study.* Rev. ed. London: Athlone Press, 1967.

Masullo, Aldo. *La Communità come fondamento: Fichte, Husserl, Sartre.* Naples: Libreria Scientifica Editrice, 1965.

Merleau-Ponty, Maurice. *Adventures of the Dialectic.* Translated by Joseph J. Bien. Evanston, Ill.: Northwestern University Press, 1973.

Mészáros, István. *The Work of Sartre.* Vol. 1, *Search for Freedom.* Atlantic Highlands, N.J.: Humanities Press, 1979.

Morris, Phyllis S. *Sartre's Concept of a Person: An Analytic Approach.* Amherst: University of Massachusetts Press, 1976.

Murdoch, Iris. *Sartre, Romantic Rationalist.* New Haven: Yale University Press, 1953.

Natanson, Maurice. *A Critique of Jean-Paul Sartre's Ontology.* The Hague: Martinus Nijhoff, 1973.

Nauta, L. W. "Dialektik bei Sartre." *Studium Generale* 17 (July 1968): 591–607.

Odajnyk, Walter. *Marxism and Existentialism.* Garden City, N.Y.: Doubleday Anchor Books, 1965.

Pagano, Giacoma M. *Sartre e la dialettica.* Naples: Giannini, 1970.

Poster, Mark. *Existential Marxism in Postwar France: From Sartre to Althusser.* Princeton, N.J.: Princeton University Press, 1975.

———. *Sartre's Marxism.* London: Pluto Press, 1979.

Presseault, Jacques. *L'Être-pour-autrui dans la philosophie de Jean-Paul Sartre.* Paris: Desclée de Brouwer, 1970.

Schaff, Adam. *Marx oder Sartre? Versuch einer Philosophie des Menschen.* Berlin: Deutscher Verlag der Wissenschaften, 1965.

Schilpp, P. A., ed. *The Philosophy of Jean-Paul Sartre.* La Salle, Ill.: Open Court, 1981.

Schwarz, Theodor. *Jean-Paul Sartres 'Kritik der Dialektischen Vernunft.'* Berlin: Veb Deutscher Verlag der Wissenschaften, 1967.

Seel, Gerhard. *Sartres Dialektik.* Bonn: Bouvier, 1971.

Sheridan, James F. *Sartre: The Radical Conversion.* Athens: Ohio University Press, 1973.

Bibliography

Silverman, H. J., and Elliston, F. A., eds. *Jean-Paul Sartre. Contemporary Approaches to His Philosophy*. Pittsburgh: Duquesne University Press, 1980.

Sotelo, Ignacio. *Sartre y la razón dialéctica*. Madrid: Tecnos, 1967.

Spiegelberg, Herbert. *The Phenomenological Movement*. 3d ed., rev. The Hague: Martinus Nijhoff, 1981.

Stack, George J. *Sartre's Philosophy of Social Existence*. St. Louis: Warren H. Green, 1978.

Suhl, Benjamin. *Jean-Paul Sartre: The Philosopher as Literary Critic*. New York: Columbia University Press, 1970.

Thody, Philip. *Jean-Paul Sartre: A Literary and Political Study*. London: Hamilton, 1964.

Verstraeten, Pierre. *Violence et éthique: Esquisse d'une critique de la morale dialectique à partir du théatre de Sartre*. Paris: Gallimard, 1972.

Warnock, Mary. *Existentialist Ethics*. London: Macmillan, 1967.

———. *The Philosophy of Jean-Paul Sartre*. London: Hutchinson, 1965.

———, ed. *Sartre: A Collection of Critical Essays*. Garden City, N.Y.: Doubleday Anchor Books, 1971.

Zehm, Günter A. *Historische Vernunft und directe Aktion. Zur Politik und Philosophie Jean-Paul Sartres*. Stuttgart: E. Klett, 1964.

Special Numbers of Periodicals

L'Arc, no. 30 (1966).

Aut Aut, "Sartre dopo la 'Critique,' " no. 136–37 (July–October 1973).

Eros, "A Commemorative Issue: Jean-Paul Sartre, 1905–1980," 8, no. 1 (1981).

Journal of the British Society for Phenomenology 1, no. 2 (May 1970).

Magazine Littéraire, no. 55–56 (September 1971); no. 103–4 (September 1975).

Obliques, no. 18–19 (1979); no. 24–25 (1981).

Other Works

Althusser, Louis, et al. *Lire le capital*. 2 vols. Paris: Maspero, 1965.

Arendt, Hannah. *Eichmann in Jerusalem*. New York: Viking Press, 1965.

———. *The Jew as Pariah: Jewish Identity and Politics in the Modern Age*. Edited by Ron H. Feldman. New York: Grove Press, 1978.

Aristotle. *Metaphysics. The Works of Aristotle Translated into English*. Edited by W. D. Ross. Vol. 8. Oxford: At the Clarendon Press, 1908.

———. *Nichomachean Ethics. The Works of Aristotle Translated into English*. Edited by W. D. Ross. Vol. 9. Oxford: At the Clarendon Press, 1925.

Avineri, Shlomo. *The Social and Political Thought of Karl Marx*. Cambridge: At the University Press, 1968.

Benoist, Jean-Marie. *La Révolution structurale*. Paris: Grasset, 1975.

Bottomore, T. B. *Classes in Modern Society*. New York: Random House, Vintage Books, 1966.

Brodbeck, May. "Methodological Individualism: Definition and Reduction." *Philosophy of Science* 25, no. 1 (January 1958): 1–22.

Camus, Albert. *The Plague*. Translated by Stuart Gilbert. New York: Random House, Modern Library, 1948.

Cua, Antonio. *Dimensions of Moral Creativity*. University Park, Pa.: Pennsylvania State University Press, 1978.

Cumming, Robert Denoon. *Starting Point. An Introduction to the Dialectic of Existence*. Chicago: The University of Chicago Press, 1979.

Danto, Arthur C. *Analytical Philosophy of History*. Cambridge: At the University Press, 1968.

De Beauvoir, Simone. *The Ethics of Ambiguity*. Translated by Bernard Frechtman. Secaucus, N.J.: The Citadel Press, 1975.

Descombes, Vincent. *Le Même et l'autre. Quarante-cinque ans de philosophie française (1933–78)*. Paris: Minuit, 1979.

Downie, R. S. "Responsibility and Social Roles." In *Individual and Collective Responsibility*. Edited by Peter A. French. Cambridge, Mass.: Schenkman, 1972.

Durkheim, Emile. *The Rules of Sociological Method*. Translated by Sarah A. Solovay and John H. Mueller. 8th ed. New York: The Free Press, 1966.

Earle, E. M. *Modern France: Problems of the Third and Fourth Republics*. Princeton, N.J.: Princeton University Press, 1951.

Fanon, Frantz. *The Wretched of the Earth*. Translated by Constance Farrington. New York: Grove Press, 1968.

Feinberg, Joel. *Doing and Deserving*. Princeton, N.J.: Princeton University Press, 1970.

Fetscher, Iring. "Zum Begriff Der 'Objektiven Möglichkeit' bei Max Weber und Georg Lukács." *Revue internationale de philosophie* 27, no. 106 (1973): 501–15.

Feuer, Lewis S., ed. *Marx and Engels. Basic Writings on Politics and Philosophy*. Garden City, N.Y.: Doubleday Anchor Books, 1959.

————, ed. *Marx and the Intellectuals*. Garden City, N.Y.: Doubleday Anchor Books, 1969.

Findlay, John. *Axiological Ethics*. London: Macmillan, 1970.

Fingarette, Herbert. *On Responsibility*. New York: Basic Books, 1967.

Foucault, Michel. *The History of Sexuality*. Vol. 1. *An Introduction*. Translated by Robert Hurley. New York: Pantheon, 1978.

French, Peter A., ed. *Individual and Collective Responsibility*. Cambridge, Mass.: Schenkman, 1972.

Friedrich, Carl J., ed. *Responsibility*. Vol. 3. *Nomos*. New York: Liberal Arts Press, 1960.

Gagnon, Paul A. *France Since 1789*. New York: Harper and Row, 1964.

Ginsberg, Morris. *Essays in Sociology and Social Philosophy*. Harmondsworth, Middlesex, Eng.: Penguin Books, 1968.

Goldmann, Lucien. *Cultural Creation*. Translated by Bart Grahl. Saint Louis: Telos Press, 1976.

————. *The Hidden God. A Study of Tragic Vision in the Pensées of Pascal and the Tragedies of Racine*. Translated by Philip Thody. New York: Humanities

Press, 1964.

Gould, Carol C. *Marx's Social Ontology*. Cambridge, Mass.: M.I.T. Press, 1978.

Granier, Jean. *Penser la praxis*. Paris: Presses Universitaires de France, 1980.

Guerard, Albert. *France. A Modern History*. Revised by Paul A. Gagnon. Ann Arbor: University of Michigan Press, 1969.

Habermas, Jürgen. *Theory and Practice*. Translated by John Viertel. Boston: Beacon Press, 1973.

Hampshire, Stuart. *Spinoza*. Baltimore: Penguin Books, 1951.

Hare, R. M. *The Language of Morals*. New York: Oxford University Press, Galaxy Books, 1964.

Harré, Rom. *Social Being*. Totowa, N.J.: Littlefield, Adams and Co., 1979.

Harris, John. *Violence and Responsibility*. London: Routledge and Kegan Paul, 1980.

Hart, H. L. A. "The Ascription of Responsibility and Rights." In *Logic and Language*. 1st and 2d series. Ed. Antony Flew. Garden City, N.Y.: Doubleday Anchor Books, 1965.

―――. *The Concept of Law*. New York: Oxford University Press, 1961.

―――. *Punishment and Responsibility*. New York: Oxford University Press, 1968.

Hayek, F. A. *The Counter-Revolution in Science*. Glencoe, Ill.: The Free Press, 1952.

Heidegger, Martin. *Being and Time*. Translated by John Macquarrie and Edward Robinson. New York: Harper and Row, 1962.

Hirschman, Albert O. *The Passions and the Interests*. Princeton, N.J.: Princeton University Press, 1979.

Hume, David. *A Treatise of Human Nature*. 2d ed. Edited by L. A. Selby-Bigge. Revised by P. H. Nidditch. Oxford: Clarendon Press, 1978.

Husserl, Edmund. *Ideas Pertaining to a Pure Phenomenology and to a Phenomenological Philosophy*. First Book. *General Introduction to a Pure Phenomenology*. Translated by F. Kersten. The Hague: Martinus Nijhoff, 1982.

Ingarden, Roman. *Über die Verantwortung. Ihre Ontischen Fundamente*. Stuttgart: Reclam, 1970.

Jaspers, Karl. *The Question of German Guilt*. Translated by E. B. Ashton. New York: Dial Press, 1947.

Jordan, Z. A. *The Evolution of Dialectical Materialism*. New York: St. Martin's Press, 1969.

Kamenka, Eugene. *Marxism and Ethics*. New Studies in Ethics. New York: St. Martin's Press, 1969.

Kierkegaard, Søren. *Philosophical Fragments*. Translated by David Swenson. Revised by Howard V. Hong. Princeton, N.J.: Princeton University Press, 1967.

Labedz, Leopold. *Revisionism. Essays on the History of Marxist Ideas*. London: George Allen and Unwin, 1962.

Landes, David. *The Unbound Prometheus: Technological Change and Industrial Development in Western Europe from 1750 to the Present*. London: Cambridge University Press, 1969.

Laslett, Peter, ed. *Philosophy, Politics, and Society.* 1st series. Oxford: Blackwell, 1970.

Lefebvre, Henri. *The Sociology of Marx.* Translated by Norbert Guterman. New York: Random House, Vintage Books, 1968.

Leibniz, G. W. F. *Essais de théodicée.* Paris: Aubier, 1962.

Lukács, Georg. *History and Class Consciousness.* Translated by Rodney Livingston. Cambridge, Mass.: M.I.T. Press, 1971.

———. *Toward the Ontology of Social Being.* Vol. 2. *Marx.* Translated by David Fernbach. London: Merlin Press, 1978.

MacIntyre, Alasdair. *Against the Self-Images of the Age.* London: Duckworth, 1971.

McKeon, Richard. "The Development and the Significance of the Concept of Responsibility." *Revue internationale de philosophie* 11 (1957): 3–32.

McLellan, David, ed. *Karl Marx: Selected Writings.* Oxford: Oxford University Press, 1977.

Macpherson, C. P. *The Political Theory of Possessive Individualism: Hobbes to Locke.* Oxford: Oxford University Press, 1962.

Mandelbaum, Maurice. "Societal Facts." In *Theories of History.* Edited by Patrick Gardiner. Glencoe, Ill.: The Free Press, 1959.

Marx, Karl. *Capital: A Critique of Political Economy.* Translated by S. Moore, E. Aveling and E. Untermann. Chicago: Charles H. Kerr, 1906–9.

———. *The Grundrisse.* Translated with a foreword by Martin Nicolaus. New York: Vintage Books, 1973.

———. *Selected Writings.* Edited by David McLellan. Oxford: Oxford University Press, 1977.

Marx, Karl, and Engels, Friedrich, *Werke.* 39 vols. Berlin: Dietz Verlag, 1956–68.

Merleau-Ponty, Maurice. *Humanism and Terror.* Translated by John O'Neill. Boston: Beacon Press, 1969.

Miller, James. *History and Human Existence.* Berkeley: University of California Press, 1979.

Morris, Charles W. *Signs, Language, and Behavior.* New York: Prentice-Hall, 1946.

Ollman, Bertell. *Alienation.* Cambridge: Cambridge University Press, 1971.

O'Neill, John, ed. *Modes of Individualism and Collectivism.* London: Heinemann, 1973.

Peirce, C. S. *The Collected Papers of Charles Sanders Peirce.* 8 vols. Vols. 1–6 edited by Charles Hartshorne and Paul Weiss. Vols. 7 and 8 edited by Arthur W. Burks. Cambridge, Mass.: Harvard University Press, 1931–58.

Popper, Karl R. *Objective Knowledge: An Evolutionary Approach.* Oxford: Clarendon Press, 1972.

———. *The Poverty of Historicism.* New York: Harper Torchbooks, 1964.

Roberts, Moira. *Responsibility and Practical Freedom.* Cambridge: The University Press, 1965.

Rotenstreich, Nathan. *On the Human Subject. Studies in the Phenomenology of Ethics and Politics.* Springfield, Ill.: Thomas Publications, 1966.

Ross, Stephen David. *The Nature of Moral Responsibility.* Detroit: Wayne State University Press, 1973.

Saussure, Ferdinand de. *Course in General Linguistics.* Translated by Wade Baskin. New York: The Philosophical Library, 1959.

Sesonske, Alexander, and Fleming, Noel, eds. *Meta-Meditations: Studies in Descartes.* Belmont, Calif.: Wadsworth, 1965.

Schaff, Adam. *A Philosophy of Man.* New York: Delta Books, 1963.

———. *Marxism and the Human Individual.* Translated by Olgierd Wojtasiewicz. New York: McGraw-Hill, 1970.

Shaw, William H. *Marx's Theory of History.* Stanford: Stanford University Press, 1978.

Silber, John. "Being and Doing: A Study of Status Responsibility and Voluntary Responsibility." In *Phenomenology in America.* Edited by James M. Edie. Chicago: Quadrangle Books, 1967.

Silverman, H., and Elliston, F., eds. *Jean-Paul Sartre: Contemporary Approaches to His Philosophy.* Pittsburgh: Duquesne University Press, 1980.

Simmel, Georg. *The Sociology of Georg Simmel.* Translated and edited by Kurt H. Wolff. New York: The Free Press, 1964.

Sokolowski, Robert. *The Formation of Husserl's Concept of Constitution.* The Hague: Martinus Nijhoff, 1970.

Spiro, Herbert J. *Responsibility in Government: Theory and Practice.* New Perspectives in Political Science. New York: Van Nostrand Reinhold, 1969.

Tiryakian, Edward A. *Sociologism and Existentialism.* Englewood Cliffs, N.J.: Prentice-Hall, 1962.

Toulemont, R. "La Spécificité du social d'après Husserl." *Cahiers internationaux de sociologie* 25 (July–December 1958): 135–51.

Veatch, Henry. *For an Ontology of Morals.* Evanston, Ill.: Northwestern University Press, 1971.

Weber, Max. *Selections.* Edited by W. G. Runciman. Cambridge: Cambridge University Press, 1978.

Weyembergh, Maurice. "M. Weber et G. Lukács." *Revue internationale de philosophie* 27, no. 106 (1973): 474–500.

Wolfson, Murray. *A Reappraisal of Marxian Economics.* New York: Columbia University Press, 1966.

Wolin, Sheldon S. *Politics and Vision.* Boston: Little, Brown, 1960.

Index

257

Collectivism, 176, 240 n. 32. *See also* Holism; Individualism; Nominalism, dialectical; Ontology, social

Collectivities, 18, 28, 29, 30, 50, 68, 76, 139

Colonialism (neo-), 57–64, 66, 79, 97, 109, 110, 111, 137, 141, 144, 202

Colonialist (settler), 55, 61, 153. *See also* Passive activity; Serial, individual

Command, 114, 118, 119, 120; -obedience, 120, 136, 147, 200; theory of authority, 120, 199. *See also* Authority; Institution; Sovereignty

Commitment, 40, 47, 80, 91, 190. *See also* Choice; Freedom, concrete; Project

Common individual, 115, 118, 122, 131, 146, 153, 159, 160, 180

The Communists and Peace, 78, 79, 80, 113, 151, 155, 156, 176, 178

Community, 20, 24, 25, 40, 98, 115, 118, 122, 189, 190, 191, 194–96, 232 n. 36. *See also* Fraternity; Mutual recognition; Reciprocity, positive; Transcendence, common

Comoedia, 78, 219 n. 23

Complicity, 55, 57, 61, 63, 68, 223 nn. 21, 27, 237 n. 12. *See also* Responsibility

Comprehension, 84, 91, 101, 107, 114, 130, 131, 134, 151, 153, 154, 159, 162, 163, 166, 167, 175, 193, 230 n. 22; preontological, 19, 233 n. 13. See also *Verstehen*

The Condemned of Altona, 64–69

Consciousness, 4, 76, 104, 130, 131, 187, 194; class, 23, 33, 74, 75, 153, 159, 163, 164, 180, 225 n. 21, 238 n. 14; collective, 19, 85, 110, 135, 175, 178; false, 235 n. 24; imaging, 4–5, 35, 41, 187; prereflective, 13, 22, 28, 87, 116, 120 n. 10, 211 n. 12, 213 n. 26; shame, 18, 19, 20, 36, 215 n. 3. *See also* For-itself

Constitution, 4; world-, 5, 14, 85; value-, 14, 34, 37

Contat, Michel, 200

Counterfinality, 95, 96, 174

Counterperformative, 38, 41

Critique of Dialectical Reason, xii, 4, 21, 23, 24, 25, 27, 39, 43, 44, 46, 48, 51, 53, 54, 57, 58, 65, 68, 71, 75, 77, 80, 81, 82, 84, 89, 90, 91, 93–150, 152, 155, 168,

169, 173, 177, 178, 180, 181, 189, 190, 192, 193, 203, 205

Critique of Political Economy, 137

Cumming, Robert D., xiv

Dépassement, 4. *See also* Surpassing; Transcendence

Desan, Wilfrid, xiii

Descartes, 87, 90, 196

Destiny, 53, 74, 84, 93, 98, 101, 102–4, 113, 122, 128, 144, 145, 148, 153, 156, 174, 186. *See also* Interest

Determinism, 8, 56, 58, 94, 97, 111, 136, 138, 158, 235 n. 29; economic, xi, xiii, 72, 74, 132, 137, 173, 174, 206; family conditioning, 84; social conditioning, 226 n. 39; soft, 73, 200. *See also* Exigency; Marxism; Necessity

The Devil and the Good Lord, 50, 65, 190

Dewey, John, 197

Dialectic, xii, 65, 75, 82, 104, 106, 123, 124, 149, 174, 180, 197, 201, 206, 207, 226 n. 42, 227 nn. 46, 47, 228 n. 3; constituted, 117, 126, 129, 179; constitutive (constituent), 117, 126; dialectical thinking, 46. *See also* Nominalism, dialectical; Reason, dialectical; Totalization

Dichotomies, 196–201

Disalienation, 188–90, 195, 217 n. 6; ethics of, 32, 33, 225 n. 32

Durkheim, 21, 22, 25, 85, 110, 126, 127, 175, 178, 182, 239 n. 17

Dyadic relation (dyad), 21, 22, 25, 26, 29, 85, 205. *See also* Ternary relations

Economic and Philosophical Manuscripts (1844). See *Paris Manuscripts*

Economism, 112, 137, 138, 158, 168, 174, 182, 186, 212 n. 23. *See also* Determinism, economic

Ego. *See* Self

Eichmann, 135, 148

The Eighteenth Brumaire of Louis Bonaparte, 72

End and means, 241 n. 41. *See also* Ethics and politics

Engels, 173, 174

Epicurus, 8

Index

McBride, William, xiii, xiv
MacIntyre, Alasdair, 132, 133
Malthusianism, 59, 155, 164, 165, 166, 167, 237 n. 7, 238 n. 16
Marcuse, Herbert, 142
Marx, Karl, 28, 58, 72, 73, 74, 75, 88, 102, 133, 136, 137, 145, 156, 168, 173, 175, 176, 177, 181, 188, 189, 192, 194, 197, 198, 203
Marxism, xi, xiii, 26, 27, 30, 71, 137, 159, 162, 172, 173, 178, 200–201; revisionist, xiii, 239 n. 4; Sartre's, xi, xiii, 173–77. *See also* Historical materialism
"Materialism and Revolution," 43, 53, 131
Means-end problem. *See* Ethics and politics
Mediation, 22, 24, 28, 29, 30, 37, 55, 57, 60, 69, 88–89, 91, 93–123, 125, 126, 129, 131, 134, 138, 141, 143, 145, 147, 161, 162, 166, 174, 177, 181, 182, 183, 185, 189, 192, 200, 207; diachronic, 110; social, 56
Merleau-Ponty, Maurice, xii, 56, 71, 72, 75, 85, 91, 109, 176, 177, 178, 179
Mészáros, István, xii, xiii
Milieu, 99, 141, 151, 166, 206; of freedom, 146; of recurrence, 101, 229 n. 6; verbal, 100, 140, 144, 162
Model of society: existentialist, 19, 21, 23, 29, 30, 47, 51, 56, 71, 125, 153, 177; praxis, 30, 95, 205. *See also* Looking/looked-at
Moral imperative (MI), 33, 35, 41, 62, 146, 152, 218 n. 16
Motive, 5; reason/motive (*motif/mobile*), 8, 211 n. 16
Mutuality, 28, 30, 120, 186, 191, 199; mutual recognition, 43, 44, 45, 46, 48, 62, 119, 184, 185, 192, 198; positive, 21. *See also* Community; Reciprocity

Napoleon III, 72, 108
Necessity, 58, 64, 67, 71, 74, 77, 78, 79, 81, 82, 94, 96, 97, 154, 162; and freedom, 70–92, 102, 156, 174, 188, 200–201; reign of, 97, 122. *See also* Determinism; Exigency; Freedom
Need, 87. *See also* Lack; Scarcity
Negation, 87–88, 91, 101, 162

Nihilation (*néantisation*), 4, 5–6, 20, 76; nihilating freedom, 7; primordial, 5–6; self-, 12. *See also* Consciousness; For-itself
No Exit, 31, 65, 70, 190, 215 n. 6
Nominalism, dialectical, xiii, 86, 91–92, 117, 126, 127, 129, 182, 183, 198, 205
Nonidentity (nonself-identity), 135; of consciousness, 6, 10, 11; freedom of, 7, 182
Nothingness: *néant*, 4; *rien*, 6
Notion (*Begriff*), 90, 228 n. 61

Oath (pledge), 116, 126, 127, 141, 142, 163, 193, 216 n. 8
Object, 192; collective, 94, 98, 103, 113, 115, 120, 122, 128, 130, 136, 144, 145, 153, 179, 188, 189, 194; of history, 70, 96, 113, 185; quasi-, 116, 118; social, 233 n. 11
Objectification, 36, 39, 67, 95, 133, 147, 242 n. 8. *See also* Alienation; Third, objectifying (alienating)
Objective, 128, 131, 141, 232 n. 34
On a raison de se révolter, 192
Ontology, social, xiii, xiv, 18, 19, 20, 21, 23, 24, 26, 30, 45, 51, 59, 69, 71, 72, 75, 92, 93, 99, 101, 112, 113, 122, 124, 151, 154, 162, 168, 177, 180, 181, 185, 190, 200, 205, 240 n. 23. *See also* Collectivism; Holism; Individualism; Nominalism, dialectical
"Open future" argument, 39, 41
Oppression, 54, 56, 59, 60, 62, 64, 69, 78, 83, 97, 100, 109, 110, 111, 134, 150, 153, 154, 158, 160, 161, 162, 163, 164, 165, 166, 186. *See also* Exploitation; Praxis, ethical primacy of
Other, 20, 22, 26, 30, 45, 47, 70, 71, 77, 78, 95, 100, 101, 104, 108, 118, 119, 120, 128, 134, 143, 144, 148, 149, 153, 159, 160, 161, 163, 166, 191, 193, 190, 201, 203, 204, 207, 215 n. 6, 219 n. 17; dialectic of, 93–104, 178, 181; -comprehension, 101, 132, 229 n. 11; -thought, 99, 163
Otherness (alterity), 6, 93, 95, 99, 103, 114, 116, 117, 122, 132, 143, 144, 149, 159, 160, 162, 188, 189, 199; free (alterity), 116, 178, 188, 190, 242 n. 8; vertical, 121. *See also* Alienation

261